# Strengthening Christ's church

# *Strengthening Christ's church*

## The message of 1 Corinthians

### Roger Ellsworth

 EVANGELICAL PRESS

EVANGELICAL PRESS
Faverdale North, Darlington, DL3 0PH, England

e-mail: sales@evangelicalpress.org

Evangelical Press USA
P. O. Box 825, Webster, New York 14580, USA

e-mail: usa.sales@evangelicalpress.org

web: http://www.evangelicalpress.org

First published 1995
This impression 2008

**British Library Cataloguing in Publication Data available**

ISBN 13 978 085234 333 3                    ISBN 0 85234 333 7

Printed and bound in Great Britain by Biddles Ltd, King's Lynn,
Norfolk

Dedicated to my dear friends,
Tod and Brenda Doty

# Contents

# Preface

Paul's first letter to the Corinthians was directed to a deeply troubled church in the midst of a very challenging world.

Founded by Paul on his second missionary journey (Acts 18) in one of the major metropolitan areas of the day, the church of Corinth would seem to have been poised to make a profound impact for Christ. But this church was in danger of squandering her opportunity as she stumbled and groped along.

What was the problem? Two words have riveted themselves in my mind as I have combed through Paul's epistle — contamination and confusion. The Corinthian church was contaminated by society's sins and confused by its thinking.

If this all sounds hauntingly familiar it is because it hits perilously close to home. Today's church finds herself in a frighteningly secular world, one in which paganism is aggressive and militant. Opportunities are great, but, alas, the church often seems to be as contaminated and confused as the church of Corinth.

Paul's medicine for Corinth will do us good. He bathes the contamination and the confusion of the church in the glory of Christ crucified. Studying in Calvary's school is always the antidote for the Christian. It is my hope that these studies will cause each reader to look with fresh wonder at that cross.

I am able to offer these studies only because I have been assisted by so many. I am indebted to several writers who have traversed this ground before me and to my beloved church family, Immanuel Baptist Church, for encouraging me in the ministry of preaching the Word. I am thankful that my wife, Sylvia, and my secretary, Sheila Ketteman, have continually urged me to write. I am grateful to the

editors of Evangelical Press for their invaluable guidance. And my
good friends, Beth Bozeman and Jim Wiens, deserve a lion's share
of praise for their diligent  assistance in preparing the manuscript.

Roger Ellsworth
Immanuel Baptist Church

# 1.
# Timely reminders

*Please read 1 Corinthians 1:1-3*

We live in a day of muddled thinking and messy living. Ours is a sick age.

Sick people need a doctor, and the church of Jesus Christ is uniquely qualified to serve as a physician to this sick age. She should be diagnosing the problem and proposing treatment. She should be putting her society in touch with the medicine that can heal. Furthermore, the church should be a living demonstration of what good health is.

But what can a physician do when she is suffering from the very illness she is trying to treat? There is no way around it. The church is often a sick physician. She is unable to treat the muddled thinking and messy living all around her because her own thinking is often muddled and her living messy. In order to function as a physician, the church must have both clarity of mind and purity of life. She must be, in the words of Jesus, both light and salt (Matt. 5:13-16).

## Salt and light

The function of salt is twofold: it preserves meat by arresting decay and provides flavour for food. Jesus gave us absolutely no choice about whether we will be salt. He has already made us his salt. The only question is whether we will be pure salt to arrest the contamination of the world around us, or savourless salt. If we are pure salt, we can effectively address the contamination of our world; if we are savourless salt, we have become so contaminated by the world that we are incapable of helping it.

The function of light is to dispel darkness. Jesus also gave us no choice about being light. The only question is whether we are going to shine brilliantly and openly from a lampstand, or flicker dimly under a covering.

Salt and light are powerful metaphors to convey the need for Christ's disciples to have both purity of life and clarity of mind. They let us know his disciples are to be free from both contamination and confusion. The letter we know as the First Epistle to the Corinthians is a clarion call to the Christians in Corinth and to Christians today to come away from contamination and confusion and to function as salt and light.

## The situation at Corinth

The Corinthians urgently needed this call. The church, founded by the apostle on his second missionary journey (Acts 18:1-18), was located in one of the great cities of that day. Situated on a narrow strip of land, only four miles across, Corinth was simultaneously a strategic centre of commerce by land and by sea.

Thriving commerce often translates into thriving debauchery, but Corinth took debauchery and licentiousness to new heights — or new depths! The other pagan cities of the day acknowledged Corinth's moral corruption by coining the word *'corinthiazesthai'* — to live like a Corinthian.[1]

Sexual immorality and perversion; covetousness and stealing; drunkenness and gluttony; pride; abusive speech; swindling — a quick journey through Paul's letter reveals Corinth had it all. Warren Wiersbe writes, 'If you want to know what Corinth was like, read Romans 1:18-32. Paul wrote the Roman epistle while in Corinth, and he could have looked out the window and seen the very sins that he listed!'[2]

A casual observer might suggest religion as the answer for Corinth, but religion was plentiful and the tide of iniquity flowed on unabated. In fact, the religions of Corinth were part of the problem. A temple to the goddess of love and fertility, Aphrodite, was there. A thousand priestesses plied the trade of prostitution as part of the religious rites. Long-haired male prostitutes were also a common sight.[3]

Only the church of Jesus Christ had the medicine this sick society needed, but, sadly, the true physicians were themselves down with the disease. Instead of their influencing Corinth for Christ, Corinth had influenced them, and the sins of society had cropped up in the church. John MacArthur says the Christians of Corinth could not get 'decorinthianized', and he proceeds to add these telling words: 'They wanted to have the blessings of the new life but hang on to the pleasures of the old.'⁴ Their salt had indeed lost its savour, and their light had indeed been covered.

## Paul's object in writing

So Paul began to write. It was not the first time he had written to this troubled church. He refers to an earlier letter (5:9), one which we do not have. Evidently, this letter was a stinging rebuke to the church for their careless living. It did not succeed in putting an end to their problems, but it did prompt a return letter from the church, in which they posed several questions. 1 Corinthians is Paul's response to their letter. It is another impassioned plea for them to deal decisively with their contamination, and it is the concerned response of Paul's pastor's heart to clear up the questions they had raised in their confused state.

More than that, Paul wanted to bring their contamination and confusion into the light of the gospel, so it would be clear that Christianity works, even in a sophisticated, cosmopolitan, pagan society like Corinth. This church was both a marvel and a mess, and Paul's concern was to help them clean up the mess so only the marvel would be left for the godless city of Corinth to see.

We have a tendency to think the opening and closing words of Paul's epistles are nothing more than mere formalities and that we can safely rush right past them. But Paul was not one to waste words, and what he says in the first three verses of this letter really drives right to the heart of the contamination and confusion of the church. These verses contain in germinal form everything the Corinthians needed to get themselves sorted out.

## Paul's authority as an apostle

First, Paul reminds them of his authority as an apostle (1:1). This was his customary way of opening his letters, but that doesn't make his words any less meaningful. Paul knew he could not be of any help to the Corinthians until they recognized his authority and submitted to it. They were in trouble because they had lost sight of this very thing. Somehow they had got the notion that they could 'freelance' in the Christian life, they could make it up as they went along. By reminding them of his apostleship, Paul was pulling them back from this disastrous mentality.

Did Paul really have authority over the Corinthians? Or was this just a figment of his own imagination? All Christians readily acknowledge Paul was an apostle, but very few seem to understand what this entailed. Some Christians don't hesitate to question whether Paul had the right to tell the Corinthians what they should believe and how they should behave. Those who argue in such a way fail to realize the unique place an apostle occupied in the economy of God.

The apostle was not one who just took up religious leadership on a mere whim, but one who had received a special commission from the risen Christ. He was the recipient and bearer of God's revelation to the churches. We might say the apostles were to the early church what the New Testament is to us. Since God had invested such authority in them it was not optional to believe them. To dispute apostolic teaching was the same as disputing with God!

### The calling of his readers

Paul was not content simply to remind the Corinthians of his authority. He goes on to remind them of their high calling. He says they are **'the church of God'**, **'sanctified in Christ Jesus'** and **'called to be saints'** (1:2).

The word 'church' was originally used for any secular assembly, but Christians took the term and made it distinctively theirs. They used it to designate those called out of the world by God for fellowship with him.

They were also 'sanctified in Christ Jesus' and 'called to be saints'. What riches there are in those two phrases! Something had happened to the Corinthians. They had been acted upon by God himself. He had 'sanctified' them. He had cleansed them from their sins and set them apart for his own use. Furthermore, he had done this through the Lord Jesus Christ. There is no cleansing from sin apart from him.

God had also 'called' them. How Paul loved this word! He himself had been 'called' to be an apostle, and the Corinthians had been 'called'. God had come to them while they were in their sins and had called them to himself.

The result of God's gracious work in their lives was that they were now 'saints'. They were God's holy ones, those he had cleansed and called to himself.

Sainthood isn't something therefore that applies only to a handful of super-Christians. All Christians are saints because they all share the common experience of being sanctified and called by God.

In using these powerful phrases, the apostle was already issuing a strong encouragement to the Corinthians to deal decisively with the sins in their midst. God's grace had made them his holy ones. Those who have such a high calling could not take sin lightly. Their calling demanded the highest moral character, and Paul's introductory words urge them to live up to that calling.

There is at the same time a vein of comfort in his words. Even though they had allowed sin to contaminate their lives, they were still God's saints. God's work of grace in the lives of his people can never finally be defeated!

In addition to calling them saints, Paul reminds them of the larger family of saints to which they belong. What was his point in this? It was to remind the Corinthians that they were part and parcel of a larger body of believers; they were not mere autonomous islands who could live without regard to the other members of the body of Christ. Paul's words imply that the Corinthians had failed to see that all the followers of Christ had a stake in how they measured up to their Christian calling. These reminders of their high calling constituted a very stern rebuke to the Corinthians for allowing themselves to be swept away by the twin tides of contamination and confusion.

## God's care for the church

Finally, Paul's introductory words also reminded the Corinthians of God's ongoing care and concern for them (1:3). We start looking at the mess this church was in and we find ourselves thinking the whole situation was irretrievable. Thank God, all was not lost. The God who had called them to himself in grace and who had given them peace through the atoning death of the Lord Jesus Christ was calling this grace and peace to their minds and still wishing them grace and peace through his appointed apostle.

Perhaps you are wondering what all this has to do with us. The sad answer is that 'Corinthianism' didn't die with the Corinthians. It is still alive and well in our churches. Like them we know what it is to throw off God's authority and become contaminated and confused by the world. We also know what it is to be so paralysed by moral laxity and doctrinal uncertainty that we fail to appreciate our privileges or live up to our potential. We also know what it is to be so stricken with the sickness of our world that we are powerless to carry the life-giving medicine of the gospel to others.

No, we don't have an apostle to whom we can write for guidance, but we do have this record of how Paul helped the Corinthians with their contamination and confusion. What does this mean? It means the God of grace and peace is still speaking to us! He doesn't write off his children as soon as we fall into the world's evil ways, or as soon as we uncritically adopt the world's thinking. He continues to be concerned about us and to call us to grace and peace. This very letter is a token of his grace, and obedience to its teachings will bring us to a posture of peace in the midst of a trying world.

# 2.
# What we have in Jesus

*Please read 1 Corinthians 1:4-9*

Contaminated and confused! That was the church at Corinth. Their problems (chapters 1-6) arose from their contamination with the world. Their questions (chapters 7-16) arose from their confusion about certain aspects of Christian truth.

As we saw in the previous chapter, even Paul's words of greeting seem to be not a mere empty formality, but calculated to go immediately to the solution of their problems. He reminded them of his calling to be an apostle, of their calling (called out of the world, called to be saints, called into fellowship with others) and of God's ongoing care and concern for them. Together these truths constituted a massive rebuke to this church for their sinful living.

The verses now before us at first glance appear to be nothing more than a fine bit of psychology. Paul appears to be congratulating them for what he can before he starts correcting them. Several commentators have observed that this is always a helpful way to approach problems.

I suggest, however, that Paul had something quite different in mind. Look at the number of times he refers to the Lord Jesus in these verses (1:4-9). For that matter, look at the number of times he refers to the Lord in the first nine verses. Some form of his name appears nine times in these first nine verses. Can there be any doubt that Paul was deliberately underscoring the centrality of the Lord Jesus? And isn't this his way of saying the Corinthians had lost sight of their Lord? Hadn't they, in fact, turned their attention away from him and become obsessed with themselves?

If this is indeed the case, Paul's opening verses constitute his attempt to turn their eyes away from themselves and back to their

Lord. Paul sought to do this by stressing for them again what they had in Christ. And what did they have? We can summarize it all in that word **'grace'**.


## Saving grace

The first thing the Corinthians enjoyed through Christ was saving grace (1:4). That simply means their salvation was entirely his doing. They had done absolutely nothing to earn or deserve it. Paul loved to dwell on this theme in all his letters. We find him writing to the Ephesians: 'For by grace you have been saved through faith, and that not of yourselves; it is the gift of God, not of works, lest anyone should boast' (Eph. 2:8-9).

The truth is, there was nothing for Paul to praise in the Corinthians. Everything they were and everything they had came to them as a gift of God's grace, and when a person receives a gift, there is nothing for him to boast about. The credit for a gift always goes to the giver, not to the receiver. So Paul opens this letter, not by praising them, but by praising God for what he had done in them.

How did God give this marvellous gift of salvation to them? Paul was always glad to trumpet out the good news: **'by Christ Jesus'**. That means God has freely bestowed salvation on his people because of something Jesus did. In other words, God does not save indiscriminately and arbitrarily, but only through Christ.

How can salvation come to us through Christ? It does so because he removed the obstacles between God and us. By his perfect life he provided the righteousness we need to stand before God, and by his death he paid the penalty for our sins. He actually bore in himself the wrath of God on our behalf. Salvation means Christ took on him our sin, and by turning from our sins and trusting solely in him, we receive his righteousness. Paul put it like this in his second letter to the Corinthians: 'For He made Him who knew no sin to be sin for us, that we might become the righteousness of God in Him' (2 Cor. 5:21). The first thing the Corinthians needed to do to overcome their problems was reflect on the saving grace of God bestowed upon them through Jesus Christ, and to reflect on it until it became real again and gratitude flooded their hearts.

**Enriching grace**

There is more to God's grace than our sins being forgiven. His is also an enriching grace (1:5-7). It had not only saved them; it had equipped them to serve God acceptably. Paul mentions just two gifts God had granted them. One was the gift of **'utterance'**, which is the ability to share the truth. The other was the gift of **'knowledge'**. This doesn't mean they knew everything there was to know. If that were the case, they would have had no need to ask Paul any questions. So what is this gift of knowledge? David Prior suggests it means that 'The church as a body has access to all the wisdom, insight, discernment, and truth which it needs; it needs no special gurus to bring it to them.'[5]

Through God's enriching grace, they were also established in the faith (1:6). The word **'confirmed'** is most interesting. It means to have something settled in our convictions. In a day when people are tossed to and fro with uncertainty, the person who knows what he believes and why he believes it is rich indeed.

The grace of God further enriched them by making them expectant (1:7). In other words, it gave them a glorious hope. They had something to look forward to: the day when the Lord Jesus Christ would be revealed in all his power and glory.

Despair abounds on every hand today. The suicide rate is ample proof of it. Ours is an 'escapist' society in which people avoid coming to grips with reality by tripping out to a fantasy world or by trying to drown their troubles in a bottle. Others avoid facing up to themselves by making a career out of blaming someone else — their husband or wife, their parents, their boss, the government.

The Christian is the only one in this world who has genuine hope. He doesn't don rose-coloured glasses and pretend everything is all right with this world. In fact, the Christian is ruthlessly realistic about the world. He sees past the outward glitter to its inward corruption. He knows the world, because of sin, is under the sentence of divine wrath, but he also knows Jesus Christ is returning some day to completely obliterate both sin and death. And he knows this because the God who graciously saves has also graciously revealed these truths in his Word. Armed with such truths, the Christian is truly rich.

**Preserving grace**

But saying the grace of God is a saving, enriching grace still doesn't exhaust it. Paul says it is also preserving grace (1:8-9). The Corinthians could depend on this grace to continue to work in them and keep them until the day they stood blameless before Jesus Christ. Paul gives two reasons for believing in the keeping power of God's grace.

*The faithfulness of God*

The first is the faithfulness of God. Notice how he puts it: **'God is faithful, by whom you were called...'**
We have already seen that salvation is due solely to the grace of God. Men can take no credit for it. It was God who called them to salvation, and it is God who calls all who are saved to be saved.
If we are not responsible for salvation in the first place, how can we be responsible for keeping it? The keeping of our salvation doesn't rest on our faithfulness, but on God's faithfulness in maintaining his work in us. That is why Paul wrote to the Philippians of his confidence 'that He who has begun a good work in you will complete it until the day of Jesus Christ' (Phil. 1:6).

*Fellowship with Christ*

The second reason Paul gives for believing in preserving grace is the fellowship of the Lord Jesus Christ. To be saved means to be called to have fellowship with Christ. That fellowship means we have both union and communion with Christ.
The doctrine of our union with Christ is precious indeed and too little stressed. Being saved means we have been joined to Christ. This union is so complete that if we were to lose our salvation and perish, Jesus himself would have to perish!
To have fellowship with Christ also involves communion. This means we are conscious of Christ's presence in our lives. We have communion with him as he speaks to us in his Word and as we speak to him in prayer. How can anyone who stands in such close relation to Jesus Christ ever perish? It is not only impossible but inconceivable!

Grace first inscribed my name,
In God's eternal book;
'Twas grace that gave me to the Lamb
Who all my sorrows took.

Grace taught my soul to pray,
And made my eyes o'erflow;
'Twas grace that kept me to this day,
And will not let me go.

This is the saving, enriching, preserving grace of God. Isn't it incredible that the Corinthians could get into such a state of coldness and sinfulness when they had been given so much in Christ? But what about us? If we are Christians, we have exactly the same things they did. God has saved, enriched and preserved us. Do our lives reflect gratitude and praise? Or do we grumble and show discontent and resentment? Are we tolerant of sins in our lives that grieve Christ? Are we childish and selfish? Have we allowed our loyalties to be so divided that God doesn't have all of our hearts? If so, the answer for us is the same as it was for them:

Turn your eyes upon Jesus,
Look full in his wonderful face,
And the things of earth will grow strangely dim
In the light of his glory and grace.

# 3.
# The problem of division

*Please read 1 Corinthians 1:10-17*

The Bible consistently stresses the beauty of unity and the danger of division. The psalmist says, 'Behold, how good and how pleasant it is for brethren to dwell together in unity!' (Ps. 133:1). And Jesus, on the night before he was crucified, repeatedly prayed for unity among his followers (John 17:11,21,23).

Evidently, the Saviour's burden for unity gripped the heart of the apostle Paul because he always seemed to find a place in each of his letters for an eloquent appeal for unity among Christians. One of his most notable pleas is found in his letter to the Philippians: 'Only let your conduct be worthy of the gospel of Christ, so that ... I may hear of your affairs, that you stand fast in one spirit, with one mind striving together for the faith of the gospel...' (Phil. 1:27).

However, the church of Corinth was anything but united. The fact is, the church resembled the society in which she lived. Corinth was divided in all kinds of ways — rich and poor, slave and free, cultured and barbaric, Jew and Gentile. The church should have been different, but she wasn't. The white skirt of the church was contaminated with the dirt of the world. The Christians in Corinth had managed to lose sight of the grace they had in Christ and had become obsessed with the grief they had in each other.

Paul refuses to tiptoe around the issue. In measured, powerful words he opens fire on this distracting, disrupting, destructive cancer of division. **'Now'** signals an abrupt shift from the positive to the negative. The words of commendation are over and the words of correction begin. **'Plead'** reveals the intensity of his feelings about this issue. It is a strong word, meaning 'to beg, to implore, or to beseech'. **'Brethren'** reminds them of the basis of their unity —

they all belonged to the same family. **'By the name of the Lord Jesus Christ'** reminds them of the authority of the one to whom they had professed their greatest allegiance. If their Master had sworn eternal hostility against division, how could they tolerate it?

After laying down this opening barrage, Paul marches up to grapple with the problem in close hand-to-hand combat. He rips away all the camouflage so the Corinthians might see the true ugliness of division and be repulsed by it. He does this by discussing the tragedy (1:10-12) and the absurdity of division (1:13). Then he turns to deal with the remedy for it (1:14-17).

### The tragedy of division

The tragedy of a divided church is twofold. She fails to achieve maturity in Christ, but succeeds in achieving notoriety in the world. Paul never grew tired of insisting upon spiritual maturity as the goal for God's people. He desired each of the Christians at Ephesus to 'come to the unity of the faith and the knowledge of the Son of God, to a perfect man, to the measure of the stature of the fullness of Christ...' (Eph. 4:13).

His desire for the Corinthians was the same. He wanted them to be **'perfectly joined together in the same mind and in the same judgment'** (1:10). The word 'perfectly' is translated 'complete' in the New American Standard Bible and it simply means 'mature'. Paul is quite obviously connecting unity with maturity, and the implication is that the Corinthians were not making much progress towards the goal of maturity in Christ. They were not of the same mind, the same judgement, or the same speech. In fact, they seemed to delight in flaunting their disunity. Paul states: **'Each of you says, "I am of Paul," or "I am of Apollos," or "I am of Cephas," or "I am of Christ"'** (1:12).

It is bad enough when a church has two warring factions, but this church had several! Evidently there was a division between the Gentile Christians and the Jewish Christians, with the former claiming to follow Paul while the latter clung to Cephas (Simon Peter). Another division apparently existed between the more intellectual members, who were enamoured of the cultured, eloquent Apollos, and the more ordinary members. A final division existed because some felt they were spiritually superior to all the rest. They considered themselves the spiritual élite, the spiritual aristocracy. This group boasted they were of Christ. This sounds so good that we are inclined to enter the fray on the side of this particular group. How could they have been in the wrong? The point is, by their boast that they were of Christ, they were denying that the other members of the church belonged to him. Furthermore, their boast was tantamount to denying that the preachers the others were following had been called by Christ. The 'Christ-boasters' were making it appear as if Christ belonged exclusively to them.

Here is the tragedy of division. Instead of moving towards the goal of Christian maturity, this church was bogged down in the swamp of childishly disputing which group was superior! But the tragedy went even further. Because of their divisions, they were causing the church and the cause of Christ to have a bad name. Paul says it had been **'declared'** to him by those of Chloe's household. It is not important for us to pinpoint precisely who this woman was. What is important is that Paul had learned of their quarrels while he was ministering in distant Ephesus! A church quarrel never has to be advertised. It always advertises itself and its circulation is greater than that of any newspaper in the area! Jesus said, 'By this all will know that you are My disciples, if you have love for one another' (John 13:35). That is the kind of advertising we should seek!

## The absurdity of division

From the tragedy of division, Paul moves to point out the absurdity of it. He spares nothing in heaping scorn and sarcasm upon them for allowing divisions. Three short, biting questions put the whole matter in perspective: **'Is Christ divided? Was Paul crucified for you? Or were you baptized in the name of Paul?'** (1:13). These questions cover all the grounds of the Christian's allegiance to Christ, namely, that Christ is, that he died to redeem us and that we are publicly set apart for his purpose by baptism.

Each Christian has these things in common with all other Christians. Paul wanted them to look long and hard at these things and ask themselves how they could be divided when they had so much to unite them. How could they allow division when they all belonged to the same Christ? They were acting as if Christ himself had been divided up and parcelled out! How could they exalt one preacher above another? Paul, tactfully using his own name, reminds them he hadn't been crucified for them, and they hadn't been baptized in his name.

Do you see his point? The Corinthians didn't belong to him or to any of the other great preachers of the day. They belonged to Christ — all of them, not just an élite few. Their salvation came through him. The preachers they claimed to follow had been sent by him. The church itself was not theirs, but his. They had lost sight of the very thing that united them — Jesus Christ! Having placed their divisions in those terms, Paul was in a position to point out the remedy for the whole mess. They had to start magnifying Christ and minimizing themselves and their favourite preachers.

## The priority of the cross

Each Christian seems to have a particular fondness for the preacher who baptized him and for the one who speaks with unusual power and eloquence. Paul had shunned both of these rôles. He had baptized only a few at Corinth, not because he wanted to disparage baptism, but because his calling was to be an apostle, whose essential task was to evangelize.

Paul also refused to embellish his message with **'wisdom of words'** (1:17). In other words, he didn't cultivate an entertaining style of preaching, nor did he try to dazzle his hearers with a display of scholarship. He confined himself to the simple proclamation of the facts of the gospel.

Paul had no desire to be exalted, but only to see Christ exalted. He clearly understood that what matters is not the one who preaches but the one who is preached; not the one who baptizes but the one into whom we are baptized. In short, magnifying Christ and his death on the cross was the burning passion and the driving force of Paul's life. He says his purpose was **'to preach the gospel, not with wisdom of words, lest the cross of Christ should be made of no effect'** (1:17). He was fired with such a holy jealousy for the priority of the cross that he could not tolerate anything that diminished the message of it. It deeply saddened him that the Corinthians were doing the very thing he hated the most.

The Corinthians were not the last ones to get so contaminated with the filth of the world that they diminished the message of the cross. We also live in a frighteningly fragmented world. Political parties, ethnic divisions, neighbourhood rivalries and family disputes are the order of the day. Christians have been called to speak the message of the cross to this fragmented world, to clearly say that the cross has the power to transcend distinctions and break down walls of partition.

But all too often the fragmenting mentality of the world is at work in the fellowship of the church, the fellowship that professes to be built around that cross.

Sometimes this fragmenting mentality manifests itself in Christians following after preachers who preside over vast religious empires while they neglect the ministry of the faithful pastor in their own church. Sometimes it manifests itself in clinging to the ministry of a former pastor instead of embracing the ministry of the current pastor. Sometimes it manifests itself in Christians bragging about their pastor and looking with disdain upon other faithful pastors in the same community.

These are only a few of the manifestations of the preacher-following syndrome. We might be inclined to dismiss these as rather trivial, but preacher-following is not trivial. Great damage always results. Christians are divided one against the other and the message of the cross is discredited before the eyes of a fragmented world.

This does not mean the office of the minister is to be demeaned. The same apostle Paul who warned the Corinthians about their shameful personality cults also urged the Thessalonians to esteem their ministers 'very highly in love'(1 Thess. 5:12-13).

But high esteem for ministers flows from the fact that they are servants of the Lord. We esteem them because they represent and serve him. We belong to him, not to ministers, and any minister worth his salt is most grieved when people look to him rather than to the Master he has been called to serve.

May God help us to see the tragedy and absurdity of division, and may he also help us to so devote ourselves to the message of the cross that everything unbecoming of the Christian gets lost in its priority.

# 4.
# The dividing-line of the cross

*Please read 1 Corinthians 1:18-25*

Corinth was a city of debate and division at the time Paul wrote his first letter to the Corinthians. John MacArthur says there were 'perhaps as many as fifty identifiable philosophical parties or movements in the city'.[6] Debating the merits of these various schools and their leaders was a favourite pastime of many of Corinth's citizens.

The grim reality which so grieved Paul was that Christians of the city had carried over into the church the same mentality and spirit that swirled around them. They were clustering around various preachers of the gospel and debating their respective merits and deficiencies as though these men were nothing more than rival heads of various schools of philosophy. They had failed to see that they had been placed in an entirely new and different realm.

The fact that something prevails in society is no justification for its prevailing in the church. Paul, therefore, focuses their attention on the different kind of wisdom at work in the church. It was not the vaunted wisdom of the world but the wisdom of God himself. Essentially, Paul poses this question: 'If human wisdom is so great, why couldn't it save you?' You see, every Christian professes to be saved solely by the death of Christ on the cross. Anyone who claims to be a Christian apart from this is only deceiving himself. In essence, Paul says to them, 'Take a look at that cross by which you claim to be saved. What do you see there? Certainly not human wisdom! As far as human wisdom is concerned, that cross is utter foolishness!' His conclusion is obvious: if they were not saved by human wisdom, why should they now be putting so much stock in it and carrying it over into the life of the church?

As far as Paul was concerned, the cross of Christ is the great dividing-line among men. While others talked about this, that, or the other division, Paul talked of only one — the division made by the cross of Christ. The Corinthians were supposed to be in agreement about that cross; therefore, there was no basis for their being divided on anything else. The true division was between them and the world. Ironically, they were acting as if they had more in common with the world and its philosophical reasoning than they had with each other.

We urgently need Paul's message because we also have a way of lifting the popular elements out of our culture and 'baptizing' them into the church. Instead of magnifying the different kind of wisdom at work in Christianity, we are often found playing it down so we can accommodate the spirit of the age. Some who constantly warn about the tyranny of a dogmatic fundamentalism have never been able to see the ever-present danger of 'trendamentalism'.

### The unbeliever's view of the cross

Let's turn our attention to what Paul has to say about the cross of Christ as the great divider of people. First, notice how the unbeliever views the cross. Paul sums up the unbeliever's response to the cross in graphic words: **'The message of the cross is foolishness to those who are perishing...'** (1:18)

Take note of how Paul characterizes the unbeliever. He is 'perishing'. That is a present participle. Christians often tell their unsaved friends to turn to Christ, or they will perish in eternal destruction, but the truth is that the unbeliever is even now in the process of perishing. The apostle John says the unbeliever is 'condemned already' and even now, 'The wrath of God abides on him' (John 3:18,36).

With this word 'perishing', we already have in hand proof of the inadequacy of human wisdom. Man's first problem is that he is utterly blind to his own condition. He has the ability to do many wonderful things. He can probe outer space, work medical wonders and make all kinds of time-saving gadgets, but he is hopelessly blind to his own nature. He constantly sees the effects produced by his evil nature: drug addiction, crime, corruption in government, deterioration of his environment, war, sexually transmitted diseases. However, he refuses to face up to his sinfulness. He looks at these and other problems and says the solution is more education. So he pours more and more money and effort into education, only to see evil flow on unabated. If man were truly wise, he would be able to see that the problem is rooted in his own nature.

The cross of Christ is God's answer to evil. It shows evil as such a serious and dreadful reality that it required nothing less than that the very Son of God should himself become a man and die. That same cross declares that his death is sufficient for man to be delivered from evil.

One would think, given man's catastrophic condition, that such news would receive a warm reception. But such wasn't the case in Paul's day, nor is it in ours. The message of the cross was greeted with scorn and derision by both segments of Paul's world — Jews and Greeks. The Jews were offended by the cross because it totally violated their preconceptions about the Messiah. Their history was replete with God performing mighty acts and various signs, and they expected their Messiah to deal in these same things. They constantly demanded that Jesus show them a sign (Matt. 12:38; Mark. 8:11; John 6:30). Their Messiah was to be a man of great might and power, not a man who died in weakness and shame on a Roman cross. The Greeks, on the other hand, could not accept the message of the cross because it defied logic. How could a man branded throughout the empire as the lowest of criminals be the Saviour of the world? The cross of Christ was in Paul's time a stumbling-block to the religious Jew and a laughing-stock to the rational Greeks, and it is no less offensive and ludicrous to unbelievers today.

## The believer's view of the cross

When the believer looks at the cross he sees something different. To him the cross is light years away from being an object of ridicule and contempt. To him the cross is nothing less than **'the power of God'** (1:18,24) and **'the wisdom of God'** (1:24).

The cross is the power of God to the believer because it is the source of his transformation which results in a new nature. This change is so great that Jesus compared it to being 'born again' (John 3:3). Paul went so far as to say, 'Therefore, if anyone is in Christ, he is a new creation; old things have passed away; behold, all things have become new' (2 Cor. 5:17).

Here is how great the change is in the believer. It begins the moment he is regenerated by the grace of God and embraces the cross of Christ, and it continues all through this life as God matures and refines him. At last it culminates in his standing 'faultless before the presence of His glory' (Jude 24). You see, just as the unbeliever is in the process of perishing, so the believer is in the process of being saved. Only the power of God is sufficient to get anyone through such a process, and make no mistake about it, this whole process is based on the death of Jesus Christ on the cross.

The cross is also to the believer the wisdom of God. How can such a thing as the cross be an expression of God's wisdom? If we were asked to devise a plan by which man could be forgiven of his sin and brought into fellowship with God, we would never have come up with the cross of Christ. But that was and is God's plan, and it is the wisest of all plans. Man's sin, if I may put it in this way, presented a dilemma for God. Because God is holy, he could not ignore sin. His nature required him to judge it. But because God is also gracious, he desired to find a way of forgiveness for sinners. The dilemma, then, was how God could judge sin and forgive the sinner. The cross of Christ is the answer to that dilemma. On the cross, God judged the sins of all who believe in his Son, Jesus. There is, therefore, no penalty left for those who believe. It has already been paid by Jesus Christ. So the believing sinner is able to sing with the poet:

Jesus paid it all;
All to him I owe.
Sin had left a crimson stain;
He washed it white as snow.

Men may ridicule and mock, but the believer knows what he has found in the cross. Paul was so confident of the saving power of the cross that he threw out a challenge: **'Where is the wise? Where is the scribe? Where is the disputer of this age?'** Had these wisest of men been able to produce anything to rival the peace, joy and hope of those who clung to the cross? Paul knew they had not and could not. We can fling out a similar challenge to our own world. Have our great thinkers been able to provide satisfying answers to life's ultimate questions? Why, if our wisdom is so great, is our world in such difficulty? The answer is that modern wisdom has failed as completely as the wisdom of Paul's day. It has failed because God, in his own wisdom, has determined that man will never be able to know him apart from the cross of Christ. Don't laugh at that cross until you are able to produce something that brings as much peace, joy and hope as it has brought to millions down through the years.

# 5.
# The character of believers

*Please read 1 Corinthians 1:26-31*

Let's suppose you have invented a new gadget, and you now want to make a fortune by selling it. How would you begin? Wouldn't you want first to get some very influential people to endorse your product? Wouldn't you want to enlist outstanding people from education, politics, sports, industry and the entertainment world to try it and give testimonials for it? Wouldn't you then want to target the intelligent, fashionable and affluent sectors of society? Wouldn't you assume their support would easily translate into support from the masses?

This is how the world does things, and many Christians are convinced it is the way the church ought to go about its business. So we have witnessed in recent years a whole host of film stars, athletes, politicians and other notables parading across Christendom's platforms to give their 'testimonies'. The logic behind this is quite clear: if leading figures endorse Christianity, we can expect the masses to do so.

God never does things the way we do. We shouldn't be surprised at this. God has told us as much: '"For My thoughts are not your thoughts, nor are your ways My ways," says the Lord' (Isa. 55:8). So when God started putting the church together at Corinth, he violated human standards and expectations by calling, not the élite of society, but the very dregs. Since they had never belonged to the élite group, one would not expect these dregs of society to feel any particular attachment to an élitist lifestyle. Irony of ironies — these Christians were actually seeking to reproduce in the church the characteristics of the élite of their society. Paul, therefore, found it necessary to remind them that their salvation was not due to human wisdom, so they should not be promoting and glorifying such wisdom in the church.

## What they were before they were saved

Paul makes this point by reminding them of three truths. First, he reminds them of what they were before they were saved. He uses three couplets to describe that state: not wise, but foolish; not mighty, but weak; and not noble, but base. The **'wise'** refers not only to those who were highly cultured and learned, but to those who took great pride in their culture and learning. The **'mighty'** refers to those who possessed power and authority and who wielded a great deal of influence in society. The **'noble'** refers to those who enjoyed high social standing by virtue of their birth. The Christians in Corinth, with only a few exceptions, were not wise, mighty, or noble. They were very ordinary people. They were, in Paul's words, foolish, weak and base. They had no position, no power and no pedigree.

What was true in Corinth has remained true down through the ages. Not many of the so-called 'upper crust' come to the saving knowledge of the Lord Jesus Christ. Thank God, Paul did allow for a few exceptions by saying 'not many' rather than 'not any'. This caused the Countess of Huntingdon, an Englishwoman of high social standing and great distinction, to observe that she owed her salvation to the letter 'M'. If Paul had said 'not any', she knew she would have been left out.[7]

It was quite absurd, in view of their low social standing, for these Corinthian Christians to have become so infatuated with human wisdom. But if the absurdity is apparent in the light of what they were before being saved, it becomes even more glaring when we stop to consider how they were saved.

## How they were saved

These people were not wise, so they didn't get their salvation by exercising their intellectual powers. They were not powerful, so they didn't get it by performing some great deed. They were not of noble birth, so they didn't get it because of birth. How, then, are we to explain such ordinary people being blessed with this greatest of all possible benefits — eternal life — while most of the wise, mighty and noble remained lost? Paul says it was because God deliberately chose to do his work in people who were, by all outward appearances, the most unlikely and the most unpromising.

The words **'calling'** (1:26) and **'chosen'** (1:27-28) make it clear that God graciously took the initiative in their salvation. And this is true with regard to every person who is saved. No one can take credit for salvation because it is God's work from beginning to end. Every child of God understands the lines of Augustus Toplady:

> Not to myself I owe,
> That I, O Lord, am thine;
> Free grace hath all the shades broke through
> And caused the light to shine.

The Bible says sinners are by nature blind (2 Cor. 4:4,6) and dead towards God (Eph. 2:1-5). What could anyone in such a state do to bring salvation? Absolutely nothing! If God had not graciously taken the initiative and moved towards us, we could never have moved towards him. Charles Wesley saw this truth and captured it in memorable verse:

> Long my imprisoned spirit lay
> Fast bound in sin and nature's night;
> Thine eye diffused a quickening ray,
> I woke, the dungeon flamed with light;
> My chains fell off, my heart was free,
> I rose, went forth, and followed thee.

**Why they were saved**

By stressing what they were before being saved and how they were saved, Paul dealt heavy blows to their practice of magnifying human wisdom. But he delivers his most decisive blow by emphasizing why they were saved. In saving them, God was essentially nullifying the very things they were magnifying, and he was magnifying the very thing they had been nullifying. In other words, God designed salvation so human wisdom and power would have no place and so **'no flesh should glory in His presence'** (1:29). If God had made salvation a matter of learning, power, or birth, men would have reason to boast and salvation would be impossible for ordinary people. But God's way takes away all these grounds and makes salvation available to all.

Consider how God has nullified the wisdom and power these Corinthian Christians were so impressed with. There is no greater wisdom than knowing God's truth and no greater power than that which delivers us from sin and makes us right with God.

It is precisely in these areas that man's wisdom and power have most miserably failed him. That is why Paul asked, 'Where is the wise man?' (1:20). In this business of knowing God and being forgiven by him, the wise man is nowhere to be found. And the same can be said of the man who wields great power and influence. But what man couldn't do with his wisdom and power, God has accomplished through his grace. He has shown that he is not only able to save the best among men, but to save the worst among them!

### Christ, the power and the wisdom of God

How did he go about doing this? Paul says it is all **'in Christ Jesus'** (1:30). Christ is the very wisdom and power of God because he has provided everything the best and worst of men need in order to know God and to stand clean before him. Paul summarizes what Christ provided in three words: **'righteousness'**, **'sanctification'** and **'redemption'**.

By 'righteousness', Paul means Christ has secured for the believer right standing before God. One has to be righteous to stand before a perfectly holy God. We have absolutely no righteousness of our own because we have broken the law of God innumerable times. But Christ, by living in perfect obedience to the law of God, has provided the righteousness God demands. That righteousness becomes what the hymn-writer, Count Zinzendorf, calls 'our glorious dress' when we repent of our sins and place our trust in Christ.

Christ is our 'sanctification'. He sets us apart for his holy purpose. He causes us to grow and matures us so we are increasingly weaned away from sin and increasingly devoted to him.

He is also our 'redemption'. There is coming a day when we shall finally be completely victorious over sin. We shall receive new bodies that will be like his glorious body (Phil. 3:21) and we shall live in a new heaven and a new earth (Rev. 21:1-4).

Therefore, in Christ we have righteousness to cover our past, sanctification to cover our present and redemption to cover our future. How great is God's wisdom and how marvellous is his power! There can be only one adequate response to that kind of wisdom and power, and it certainly isn't the parading and acclaiming of human leaders. God designed his salvation to eliminate that option completely. The only adequate response is, in the words of the apostle Paul, to **'glory in the Lord'** (1:31).

# 6.
# The character of preaching

*Please read 1 Corinthians 2:1-5*

The Corinthian church was tangled in the nasty business of exalting one preacher over another. To counter this, Paul argued first that the nature of the gospel is such that there is nothing for man to glory in. Then he argued that the nature of the believer's experience is such that there is nothing for him to glory in. Now Paul says the nature of preaching is such that there is nothing for man to glory in. Saving power is not to be found in the preacher of the Word any more than it is in the hearer of the Word. So Paul says exalting one preacher over another constitutes a complete misunderstanding of what preaching is all about.

Preaching is not intended to be something which glorifies men. It is not something to be used by men to gain the admiration and praise of their hearers. John Stott makes this painful point quite well: 'We must never show a reverence to ecclesiastical dignitaries which is due to God alone. Preachers are especially exposed to the danger of flattery. I fear that the whole frame of mind in which some Christian people go to church is wrong. They do not go to worship God or to hear God's Word. They go to hear a man. So it is not the message to which they listen, but the oratory.'[8]

What, then, is true preaching? According to Paul it consists of three elements: having the right message, the right method and the right motive.

## The message

Paul summarizes the right message in two phrases: **'the testimony of God'** and **'Jesus Christ and Him crucified'**. Together these phrases cover the source and content of the message.

*The source of the message*

'The testimony of God' reveals the divine authority behind the preacher's message. God's testimony is what he has revealed concerning himself. If our message is the testimony of God, then our trying to improve it by human wisdom and eloquence is like holding up a candle to help the sun shine.

It is not a matter of eloquence being inherently wrong. History is replete with accounts of eloquent preachers being mightily used of God. But the preacher must never allow himself to think his eloquence is sufficient to convert souls. The power to convert resides in the gospel, not in our eloquence (Rom. 1:16). If God's power resides there, so should our confidence.

Here lies the explanation for the weakness we see in our churches today. Our pulpits are filled with preachers who question the divine authority of the very message they are proclaiming. Is it any wonder our churches are filled with people who will not stand for anything and fall for everything?

Why is there is so little conviction of truth among church members in general and preachers in particular? The answer is that we, like the Corinthians, have been overly impressed with the intellectual accomplishments of our age. We seem to think the Bible is unable to compete with the latest scientific, technological knowledge. And our society is quick to detect our timidity about our message and eager to show the disdain it feels for people who still profess to believe in the truth of the Bible. They dismiss us with a knowing glance and a rueful shake of the head as though we didn't have a clue to the latest facts and, therefore, are deserving only of their pity.

In such a climate, it is all too easy to become self-conscious and embarrassed and even to think the cardinal doctrines of Christianity might be wrong. Before we know what has happened, we have succumbed to the subtle temptation to adjust our message to the so-called 'assured results of modern scholarship'. We may even find ourselves excusing our compromise of Christian truth by arguing that Paul didn't have to contend with our situation, and he would, if he were in our shoes, be in the vanguard of making Christianity acceptable and relevant.

But wait a minute. Think again of what it meant for Paul to renounce wisdom and eloquence at Corinth of all places. Corinth boasted that its institutions of learning and its philosophers excelled those of Rome and Athens. And Paul came to Corinth from Athens where his preaching of the gospel had been received with scepticism and ridicule (Acts 17:16-34). If ever there was a time for Paul to reconsider his message and adjust it to the prevailing intellectual climate, it was after he left Athens and before he arrived in Corinth. Paul knew full well if there was one place where excellency of speech and philosophy would be impressive it was at Corinth. We may even surmise that Paul spent a sleepless night wrestling with this very problem before launching his ministry there. However, when Paul began to preach in Corinth, it was without any of the appealing embellishments so popular there. It was the same old gospel he had preached everywhere else.

How are we to explain such stubbornness on the part of Paul? The answer is right here in these verses. Paul was convinced his gospel was God's own testimony and, as such, it was essential for Corinth. I, for one, don't expect to see real power return to our churches until Paul's conviction returns to our pulpits!

## The content of the message

Paul, then, believed in the divine authority of his message, that it had originated with none other than God himself. But what is this message? Paul summarizes it as 'Jesus Christ and Him crucified'. Paul isn't saying he preached only on the crucifixion of Christ as a historical event, but everything he did preach had Jesus' death as its point of reference. No other doctrine has any meaning apart from that because it is through Christ's death that God saves his people. The right message is the good news of salvation through the crucified Christ.

## The method

One can have the right message and still not be doing true preaching. A preacher must also have the right method. In short, the Christ of Calvary must be preached in the power of Pentecost. Paul's preaching at Corinth is an example of the correct method for all preachers. It featured neither eloquent style nor philosophical content. The omission of these elements was not a mere blunder or oversight on

Paul's part, but was his deliberate choice. He purposefully omitted eloquence and philosophy and came preaching **'in weakness, in fear, and in much trembling'**. In other words, Paul preached with a keen sense of his own inadequacy and utter dependence upon the Lord to carry the truth of the gospel home to human hearts.

Has it ever occurred to you that Paul would never be hired to pastor most of our churches today? We have a liking for the preachers who have wit, flash, charm and eloquence. Paul wouldn't rate very highly in this day and age because he just didn't have enough going for him. But one thing Paul did have — when he preached, the power of God fell! That alone puts him miles ahead of the powerless glamour boys in most pulpits. One look at the power of God attending Paul's preaching, and we surely feel compelled to pray, 'Oh, Lord, give us an epidemic of weakness, fear and trembling!'

How can we see a return to this much-needed power? The first step, as Stott suggests, is to humbly acknowledge our desperate need for it! [9]

Then we must make living holy lives our daily priority. It has been said before, but it bears repeating — the church is looking for better methods, but God is looking for better men. Only when holiness becomes our burning passion can we legitimately expect the Spirit of God to come upon us with the power Paul knew. True preaching combines the right message, which is Christ crucified, with the right method, preaching in the power of the Spirit. But there is still more. The preacher must also have the right motive.

## The motive

Paul says his motive in preaching to the Corinthians was that their faith **'should not be in the wisdom of men but in the power of God'**. In other words, Paul was saying he purposely designed his preaching to keep his hearers from trusting in his ability as a preacher. By glorying in various preachers, the Corinthians were doing the very thing Paul was most anxious to avoid! It is easy to see why Paul was intent on their faith not resting on him. Faith that depends upon a polished preacher and a clever argument is always at the mercy of a more polished preacher and a more astute argument. But faith that rests on the power of God will never have to worry about being outmoded.

## The secret of powerful preaching

We may summarize what Paul has said in the following truths. First, the way to convert people to Christ is to set forth the truth of the gospel. Secondly, the proper way to state the truth of the gospel is with a deep sense of insufficiency, realizing the success of the gospel depends, not on the skill of the preacher, but on the power of the Spirit. Thirdly, there is only one faith that converts sinners from the error of their ways and sets their feet on the path of life. That is the faith which comes to men through the power of God as the truth of God is preached.

C. H. Spurgeon captured those three lessons in these immortal words: 'The power that is in the gospel does not lie in the eloquence of the preacher; otherwise men would be converters of souls. Nor does it lie in the preacher's learning; otherwise it would consist in the wisdom of men. We might preach till our tongues rotted, till we should exhaust our lungs and die, but never a soul would be converted unless there were mysterious power going with it — the Holy Ghost changing the will of man.'[10]

# 7.
# A different kind of wisdom

*Please read 1 Corinthians 2:6-9*

The last half of the second chapter of 1 Corinthians brings before us two of the most important themes in all of the Bible: how the gospel is the wisdom of God, and how the work of the Holy Spirit is essential for man to understand the gospel. Failure to understand these two themes has created all sorts of havoc in society and in the church.

### The wisdom of God

Let's take up the first of these: how the gospel is the wisdom of God. There is no difficulty in understanding why Paul deals with this issue. He has been systematically dismantling the Corinthians' infatuation with human wisdom. He knew this was the root of the divisions in the church, and he didn't hesitate to unleash a blistering attack on it. Moreover, he has firmly declared his commitment to preach the gospel without any reliance on human wisdom.

Paul was an extremely brilliant man, and he knew his discussion up to this point had left a door open for some of his detractors. He knew some would be inclined to ask if he was trying to infer by his rebuke of human wisdom that there is no wisdom to be found in the gospel. In other words, Paul knew some of the Corinthians would say, 'Paul, if there's no room for wisdom in the gospel, what chance do we have of convincing people to accept it? Won't they rightly regard it as worthy of nothing but their contempt?'

In this passage, then, we have Paul closing the door he has left open. He says, in effect, that the gospel doesn't have to take a back seat to any other teaching in this matter of wisdom because it contains the very wisdom of God himself. His teaching up to this point has not been that there is no wisdom at all in the gospel of Christ, but only that it is a totally different kind of wisdom.

Do you see how vitally relevant it is for us to consider this passage? Isn't it true that many are dismissing the gospel because they see absolutely no wisdom in it at all? The reason they see no wisdom in it is because they are looking for the wrong kind! They are approaching it in terms of human wisdom, and they turn away from it without ever understanding that their human wisdom simply isn't sufficient when it comes to the things of God.

## The insufficiency of human wisdom

Man has his science and technology, his psychology and sociology, and he wants to judge the gospel of Christ on the basis of his knowledge in these areas. The problem is that this knowledge has absolutely nothing to do with the gospel. Oftentimes the church gets confused at this point and begins to fret over the fact that she seems unable to reach the intellectuals. When the church does this, she is simply failing to realize that the brilliant scientist with his Ph.D. is no better equipped to understand the gospel than the man in the street!

Stop and think about man's wisdom for a moment. How does he come by it? First, there are those things he concludes from observation. This is the 'stock in trade' of the scientist. He carefully observes how certain things cause certain consequences, and he draws his conclusions and writes out his scientific laws. In other words, he uses his eyes and his ears. Man also knows various things by intuition. Here we enter the realm of the poet. The poet knows what it is to have bursts of inspiration and flashes of insight. He functions on the basis of his heart.

Are you ready for what Paul says? Here it is: man's observation and intuition are utterly useless when it comes to the gospel of Christ. He says, **'Eye has not seen, nor ear heard, nor have entered into the heart of man, the things which God has prepared for those who love Him.'**

Why is this the case? Man is by nature totally depraved. That doesn't mean he is as bad as he can possibly be, but that there is no part of his existence that has escaped being tainted and tarnished by sin. His mind is darkened so that he cannot perceive the truth of God. His affections are degraded so he is unable to love the things of God. Even his will hasn't escaped the debilitating touch of sin. Left to himself, no one would even seek God (Rom. 3:10).

Do you want proof that man's wisdom is completely inadequate when it comes to the truth of God? Paul is ready to oblige. He says the **'rulers'**, or 'princes', of his own day had proved it beyond dispute. Who were these 'rulers'? They were those everyone regarded as wise. They were the leaders in every realm. If someone had been looking for people to figure out a complicated matter, he would have put his money on these folk. But what did they do with all their wisdom? Paul says they crucified **'the Lord of glory'**.

Isn't that amazing? Jesus Christ was the very Lord of glory and yet the smartest people of the day didn't recognize him. If they had recognized him, they would never have crucified him. He furnished them with all kinds of proofs and evidences, but they regarded him as an impostor and crucified him. So much for the track record of human wisdom!

### Truth that God himself must reveal

Why is human wisdom so totally helpless in this business of knowing the truth of God? Paul says it is because the truth of God is a mystery (2:7). We are all familiar with television mysteries in which some super-sleuth carefully observes, enquires and deduces until he or she has the answer in hand. But Paul isn't talking about this kind of mystery because he has already ruled out human observation and deduction as being sufficient. So what does this word 'mystery' mean? In the Bible a mystery is truth which is completely inaccessible to the unaided human mind. It is truth which God must reveal, or it would never be known. Human wisdom isn't sufficient to understand the gospel because it is a mystery. It consists of truth that God himself must reveal.

Paul mentions three things about the gospel that show how it contains the wisdom of God. The first is that *it was all planned before the world began*. Before there was a Garden of Eden, before there were any animals, before there was an Adam or an Eve, there was the gospel of Jesus Christ! The apostle Peter says Jesus was 'foreordained before the foundation of the world, but was manifest in these last times for you' (1 Peter 1:20). Would you have known that if God had not revealed it?

The second thing Paul says about the gospel is that *it was designed for the glory of all those who believe it.* God planned the gospel so believers could be forgiven of their sins and could eventually share all of his glory in heaven. The fact is that believers don't have to wait until heaven to know something of the glory of being delivered from their sins. There is tremendous glory in knowing the truth of the gospel and anticipating heaven.

> The men of grace have found
> Glory begun below;
> Celestial fruit on earthly ground
> From faith and hope may grow.

No wonder Paul couldn't quite contain himself and spoke jubilantly of 'the things which God has prepared for those who love Him'! Think about all these marvellous benefits the believer enjoys. Would any of us have known anything about any of them if we had been left to discover them on our own?

The third thing Paul says about the gospel is that *it centres on the Lord Jesus Christ.* Paul says the wise men of his day crucified 'the Lord of glory'. Have you stopped to think about that phrase? I'm sure Paul chose it quite deliberately for the express purpose of reminding the Corinthians of the very heart of the gospel. Jesus, you see, was no mere man. He was nothing less than the Son of God come from heaven. Before he ever stepped into this bleak world, he existed along with God. Not only was he with God, he was fully God himself. He was, as God, surrounded by all the glories of heaven and praised by the angelic hosts. But he left it all to become one of us.

Much of his time here he appeared as though he was nothing more than a man. He grew hungry, tired and thirsty. These are the things the religious leaders and princes saw. But the disciples of Jesus saw much more. When they looked at Jesus they saw his humanity, but they also saw the glory of God himself shining through the veil of that humanity. They saw so much of that glory, they couldn't help but know that this was indeed the very 'Lord of glory'.

Would you have ever in a million years figured out a plan of salvation such as this? God's own Son left the glories of heaven to render perfect obedience to God and to bear the wrath of God against sinners by dying on the cross. This is the very wisdom of God himself at work and you will never be able to understand it on your own. How could God become man? How could he be born of a virgin? How could his death satisfy a just and holy God? How could he possibly have risen from the dead? How can God be three, yet one? Try to figure these things out on your own and you will fail because they are completely in a different realm! But forsake your own wisdom and cast yourself wholeheartedly upon these truths, and you will find in Paul's own words 'joy unspeakable and full of glory'.

# 8.
# God's wisdom revealed by the Spirit

*Please read 1 Corinthians 2:9-16*

The gospel is a mystery. That means we are incapable of comprehending it with our own wisdom. Take the most brilliant man you can find and he will be utterly unable to understand the gospel on his own.

Are there any, then, who comprehend the gospel? Multitudes throughout history have claimed to understand it, as do multitudes today. How is it possible for these people to comprehend the gospel when untold millions have been, and are, completely in the dark about it? The answer is that those who comprehend it have been 'initiated' by the Holy Spirit himself. Paul says of the truths of the gospel, **'But God has revealed them to us through His Spirit'** (2:10). Later he adds: **'Now we have received, not the spirit of the world, but the Spirit who is from God, that we might know the things that have been freely given to us by God'** (2:12).

Believers, then, understand the gospel because they have been initiated into it by the Holy Spirit. This point is made clear by William Barclay's definition of a mystery : '... something whose meaning is hidden from those who have not been initiated, but which is crystal clear to those who have'.[11]

Paul stresses three things about the Holy Spirit's work in initiating believers into the gospel. First, he points out the basis of this work. Secondly, he reveals the instrument the Holy Spirit uses to accomplish this. Finally, he shows the result of the Holy Spirit's work of initiation.

## The basis of the Spirit's work

We may summarize what Paul says about the basis of the Holy
Spirit's work of initiation in two words — competence and correspondence. The competence of the Holy Spirit for revealing the
truth of God arises from his perfect comprehension of that truth. And
his perfect comprehension of that truth arises from his correspondence to the nature of God.

The perfect comprehension of the Holy Spirit is set forth when
Paul says the Holy Spirit **'searches ... the deep things of God'**
(2:10). This means the Holy Spirit has explored and examined the
deepest recesses of the mind of God. There is absolutely nothing
about God that the Holy Spirit has not fathomed.

Did you catch that phrase, **'the deep things of God'**? That is how
Paul describes this gospel that remains hidden from man's wisdom.
Christians seem to fall into two extremes on the depths of God's
truths. For some, the gospel is too deep and they wonder why
preachers and teachers cannot keep things simple. For others, the
gospel is too simple. These feel they have outgrown it and are
always looking for something more exotic and profound. Paul's
phrase is a rebuke to both. The gospel is not so simple that it contains
no depths. However, the depths it does contain are such that there is
no need to look for something more profound.

The reason the Holy Spirit is able to comprehend these 'deep
things' perfectly is the exact correspondence between him and God.
How exact is this correspondence? Paul says it is as complete as the
correspondence between a man and his own mind (2:11). It is so
complete that no one else knows what a man is thinking unless he
chooses to reveal it. Matthew Henry says, 'The man knows his own
mind because his mind is one with himself. The Spirit of God knows
the things of God because He is one with God.'[12]

Here we come face to face with the Bible's teaching on the
Trinity. God is one God, but three persons — Father, Son and Holy
Spirit. Because he is God himself, the Holy Spirit knows the things
of God exhaustively and reveals them accurately.

## The instrument the Spirit uses

Paul was not content simply to explain why the Holy Spirit is
capable of revealing God's truth. He also went into detail about the

way in which the Holy Spirit accomplishes this. He says, **'These things** [i.e. the truths revealed by the Holy Spirit] **we also speak, not in words which man's wisdom teaches but which the Holy Spirit teaches, comparing spiritual things with spiritual'** (2:13).

To understand this we need to start with that phrase, 'We also speak.' Sometimes in this passage Paul's 'we' refers to believers in general, but to whom does it refer here? There really can be very little doubt Paul is talking about himself as an apostle of Jesus Christ. We have to remember this chapter begins with his declaration of how he had chosen to conduct his ministry as an apostle. That sets the tone for everything that follows. Of course, what Paul says here of himself applies equally to all the other apostles, so it was quite natural for him to say, 'We speak.'

Paul, then, is claiming that the Holy Spirit revealed the truth of God through the ministry of the apostles. A little later, he claims the apostolic office amounts to having **'the mind of Christ'** (2:16). Paul and the other apostles knew the content of Christ's mind: his thoughts, his plans and purposes and the self-sacrificing spirit that motivated him (Phil. 2:5-11). All of this the apostles knew, not because they had been able to figure it all out by their own intellectual prowess, but because it had been given to them by the Holy Spirit.

But what does this have to do with us? The apostles are long gone. If there are no apostles today, how is it possible for the Holy Spirit to initiate us into the truth of the gospel? The answer is that the apostles themselves committed to writing the revelation they received from the Spirit of God. In the New Testament, we have the essence of what the apostles received, what Paul calls the **'words which the Holy Spirit teaches, comparing spiritual things with spiritual'**.

Another way of putting it is to say the New Testament consists of spiritual truths placed in spiritual words. Do you realize what you have in that Bible of yours? It is nothing less than the finished product of the Spirit of God revealing the truth of God! It is the Spirit of God himself opening up before our eyes the deep things of God! It is the Holy Spirit leading us into the innermost chambers of the knowledge of God! It is 'the mind of Christ' revealed to us! How blessed we are to have the Word of God!

This Word of God is the tool the Spirit uses when he initiates someone into the gospel. And other Scriptures assure us this is so. Paul declares to the Romans, 'So then faith comes by hearing, and hearing by the word of God' (Rom. 10:17). James adds, 'Of His own will He brought us forth by the word of truth' (James 1:18). And Peter agrees that we are born again 'through the word of God which lives and abides for ever' (1 Peter 1:23).

Christian, stop and think about it for a minute. How did you learn of your sin? Wasn't it from the Word of God? How did you find out that God is holy and your sinful nature caused you to stand justly condemned before him? Wasn't it from the Word of God? How did you discover that this same God is a God of matchless grace and that he has made through his Son's death on the cross a way for you to be forgiven of your sins? Wasn't it through the Word of God?

William R. Newell captured all of this in his much-loved hymn, 'At Calvary':

> Years I spent in vanity and pride,
> Caring not my Lord was crucified,
> Knowing not it was for me he died
>     On Calvary.
>
> By God's Word at last my sin I learned;
> Then I trembled at the law I'd spurned,
> Till my guilty soul imploring turned
>     To Calvary.

## The result of the Spirit's work

That brings us to consider, finally, the result of the Spirit's work of initiation. In short, it creates what Paul calls the spiritual man. This person is marked by two qualities: he **'judges all things'**, but he cannot be judged by anyone else (2:15).

What does Paul mean by saying the spiritual person 'judges all things'? His point is that the believer operates in two realms — the natural and the spiritual. The natural man's discernment is limited to the things of this world (2:14). The believer, like the unbeliever, is able to discern the things of this world, but there the similarity ends. The believer, drawing from what he knows of spiritual things, has a completely different attitude to, and judgement of, this world. He sees through the world and recognizes it for what it really is.

What about the second quality of the spiritual person? Paul says the believer is 'rightly judged by no one'. What does that mean? Simply, the believer is a puzzle to the unbeliever. The believer, because he operates in two realms, can understand the unbeliever; however, the unbeliever, operating in only one realm, cannot understand the believer. He sees the believer going to church and he fails to understand the attraction of it. He might even go to church himself to see what the believer finds there, and when he gets there he finds himself absolutely befuddled by it all. The singing of praises to God, the praying to God, the preaching of God's Word — it all seems utterly absurd to him. He sees the believer denying himself the pleasures of sin and he is mystified.

Do you find yourself here? Are you puzzled and mystified by Christianity? If so, it is because you are still in the darkness of sin. The Holy Spirit hasn't performed his work in you. But don't despair. If you find yourself desiring to know more about God and desiring to have what the believer has, that is an indication that the Holy Spirit has begun his work in you. Ask the Spirit of God for his help! Renounce your sins! Trust completely in Jesus Christ! Do these things and you will be brought into this family that understands the glorious wisdom of God.

# 9.
# The responsibility of the minister

*Please read 1 Corinthians 3:1-9*

Are you ready for a profound theological principle? Here it is: fuzziness leads to friction! The church of Corinth had plenty of friction. One group of members had selected one preacher as their favourite and were clustering around him, while other members had selected another and were clustering around him. It appears there were at least four factions or 'clusters' in the church, each one considering itself to be superior to the others and looking upon the rest with disdain and suspicion.

Paul wanted them to know it was not spiritual superiority that created all this friction. On the contrary, it was all due to fuzziness in their thinking in two critical areas: the nature of the gospel and the nature of the gospel ministry.

I wish I could say the Corinthians were the last group of Christians to be perplexed and confused on these two subjects, but I can't. Satan has always concentrated on befogging the minds of the saints on these central themes, and he has certainly been very active in this respect in our day. This is the day of fuzzy preachers preaching a fuzzy gospel to fuzzy believers.

Paul's discussion up to this point has been designed to lift the fog from the nature of the gospel. In chapters 3 and 4 he turns to lift it from the nature of the ministry. He does so by making use of several metaphors, two of which appear in the passage before us.


## The minister as a servant

First, he pictures the minister as a servant in God's family (3:1-5). Paul puts it in these words: **'What then is Apollos? And what is**

**Paul? Servants through whom you believed, even as the Lord gave opportunity to each one'** (3:5, NASB).

What does it mean to be a servant? Doesn't the word 'servant' convey the idea of inferiority? A servant is under someone's authority. And doesn't the word also carry the idea of instrumentality? The servant exists to carry out the wishes of the one who exercises authority over him. The inferiority of the servant is conveyed by Paul's use of 'what' instead of 'who'. No, this wasn't just a slip of the pen. Paul always chose his words deliberately, and his use of 'what' was his way of minimizing the personalities of the preachers and laying stress on their lowly position. Even if Paul had not chosen the word 'what', his point would still have been clear. The word 'servants' is in itself sufficient to convey inferiority. It is the word *'diakonoi'*, which means 'table waiters'. It is, by the way, the word from which we translate our word 'deacon'. Having stressed the minister's inferiority, Paul turns to his instrumentality by saying they are 'servants through whom you believed'. Please notice Paul doesn't say they are servants *from* whom you believed, as if preachers were the originators or authors of faith. Neither does he say they are servants *in* whom you believed, as if preachers were the objects of faith.

That word 'through', then, shows us ministers are instruments or channels for God to do his work. Preachers do not provide or apply the gospel, they simply serve as a mouthpiece for it. That is how it is with the servant. He exists simply to implement the wishes of his master. The master assigns a task and the servant performs it.

Although Paul doesn't use the word 'servants' until the fifth verse, he seems to have the metaphor in mind at the outset of this passage. He pictures himself as a table waiter for the Corinthians and describes the service he provided for them.

At the beginning of his ministry among them he served milk. This was necessary because they were mere babes in Christ. It was perfectly natural for them at that time to desire milk. Peter's words come to mind: 'Like newborn babes, long for the pure milk of the word, that by it you may grow in respect of salvation' (1 Peter 2:2, NASB).

By **'milk'**, neither Peter nor Paul was indicating that new Christians need different doctrine from the mature Christian. Each needs the same doctrine, but new Christians need it in a simpler form. 'For the same Christ,' says Calvin, 'is milk for babes, and solid food for adults.'[13] More than enough time had passed for the

Corinthians to stop drinking milk and start eating meat. And Paul, as their servant, was prepared to serve them meat, but they were still unable to receive it.

It is fine for babies to be babies, but it is a tragedy for adults to act like babies. And that was what was happening at Corinth. Their division into camps and the jealousy and strife between these camps gave sufficient evidence of their childishness. Paul says they were 'carnal' and 'behaving like mere men'. This simply means they were guided by the same principles as unbelievers, rather than being guided by the Spirit of God.

Paul's words have been misconstrued by some to mean that there are three basic groups of people: the unsaved, or the natural man (1 Cor. 2:14); the saved, or the spiritual man (1 Cor. 2:15); and the carnal man. The latter is supposedly a person who is a believer but lives like an unbeliever. Much harm has been done by this particular teaching. Many are quite happy to occupy the level of this so-called 'carnal' Christian. They are content to believe they can live like an unbeliever and still go to heaven when they die. Paul's point was that the Corinthians were acting carnally at this particular time in their lives. He wasn't suggesting that carnality was the general tenor of their lives. If we are carnal habitually, it is because we have never been converted.

The minister, then, is responsible to serve others, but he is not able to make babies into adults overnight, nor is he able to keep adults from acting like babies from time to time. That seems to be the essence of what Paul was saying by using the metaphor of the servant.

### The minister as a farmer

Having said these things, the apostle changes metaphors and refers to the minister as a farmer in God's field (3:6-9). The church is God's farm or field (v. 9), and in this field God has many labourers. Some are planting while others are watering, but all are engaged in the work of farming. So there is diversity within unity here. Ministers have different gifts but are all engaged in the same task. They can take no credit for the planting or the watering because God is the only one who can cause growth (3:6).

This understanding of the minister's work is sorely needed. We are inclined to think the minister is responsible for the increase. This thinking has practically turned our churches into business institutions, with the people as stockholders, committees as boards of directors and the minister as the chief executive officer. Sadly enough, pastors have been so consumed with growing large, prestigious churches that they have actually encouraged the business pattern.

As far as the Bible is concerned, the minister's job is not to be successful, but to be faithful in spreading the gospel. Some will be more adept at planting while others will be better at watering, but whatever his rôle, the minister is to be faithful and simply trust God for the results.

When the farmer goes out in the spring he has no idea what kind of harvest he will reap in the autumn. He just goes about his business of planting and cultivation. He doesn't get too worked up over the weather because 'He who observes the wind will not sow, and he who regards the clouds will not reap' (Eccl. 11:4). The farmer, therefore, simply works hard and leaves the rest to God.

If the minister functions in this way, God will reward him **'according to his own labour'** (3:8). Thank God it is our labour, not the results of it, that forms the basis for reward. Benjamin L. Warfield writes, 'What a consolation this is to the obscure workman to whom God has given much labour and few results...'[14]

These metaphors are designed to show how foolish it is to exalt one preacher over another. Richard Lenski states: 'The Corinthians acted as if these ministers were theirs, to be measured and weighed at pleasure, to be exalted or to be lowered, to be rewarded with praise or to be chastised with criticism. Paul takes these ministers out of their hands, they are God's, doing his work under his special call and commission.'[15]

The proper way to honour ministers is look to the God who sent them. If you are not a Christian, look to him in repentance and faith. He will forgive you and place you in his family. If you are a Christian, look to him for grace to grow into maturity. The true preacher is happiest when his hearers look beyond him to the God he loves and serves.

# 10.
# The preacher as a builder

*Please read 1 Corinthians 3:10-15*

The popular interpretation of this passage has it addressing the individual Christian. Each Christian, according to this view, is building some sort of Christian life. Some are using good materials, while others are using inferior materials. At the Judgement Seat of Christ, each Christian's building will be tested by fire; those who built well will be rewarded while those who built poorly will suffer loss.

While this passage contains teachings that are applicable to individual Christians, it must be noted that their primary application is to the gospel minister and the way in which he goes about his ministry. In the first nine verses, Paul employed the metaphors of servant and farmer to convey the true nature of the minister's work. Now he moves to the minister as a builder. Twice in this chapter Paul likens the Corinthians to a building (3:9,16) and he calls himself **'a wise master builder'** (3:10). The others who had ministered at Corinth were building on the foundation he had put in place, and Paul wanted them to be very conscientious about the kind of building they were putting up.

## Building on the foundation

What is necessary for a minister to do a good job of building? First, he must build on the foundation. Those who deal with this passage quite often slip into saying the minister must build on the *right* foundation, as if there were several from which to choose. But Paul says no such thing. The fact is, there is only one foundation and that is Jesus Christ. Paul says, **'For no other foundation can anyone lay than that which is laid, which is Jesus Christ'** (3:11). The choice for the minister, then, is not between several foundations but between the only foundation and no foundation at all.

We all know what would happen if we were to build a house without any kind of foundation. It wouldn't stand very long, and it certainly wouldn't be very sturdy while it did stand! So it is with the ministry that is not built on Christ. It will not be very sturdy and will collapse somewhere along the line. If it doesn't collapse here, it will in eternity.

All of this can also be applied to the individual. In the Sermon on the Mount, Jesus says some build their house on a rock while others build on sand. In other words, some have a foundation while others do not. Those who have the foundation are the ones who are able to endure the storms of life and those without the foundation collapse. What is the foundation? It is the same as in Paul's writings — the teachings of the Lord Jesus or, if you like, Jesus himself (Matt. 7:24-27). Nothing of lasting value can be built apart from Jesus Christ! That is the great truth insisted upon by Scripture, no matter where we turn.

## The materials used for building

But having said there is only one foundation for the minister to build upon, Paul turns his attention to the kind of materials the minister should use in building on this foundation (3:12-15). He divides the materials into two kinds: the valuable, lasting materials — gold, silver and precious stones, and the worthless, perishable materials — wood, hay and stubble. We understand, of course, that Paul is using these materials in a representative or symbolical way. He is not suggesting we build our church buildings out of gold, silver and precious stones! He is thinking about how the church is built in a spiritual sense.

But just what do these materials represent? Many think they represent people, and Paul is, therefore, urging ministers to build the church out of people who truly know the Lord. While this is unquestionably a biblical emphasis, I think it misses the point. One of the great rules of biblical interpretation is to let Scripture interpret Scripture. As far as this passage is concerned, we should look at other scriptures that use these building materials in a metaphorical sense. When we do so, we find gold, silver and gems are often used as emblems for the Word of God (Ps. 19:10; 119:72; Prov. 2:1-5; 3:13-15; 8:10-11). Compared to the Word of God, all other teachings are mere chaff (Jer. 23:28).

I suggest, therefore, that these building materials represent the teachings or doctrines of the minister. The gold, silver and precious stones represent, in the words of John Gill, 'the great, momentous, and valuable truths of the gospel, which agree with and are suitable to the foundation they are built upon'.[16]

The Word of God, then, is the primary component in the work of the minister. It is food for the family (3:1-4), seed for the field (3:5-9) and materials for the building.

But what about the wood, hay and stubble? They represent doctrines that are not completely false — because they are, after all, built on the foundation of Christ — but rather 'mixed' doctrine. In other words, the true doctrines of Christ are mixed with all sorts of cheap, empty trivialities and vain speculations.

This, you see, was the root of the problems at Corinth. The people in the church had mixed teachings from the various schools of philosophy with the gospel. They hadn't denied the gospel, but they certainly had diluted it. Paul's desire was to help them see what had already happened and to put them on their guard against any preachers who would serve up a diluted gospel in the future.

Do we have any preachers building with wood, hay and stubble? Are today's preachers prone to dilute the gospel with human wisdom? Isn't it true, for instance, that many preachers quote the so-called 'findings' of modern psychiatry with as much, if not more, confidence as they quote the Bible? Don't many preachers downplay themes like the holiness of God and the sinfulness of man and dwell instead on how to cope with life's minor aggravations and irritations? Isn't it true that many preachers cultivate a style that is more like a comedy act than the preaching of the gospel?

The problem is not that these preachers do not believe in the gospel, but rather that they consider the gospel to need help in reaching sophisticated people. Yes, Paul called the gospel 'the power of God to salvation' (Rom. 1:16), but Paul didn't have to compete with modern knowledge and technology! Such seems to be the thinking of many a preacher.

### 'The Day will declare it'

Preachers who mix worldly wisdom with the preaching of the gospel don't realize they are building defectively; however, that is exactly what they are doing, and some day it will be made clear to them. Defectiveness in building cannot remain hidden very long. Paul says a day is coming when **'Each one's work will become manifest; for the Day will declare it, because it will be revealed by fire; and the fire will test each one's work, of what sort it is'** (3:13).

What is this day? Some interpreters think it is the day of trial or crisis, and they refer to Peter speaking of the 'fiery trial' (1 Peter 4:12). No doubt, the trials and troubles of life do make us feel we are walking through fire and only the true gospel is sufficient to help us face such things. Defective doctrine always fails when it runs up against the hardships of life.

However, most interpreters think Paul is referring to the day when all Christians must stand before the Lord to give account of themselves. On that day, those who have preached defective doctrines will **'suffer loss'**, that is, they will lose any reward for their ministry, but they themselves will be **'saved ... through fire'** (3:15). The picture here is of the building the minister has built going up in flames while he escapes with his life.

The minister who has built well, on the other hand, will receive a reward (3:14). What is the nature of this reward? Some always associate rewards with crowns, and they visualize Christians strolling around heaven with stacks of crowns on their heads. But the greatest of all possible rewards is simply to hear the Saviour say, 'Well done, good and faithful servant' (Matt. 25:21).

Ours is the day of casual ministers preaching trivial sermons to nonchalant church members. How we need Paul's words! They ought to shake us and drive us to our knees! It could be that the spiritual awakening we so desperately need will begin with preachers realizing afresh the awesome responsibility that is theirs!

The responsibility for building with good materials rests primarily upon the preacher, but it does not rest exclusively on him. Each Christian has the responsibility to be discerning and watchful so he can detect and shun the defective minister and can cherish and support the faithful servant of God.

# 11.
# Destructive ministers and deceived believers

*Please read 1 Corinthians 3:16-23*

The church is like a building and ministers are like builders. The foundation on which the church is built has already been provided and the builders, therefore, must simply concern themselves with building on it. What is this foundation? It is none other than the Lord Jesus Christ himself. It is important for the minister not only to realize that Christ is the foundation of the church, but also that there is no other possible foundation. Paul says, 'For no other foundation can anyone lay than that which is laid, which is Jesus Christ' (3:11).

Even having Christ as the foundation is no guarantee the building itself will be what it ought to be. According to Paul, there are three dangers that threaten the building of the church. One, as we saw in the previous chapter, is defective builders. These are ministers who build on the foundation of Christ but do so with inferior materials. They bring in doctrines that do not correspond to the foundation. The passage before us now brings us face to face with the other dangers: destructive ministers and deceived believers.

## Destructive ministers

The danger of destructive ministers is forcefully brought before us in verses 16 and 17. It is easy to read through these two verses with the idea that Paul is still talking about ministers building defectively, but close examination reveals that he isn't. When the day of accounting comes, defective builders will suffer loss but will themselves be saved (3:15). The destructive ministers, on the other hand, will be destroyed (3:17).

Destructive ministers — what an unsavoury thought! So unpleasant is it that many have virtually denied the possibility of it. They seem to assume false preachers are easily detected and, never having detected any, they conclude that they do not exist. Others believe there are destructive ministers, but they all belong to denominations other than their own. In their opinion, Satan couldn't be clever enough to slip false preachers into their own denomination.

No matter how much we want to avoid this issue, it simply will not go away. The sad truth is that the church has always been afflicted with ministers who do not build anything at all, but simply wait for others to build so they can move in to tear down. It is also true that no church is automatically immune to the danger of destructive preachers.

How do these preachers go about their destructive work? They deny the central truths of the gospel, those truths which God has promised to use to build up the church. The sinfulness of man, the holiness of God, the atoning death of Jesus Christ on the cross, the absolute necessity of the work of the Holy Spirit in the hearts of men, the changed conduct of those who receive Christ — these are the truths God himself has revealed and blessed down through the years.

It is these very truths that cause the destructive minister no small amount of consternation, and he begins to modify and trim them to suit himself. By the time he has finished, man is not sinful but basically good. Any evil he does is due to some flaw in his education or environment. And God is so full of sentimental love for man that he couldn't possibly condemn sin. The cross of Christ, therefore, has nothing to do with sin, but only expresses the love of God. So it goes on until Christianity is completely gutted and all that remains is the empty shell.

How are we to explain ministers who are set apart to preach the gospel yet do such violence to it? Paul gives us the answer. He says the basic problem with destructive ministers is twofold: they are overawed with the wisdom of their own age and they have absolutely no appreciation for what is sacred.

Again in this passage (3:18-20), Paul sounds the alarm about accepting human wisdom at face value and setting it above the wisdom of God. This is exactly what destructive ministers do. Never mind what the Bible says, their concern is what the latest poll says!

While they warn incessantly about the dangers of 'fundamental-ism', they are completely oblivious to their own obsession with the latest trends.

The moment we paste the label 'sacred' on the wisdom of the world, we remove it from where God placed it. God's Word claims sacredness for itself (2 Tim. 3:15), but the destructive minister doesn't hesitate to seize any scripture and twist it to suit his whims. Any passage that disturbs him can easily be dismissed as nothing more than the biblical author reflecting the limited views of his own age.

The church itself is sacred or holy, so Paul declares in this passage. Individual Christians are indwelt by the Holy Spirit. Therefore, the church as a whole is indwelt by the Spirit and is the temple of God (3:16-17). But the destructive minister doesn't hesitate to bring into the church his own scepticism and doubt and unleash them! Any minister who is overawed by his own wisdom and lacking in awe for what is holy can do nothing other than distort the Bible and destroy the church!

## Deceived believers

Nothing is easier, however, than bewailing the presence of defective and destructive ministers in the church. Christians almost seem to enjoy rehearsing all the corruption in the ministry today. If the Corinthians were in the mood to do the same, Paul's next words surely brought them up short. He knew these ministers had begun to flourish in the life of the church because God's people had not been as discerning as they should have been. So he turns from the ministers and trains his sights on believers in general. His phrase, 'If anyone among you . . .', takes in the whole church and begins his emphasis on deceived believers (vv. 18-23).

### Exalting human wisdom

In this section, Paul seems to suggest the Corinthians themselves had flung wide open the door through which the defective and destructive ministers were pouring. First, they had been deceived into cuddling up to the wisdom of their day and, in doing so, had placed it above the Word of God. That was tantamount to rolling out the red carpet for false preachers. We tend to think the pew always follows the pulpit; that is, that preachers preach and the people believe and act accordingly. Often, however, it is just the opposite and the pulpit follows the pew. Let preachers discover the people value anything less than the Word of God, and, eager to appear successful, they will fill the pews by giving the hearers what they want. Demand determines supply!

Paul, aware of this tendency, issues the stern reminder that the appealing wisdom of this world is utter foolishness as far as God is concerned, and he will eventually trip up those enamoured of wisdom. How? By using the very wisdom they so admire (3:19). If we trust human wisdom and place it above the Word of God, we are writing our own ticket to misery and woe! On the other hand, if we have a low opinion of our own wisdom and will submit to God's wisdom as it is revealed in Holy Scripture, we will find true satisfaction (3:18).

## Exalting man

Paul also implies that the Corinthians had opened the door to defective and destructive ministers by glorying in men (3:21-23). They looked upon their preachers in much the same way as people today look upon athletes and film stars. What can a preacher do when he is thrust into a situation in which he must 'outdo' others in order to be popular and have a following? Quite obviously, he begins to look for something new or different that will set him apart from the others. One way to gain notoriety as a preacher is to discover and begin preaching a new doctrine. The problem is that the whole idea of new doctrine runs counter to the nature of God's truth, which is, according to Jude, 'once for all delivered to the saints' (Jude 3).

## The privileges they failed to appreciate

The thing the Corinthians had failed to see was that by glorying in preachers they were cheating themselves. Paul says it was foolish for them to exalt one preacher when God had given them all! In fact, he goes so far as to say that not only preachers, but the world, life, death, things present and things to come all exist for the benefit and welfare of the church!

Paul's words make us scratch our heads in amazement. How could he say everything, including death itself, belongs to the church? Matthew Henry explains: 'Life is yours, that you may have season and opportunity to prepare for the life of heaven; death is yours, that you may go to the possession of it. It is the kind messenger that will fetch you to your Father's house. Things present are yours, for your support on the road; things to come are yours, to enrich and regale you for ever at your journey's end.'[17]

What a privilege it is to be a child of God! And how little we understand about this privilege!

But how does one get to be a child of God? How does one secure this highest of all privileges? Paul wraps it all up in one neat little package: **'And you are Christ's, and Christ is God's'** (3:23).

The Christian is one who has submitted to Jesus Christ. He belongs to Christ! And Christ is the one who voluntarily submitted himself to God's plan of salvation. He left the glories of heaven, became a man, lived a perfect life, received on the cross the penalty for sinners, and arose from the grave — and he did it all in submission to God's plan to redeem helpless sinners. Submit to this Christ who submitted himself to God, and you will ultimately discover the truth of Paul's statement: 'All things are yours.'

# 12.
# The minister as a steward

*Please read 1 Corinthians 4:1-6*

How should Christians regard preachers of the gospel? That is the question to which Paul turns in this passage. It is easy to see why it was necessary for him to take up this matter. He has devoted considerable space to urging the Corinthians not to exalt one preacher over the others and to warning about defective and destructive ministers. He knew some would misconstrue his words and conclude preachers are indeed a sorry lot and are not worthy of even a smidgen of respect. In other words, Paul was aware of the pendulum mentality. He knew some would, in the light of his words, swing all the way from preacher worship to preacher disdain.

That is exactly where many Christians find themselves today, and it is not surprising. The ministry has always seemed to attract scoundrels and scandals, but never to the degree we see today. Preachers seem utterly committed to destroying the very cause they are called to espouse by plunging headlong into moral collapse, doctrinal error, dictatorial leadership, shady business dealings and sheer laziness.

But, thank God, these things are not true of all preachers! Many fail to keep this in mind, and blanket statements about preachers abound. Tragically, many preachers who are sound in doctrine, pure in life and energetic in service find themselves tarred with the same brush as worthless preachers. People in general are not capable of distinguishing between unworthy and worthy preachers; however, God's people should be able to distinguish between them and should shun the unworthy while supporting and loving the worthy.

Paul wanted the Corinthians to have discernment at this point. He wanted them to see there was nothing wrong with prizing preachers of the gospel. True, preachers are not to be elevated beyond what they are. Paul says we are not to think of preachers **'beyond what is written'** (4:6), but preachers are still to be prized and valued. The wrong comes in exalting one preacher over another when both are sound in doctrine and pure in life. When that happens, the followers of one preacher always become **'puffed up'** against the followers of other preachers (4:6).

Our discernment will be sharpened on this vital matter of how to regard the preacher by paying careful heed to what Paul says in this passage. First, he brings before us the responsibility of the minister (4:1-2), and then he turns to deal with the accountability of the minister (4:3-5).

## The minister's responsibility

He gathers up the responsibility of the minister in two phrases: **'servants of Christ'** and **'stewards of the mysteries of God'**.

### Servants of Christ

The Greek word translated 'servants' is *'huperetes'*. The same word is used in Luke 4:20 and Acts 13:5, where it is translated 'attendant' or 'assistant'. R. C. H. Lenski says, 'To the Greeks the term meant only an attendant or helper who assists a higher master. In this case, Christ is that master. Every apostle and every minister and pastor is only an underling, a helper, or an attendant of Christ. His sole function is to take orders and at once and without question to execute them. His will is only that of his Master.'[18]

If Paul was trying to create respect for preachers, he certainly went about it in a strange way! This picture seems only to encourage people to despise and disdain ministers! That must be the inevitable conclusion if we just focus on the word 'servants', but how the picture changes when we take into account the other half of the phrase, 'of Christ'!

The point is that the preacher has no worth or value in and of himself, but his office still has great value because he is serving none other than the Lord Jesus Christ himself! The minister is not great, but he represents and serves a great Saviour!

*Stewards*

Paul also calls ministers 'stewards of the mysteries of God'. We have already encountered the word 'mystery' (2:7). It refers to truth which can never be discovered by man himself, but can only be known by God revealing it.

But what does this word 'steward' mean? This word takes us back to a very common part of the culture of that time. John MacArthur says the steward was 'a person placed in complete control of a household'. He goes on to say, 'The steward supervised the property, the fields and vineyards, the finances, the food, and the other servants on behalf of his master.'[19]

*The preacher's task*

When we put the words 'servant' and 'steward' together, this is what we have: the preacher is one who dispenses to the family of God the truths revealed by God and he supervises the family according to the wishes of the master. The indispensable ingredient for being a steward was faithfulness to the master of the house (4:2). The steward had absolutely no authority of his own but simply administered the household in accordance with the wishes of the master.

How preachers and churches need to get this picture firmly in mind! God has revealed a body of truth in Scripture. It is the job of the preacher to see to it that the church receives a balanced diet from what the Lord has provided in Scripture. It is not the place of the preacher to make up his own truth but simply to preach what the Lord has revealed. If the preacher thinks he knows more than the Lord and departs from the truths revealed by the Lord, he is unfaithful and not fit to be a preacher. Many preachers are failing right here. They concern themselves with what the people want to hear, and not with what God wants the people to hear. A good preacher will have the utmost faith in the wisdom of the Master, and he will always seek to be utterly faithful to dispense what the Master has provided. He will constantly strive to reach the point where he can honestly say with Paul, 'For I have not shunned to declare to you the whole counsel of God' (Acts 20:27).

## The minister's accountability

This brings us quite naturally and inevitably to Paul's emphasis on the accountability of the minister (4:3-5). Why does the good minister concern himself with faithfulness to God? Because he knows he must someday give account of himself to God.

When the preacher keeps his eye on the final reckoning with the Master, certain things automatically occur. First, he learns to discount *congregational pressure*. Paul was able to say the evaluation of the critical, judgemental Corinthians was **'a very small thing'** to him (4:3). He wasn't trying to be arrogant, and he certainly wasn't saying he had no sensitivity to others. He was simply registering his deep conviction that he could not serve God effectively if he constantly concerned himself with what people thought of him. This doesn't mean the preacher is above criticism, but it does mean he must not let criticism from others be the determining factor in what he preaches and in how he conducts his ministry.

The final reckoning with the Master will also cause the minister to discount *cultural pressures*. Paul also calls 'a very small thing' the judgement of 'any human court'. The Greek word for 'court' is *'hemera'*, which is usually translated 'day'. This has led some to conclude that Paul was referring to the thinking of his day, that is, the thinking of his culture.

If that is the case, it comes as a very timely word to the modern crop of preachers who are so eager to scoop up and carry into the pulpit the latest survey and the newest trend. Such preachers forget the thinking of the world is always changing, and if one becomes married to the latest intellectual fad, he will be forever in the divorce court!

Finally, the day of reckoning with the Master will cause the preacher even to discontinue *personal pressure*. Paul goes so far as to say, **'In fact, I do not even judge myself'** (4:3). Paul is not saying he never thought about his ministry, or he never tried to evaluate it. If that were the case, he would not have been able to go on to say he knew nothing against himself (4:4). His point is simply that it is extremely difficult for the preacher to make an accurate assesment of his own faithfulness. Paul knew nothing against himself; that is, his conscience was clear. But he also knew a clear conscience was no guarantee he was pleasing to the Lord. One can be pleased with oneself and still not be pleasing to the Lord!

This business of self-examination is like walking a tightrope. The Bible does urge all Christians to examine themselves and search their hearts, but too much introspection can negate usefulness. A plant will not grow if it is constantly being pulled up to see if it is growing, and we cannot serve the Lord if we are constantly analysing our service. Paul would have us simply serve the Lord to the best of our ability and leave the rest to him.

Congregational pressure, cultural pressure, personal pressure — all are tainted with human fallibility and frailty and cannot be trusted to be completely accurate. In the last analysis, only one thing matters: how the Lord looks at us. That is why Paul tells the Corinthians not to judge **'before the time'**. He was referring to the time of the Lord's judgement, when the **'hidden things of darkness'** will be brought to light. In other words, God's judgement will reveal what no one else can fully discern: the secret motives of the heart. On that day, the faithful minister will have all the praise he needs, praise from the Master himself! How foolish it is for ministers to live for human praise when they have the promise of God's praise! And how foolish will those feel who preached for human praise when, on the day of reckoning, they find themselves deprived of God's praise!

# 13.
# The curse of pride

*Please read 1 Corinthians 4:6-13*

If pride can be called an illness, it is safe to say the Corinthians had an epidemic on their hands. Three times in this chapter Paul accuses them of being **'puffed up'** (4:6,18,19) and, for good measure, he repeats the charge in the next chapter (5:2).

The word Paul uses in these verses comes from the Greek word for 'bellows'. A bellows is a collapsible device used for pumping air into something. So Paul is saying someone had taken the bellows to the Corinthians and now they were inflated and swelled up. Who had done this to them? We may take a hint from the only other time this word appears in Paul's letters. In Colossians, Paul warns about the false teacher who is 'vainly puffed up by his fleshly mind' (Col. 2:18).

The same was true of the Corinthians. No one had used the bellows on them. Their own minds were the bellows that had pumped them up with pride and arrogance. They had become inflated with the so-called 'wisdom' of their day and had carried it over into their Christianity. Specifically, they had mimicked their culture by carrying into the church the practice of various schools of thought clustering around various teachers. Each school, of course, considered itself superior and looked with disdain on the other schools.

Paul wanted to break all this down, so he reminded his readers of the nature of the gospel and of the gospel ministry. In this passage, Paul turns the searchlight away from these things and onto the Corinthians themselves, so they could see how critically ill they were with pride and how they could be healed of it. His main point is that pride is never more sickening than when it shows up in the life of the Christian. It is totally out of place there because it contradicts the teaching of grace.

## Three questions

To puncture their presumption and pride, Paul pulls three sharp arrows from his quiver. First, he asks, **'For who makes you differ from another?'** As Christians, they were different from others and had been brought into a superior position, but this was no credit to them. They were not saved by their own doing, but solely by the grace of God. So Paul is reminding them they owe everything to God.

The second question Paul asks is, **'And what do you have that you did not receive?'** The first question seems to relate specifically to salvation, but this one embraces all of life. There is absolutely nothing in life we can take credit for. John MacArthur observes: 'If we have good parents, God gave them to us. If we live in a good country, God gave it to us. If we have a good mind or creative talent, God gave it to us. We have no reason to boast either in people or possessions... Everything we have is on loan from the Lord, entrusted to us for a while to use in serving Him.'[20]

Paul's third question really drives the point home: **'Now if you did indeed receive it, why do you glory as if you had not received it?'** People who receive a gift are not given any credit for it. The credit always goes to the one who gave the gift. No one ever acknowledges a gift by saying, 'Thank me.' We all realize there would be no gift if it were not for the giver, so we always give the credit to the giver. The Corinthians had not only received salvation from the Lord, but they had also received from him the various preachers they were following. There was nothing for them to get high and mighty about. The credit for the salvation and the preachers all belonged to the Lord. Instead of looking down their noses at those who followed other preachers, they should all have joined together in giving God the glory.

Their pride, then, had caused them to deny their own gospel. It also had caused them to lose sight of the nature of the Christian's life in this world (4:8-13).

**A false view of the Christian life**

Paul says they had been acting as if they were already full, already rich and already reigning. In other words, they were acting as if they had already arrived. As far as they were concerned, there was no struggle or difficulty in the Christian life. By looking at them, one would get the distinct impression that the Christian life was one of ease and enjoyment, that there was no serving or sacrificing to be done. The whole Christian life to them was one long celebration. They were acting as if the kingdom of Christ had already triumphed to the extent that no battles remained.

How did this come out of pride? Perhaps they had fallen prey to an early form of 'deeper life' or 'victorious Christian living' teaching. The church has been overrun with this type of emphasis in the past several years. The essence of it is simply that God doesn't intend his people to suffer or make sacrifices, but always to be robust in health, have plenty of money and be free from struggles. Give the slightest hint these things are not true of you and you will be advised that you are lacking in faith and need to 'trust the Lord' or 'claim the victory'.

To hear these people tell it, Christianity is a very simple business. I sometimes think the whole problem with modern Christianity is that word 'just'. We keep saying, 'Just pray,' 'just trust,' 'just serve,' or 'just rejoice,' as if it were all child's play. However, anyone who has looked hard at both the Bible and his own roller-coaster spiritual life knows praying, trusting, serving and rejoicing can be very costly and demanding.

We hear often about the danger of seduction. The world, the flesh and the devil are always ready to lead us into disobedience. There is also, however, the danger of reduction — the temptation to reduce the Christian faith to something it is not. In other words, we must resist the temptation to leave out sanctification. Some want to go immediately from justification to glorification, but the Bible says sanctification comes between the two and is not a simple matter.

**The experience of the apostles**

Paul says he and the other apostles were not finding the life of faith to be simple. They were not full, rich, or reigning. In wistful irony, he says he only wishes it were all true and the Corinthians really were reigning! That would mean the battle was over and he could lay his armour by and reign too (4:8). Paul knew all too well that the battle was far from being over, and while the Corinthians were playing the part of conquering kings, he and the other apostles felt more like condemned prisoners. He says the apostles were **'as men condemned to death'**. They had been made **'a spectacle to the world, both to angels and to men'** (4:10).

A spectacle to us is any unusual, eye-catching display, but Paul had something quite different in mind, something very familiar to his readers — the spectacle of a victorious Roman general returning from battle. The general, of course, came into the city first, riding in his chariot. He was followed by a procession of chariots and soldiers. Last in the procession were the prisoners of war. The crowd would cheer the general and his soldiers as they passed by and would jeer and taunt the poor prisoners as they filed past. Paul says being an apostle was like being one of those prisoners.

This picture was so foreign to the Corinthians that Paul thought it necessary to flesh it out with details by summarizing the experience of the apostles. We may gather up what he says in three categories. First, the apostles had to bear *personal indignities*. Being a prisoner meant one was regarded as a fool, weak and without honour. Paul says the same was true of the apostles. While the Corinthians acted like wise, strong and honourable kings, Paul and the other apostles had to be content to be considered **'fools for Christ's sake'** (4:10).

Secondly, the apostles had to endure *physical deprivation*. Kings know little or nothing about hunger, thirst, tattered clothes, rough treatment, homelessness and hard work, but prisoners do. And faithfulness to his calling had caused Paul to get well acquainted with each of these (4:11).

Finally, the apostles had to tolerate *social ostracism*. Paul speaks of being reviled, persecuted, slandered and regarded as filth, like the stuff that is scoured off a dirty dish or pot (4:12-13). Prisoners were treated in this way and so were the apostles.

Why did Paul bring all this up? Was this just a little ego-trip for him? No. His purpose was to help the Corinthians to see their wretched pride and to repent of it. How did all this help them to see their pride? Look at it in this way. If the apostles, who were the foundation on which the church was to be built (Eph. 2:20), were serving, suffering and sacrificing in deep humility, how much more should their converts have been doing the same! But Paul says the Corinthians were reigning as kings without the apostles reigning with them (4:8). The Corinthians were acting as if they had passed the apostles by, and Paul wants to know how they could have reached the goal while the apostles were still on the road!

There is much here for us to ponder. Are we like the Corinthians? Are we all swelled up with pride? If we are, it is because we have forgotten what grace and the Christian life are all about. Grace means there is nothing for us to boast about because everything we have has been given to us. The Christian life means we have to face difficulties and trials. By all means, pray, trust and rejoice, but never forget these things do not remove all the difficulties. They only give us strength in the midst of them.

# 14.
# The spiritual father

*Please read 1 Corinthians 4:14-21*

In this passage, Paul abruptly changes his tone. The storm of sarcasm subsides and is replaced by the gentle, soothing tones of a father reasoning with his erring children.

This passage is troubling to many. They recall the words of Jesus: 'Do not call anyone on earth your father; for One is your Father, He who is in heaven' (Matt. 23:9). Here, however, Paul doesn't hesitate to designate himself as the father of the Corinthians (4:15). Is the apostle brazenly and flagrantly contradicting his Lord, or is there another explanation?

The key to resolving this dilemma is to remember Jesus was addressing scribes and Pharisees who were very fond of distinctions and honours, even to the point of usurping the glory that is due to God. Paul's claim to spiritual fatherhood is completely different. His 'fatherhood' was consistent with, and in submission to, Christ's authority, not in competition with it. Three times in this passage Paul uses the phrase **'in Christ'**, and he also uses the phrase **'if the Lord wills'**. These phrases make it obvious Paul was living in submission to his Lord, and his fatherhood was in a secondary sense only.

There is, then, a legitimate kind of spiritual fatherhood, and we urgently need to understand it and begin practising it because of the state of our churches. Isn't it obvious that most churches show very little spiritual power? What is the explanation for this state of affairs? Is it all due to the pressures of the times, or our ineptness in discovering the right programme to appeal to the modern mind? I seriously doubt if Paul, John and the other apostles would explain our spiritual bankruptcy in these terms. They would point to our own spiritual impotence as the explanation. They would say our problem

is that most of us have never reached the level of spiritual fatherhood. Let's look, then, at the characteristics Paul exhibited as a
spiritual father and resolve that we shall seek to reach this same
level.


## Producing spiritual children

The first characteristic of the spiritual father is that he begets
spiritual children (4:14-15). It was through the ministry of Paul that
most of the Corinthians were converted, so he doesn't hesitate to
refer to them as his **'beloved children'**. Many other preachers had
come to Corinth and taught there, but Paul alone occupied the
special place as the one through whom they were converted. Paul
writes, **'Though you might have ten thousand instructors in
Christ, yet you do not have many fathers; for in Christ Jesus I
have begotten you through the gospel'** (4:15).

Paul was not claiming to be the author of their faith, as though he
had the power to save people. No suggestion could have been more
repulsive to this man who loved to point out that we are saved by
nothing less than the sheer grace of God himself (Eph. 2:8-9; Titus
3:5). Paul knew, however, that God, in his wisdom, has chosen to
use human instruments in the spreading of the gospel, and he was
simply saying he had been that human agent in Corinth.

If God uses human instruments to spread the gospel, we can all
be spiritual fathers. Even women? Yes! If Paul could be a gentle,
nursing mother (1 Thess. 2:7), women can be spiritual fathers!
Every child of God ought to be producing spiritual offspring! How
are you doing in this area? Do you have any spiritual offspring? John
MacArthur writes, 'A father, by definition, is a man who has
children. He is the agent of God's creating a life. A man can be a man
without having children and even a husband without having children. But he cannot be a father without having children. A Christian
cannot be a spiritual father without being used of God to bring life
to spiritual children.'[21]


## Setting an example

The second characteristic of the spiritual father is that he demonstrates the spiritual life (4:16-17). A man cannot be a father very

long before he becomes conscious of little eyes watching his every move. It is then that the awesome responsibility of fatherhood comes crashing down upon him. His children are talking like him and acting like him! They want to go where he goes and do what he does! Just as it is natural for children to want to imitate their father, so it is quite natural for spiritual children to want to imitate their spiritual father. He then begins to feel the awesomeness of being an example.

Paul was so confident of his own walk with the Lord that he could urge the Corinthians to imitate him. What if our spiritual children began to copy us? What kind of Christians would they be? Would they read the Bible? Would they pray? Would they be faithful to attend worship? Would they be giving generously to the Lord's work? The old question just refuses to go away: 'If every church member were just like me, what kind of church would this church be?'

It is possible, of course, for us to set a proper example, only to see our children obstinately refuse to follow it. We all could cite instances of godly parents with rebellious children. The same holds true in the spiritual realm. The spiritual father can see his example completely disregarded by his children. The Corinthians were showing so many signs of being rebellious children that Paul thought it necessary to send Timothy to remind them that their spiritual father's ways were 'in Christ'. They were to follow Paul because he was following Jesus Christ.

In announcing this plan, Paul refers to Timothy as his **'beloved and faithful son in the Lord'** (4:17). Don't think Paul's words were accidental. He was intentionally contrasting Timothy with the Corinthians. In essence he was saying, 'I, your spiritual father, am sending a faithful son to all my rebellious sons to tell them to be faithful too.'

If Paul couldn't escape the trauma of having rebellious children, we may rest assured not all our spiritual children will follow our example. We must, however, still set the example. Let's continually ask ourselves if we are following Christ in such a way that we can sincerely urge others to follow us.

## Exercising discipline

Being a spiritual father is a demanding business. Not only does it demand we beget children but also that we set the proper example for them. Even then we have not fulfilled all our responsibilities, because the spiritual father also exercises spiritual discipline (4:18-21).

As noted, the Corinthians were puffed up with pride, and pride in the heart invariably spills out of the mouth. They were always talking themselves up and others down. Specifically, they were talking Paul down by saying he was not reliable (4:18).

Parents know there are some things they cannot let their children get away with; arrogance is one of them. It may seem cute for a while but the cuteness wears off very quickly. As a good parent, Paul wasn't about to let the Corinthians get away with their arrogant talking. The best way to humble a proud big-mouth is to show him up. Paul promised to do exactly that to his readers by first coming to them (4:19). That would prove his reliability and would stop them from talking him down. Once there, Paul would stop them from talking themselves up by investigating, not their puffed up words, but their **'power'** (4:19). That means he was going to set about to determine whether their lives matched up to their talk, and he offered this word of explanation: **'For the kingdom of God is not in word but in power'** (4:20).

How we need to take these words home to our hearts! If Christianity could be made a success by merely talking the right way we would have put Satan to flight long ago. But Christianity is not just talking right, it is living right!

Paul, then, as their father, could come to them in gentleness or in firmness; the choice was up to them (4:21). It's true, of course, that none of us has the authority of an apostle, but we still can learn from this portion of the passage. We still need to have enough concern for our brothers and sisters in Christ to be firm with them when the situation demands it.

We don't have much taste for this kind of thing. This is the day of 'Mr Nice Guy' Christianity and the prevailing motto is 'Live and let live.' So when a brother in Christ falls into error, we just turn our heads and look the other way, conveniently ignoring the words of Jesus: 'If your brother sins against you, go and tell him his fault between you and him alone. If he hears you, you have gained your brother' (Matt. 18:15). If this is proper procedure for dealing with any sinning brother or sister in Christ, it is certainly proper for the spiritual father to confront a spiritual child with sin in his life.

Begetting spiritual children, setting an example in spiritual life, exercising spiritual firmness — these are all part of what it means to be a spiritual father. And if the church is to recover spiritual power, we must all make it our goal to display these vital characteristics.

# 15.
# Sexual immorality and church discipline

*Please read 1 Corinthians 5:1-2*

The church of Corinth was contaminated by society in two ways. First, they had carried over into the church the same kind of fragmentation and division that was so prevalent in Corinth. The first four chapters of this letter are devoted to this problem. Secondly, they had allowed into their church the sexual immorality that was running rampant through the city. Paul deals with this issue in chapters 5 and 6. All of chapter 5 and the first half of chapter 6 are devoted to a particularly reprehensible case of sexual immorality and the need for the church to discipline the offender. The last half of chapter 6 consists of general principles that form the basis for Christian morality.

Few subjects are more distasteful to modern Christians than the one Paul drops into our laps in this passage. The subject of sexual immorality? No. The subject of church discipline! In the U.S.A. at least, we are so accustomed to sexual innuendo, sensuous television programmes, erotic films and blunt talk from sex therapists that we are well beyond blushing at any frank, open discussion of sexual immorality. But let someone mention church discipline and we immediately pale and become squeamish.

## Why discipline is unpopular today

Why is this so? Much of it is due to the softness of Christians in general and of Christian leaders in particular. We don't want to jeopardize church attendance and finances by offending anyone, so we conveniently look the other way even when flagrant sin crops up in the church.

In addition to our own softness, we now have the added problem of an intolerant society. In short, those outside the church now want to dictate what goes on inside the church. Most people believe the church has no right to discipline its members, and some have even gone to court to prevent the church from doing so. We are perilously close to reaching the day when churches will not be allowed to set their own standards for membership, let alone require strict adherence to those standards. Don't think the separation of church and state in the U.S.A. will preclude such a thing from happening there. In our day, that principle has come to mean the church has to stay out of government, not that the government has to stay out of the church! If the government decides it has a vested interest in promoting 'equality' for a particular minority, it may well require churches to change their policies on membership and ordination or forfeit their tax-exempt status.

**Ignorance**

How are we to explain the softness of the church and the intolerance of society? Ironically, both entities are monstrously ignorant about the same things.

First, they are ignorant about *the nature of the church*. Church members and non-members seem to have the idea that the church is merely another human organization that sets its own rules and can, therefore, change them to suit the mood of the time. The idea that the church has received a revelation, a deposit of truth, from God and is to be the custodian of that truth has all but vanished.

Secondly, church and society are also ignorant about *the meaning of church membership*. Joining a church used to mean one was agreeing with that church's doctrinal position and was voluntarily submitting oneself to living according to its teachings. In other words, joining a church was tantamount to voluntarily submitting oneself to live under its authority. Now it is common for people who have joined a church to say the church has absolutely no right to tell them how they ought to live. If someone doesn't want the church telling him how to live, the logical thing to do is to remove membership from that church. Incredibly, however, people who object to the church telling them how to live also insist they have a right to be members of that church.

The Roman Catholic Church has been grappling with this

problem since one of the bishops stated that Catholic politicians who could not line up with the church's position on abortion were putting themselves in danger of excommunication. This statement created a great public outcry, which essentially consisted of people saying they have a right to belong to the church regardless of their beliefs, and the church has no right whatsoever to set standards or to demand compliance with them.

The greatest ignorance shared by church and society, however, is ignorance of *the nature of God himself*. The whole notion of church discipline assumes God is holy and he expects his church to reflect his holiness. People in general, and Christians in particular, have more or less agreed to sweep the holiness of God under the carpet and to emphasize nothing but the love of God. Of course, God is love, and we can never emphasize his love enough, but even his love is a holy love. In other words, God's love for the sinner never compromises his holiness. He doesn't forgive the sinner without judging the sin. The death of Jesus on the cross is the supreme example of God's holy love. The cross was love in that Christ died for sinners, but it was holy in that Christ received in his own body the judgement of God upon sin.

All of this ignorance about church discipline makes it essential for us to weigh carefully what Paul has to say in this section of his letter. In the first two verses, he sets the stage for his entire discussion. He mentions two things: the act which necessitated discipline and the attitude which had negated it. Essentially, then, Paul is dealing with two problems in this section on discipline: the immorality of one of the members and the indifference of all the others.

## The act which necessitated discipline

The immorality of the one member Paul summarizes in a single, blunt phrase: **'A man has his father's wife'** (5:1). We may safely conclude from Paul's use of 'father's wife' that the offending member was not committing immorality with his own mother but with his stepmother.

What was the precise nature of their relationship? We cannot be sure. Leon Morris elaborates: 'Whether it means that the offender had seduced his stepmother, or that she was divorced from his father, or that the father had died, leaving her a widow is not clear.

What is quite clear is that an illicit union of a particularly unsavoury kind had been contracted.'[22]

There was no need for Paul to supply any more details because everybody in the church knew exactly what he was talking about! In fact, everybody in the city of Corinth knew about the immorality in the church. The phrase **'actually reported'** may also be translated 'reported commonly' (AV). This caused the Dutch commentator, F. W. Grosheide, to observe: 'Anyone at Corinth who spoke of the church in that city mentioned the fornication among the Christians.'[23]

Not only did the citizens of Corinth know about the immorality within the church, they were shocked by it. Paul says this kind of sin was **'not even named among the Gentiles'** (5:1). That is quite a statement! This particular sin was so repulsive and vile it was not tolerated or practised in a city that was as sex-obsessed as our own society.

### The attitude that negated it

If this sin so shocked the city, we should expect it to have been even more shocking to the church. Such was not the case! Paul describes the reaction of the church: **'And you are puffed up, and have not rather mourned...'** (5:2).

The appropriate response of the Christian to sin, then, is to feel grief about it. The Corinthians, however, were not mourning. Instead they were 'puffed up'. Their pride had desensitized them to the enormity of sin. We know there was a group in the church who considered themselves to be the spiritual élite. They imagined themselves to be spiritually enlightened to a degree far surpassing the others. One of the 'insights' these people claimed, as we shall see, was a doctrine of Christian 'freedom'. They believed Christ's salvation had set them free from the law to such an extent that they could disregard even the Ten Commandments. When this particular episode of sin was brought to their attention they probably said something like this: 'If this brother feels free to live this way, that's his business. I wouldn't choose to live this way myself, but I believe we have no right to judge him.'

In the church of Corinth, then, the flagrant act of one was tolerated because of the flippant attitude of many! It is easy to look back, see the deficiencies of the Corinthians, and take them to task. It is much harder to see our own deficiencies. We haven't dealt honestly with this passage until we think long and hard about ourselves. Perhaps we can't think of anything in our church that matches the immorality of the Corinthian church. If that is the case, we should be thankful to God! But we still cannot just heave a sigh of relief and walk away from this passage. What about our attitude towards sin? Are we shocked by it? Or do we now simply smile tolerantly at the very sins that once caused us to recoil in horror? The fact that we do not know of any flagrant sin doesn't mean there is no sin in our lives. Do we grieve over the sins that are there? Today's 'small' sin can easily become tomorrow's flagrant sin. If we would but grieve over our own sins before they become flagrant, we could spare the church the agony of having to deal with our sins afterwards.

# 16.
# A prescription for immorality and indifference

*Please read 1 Corinthians 5:3-8*

In most of his letters, Paul functions as a spiritual doctor, diagnosing various illnesses in the churches, prescribing treatments and discussing possible side-effects. Nowhere is Paul's doctoring more apparent than in the chapter before us.

We have looked at his diagnosis (5:1-2). It was short but not sweet. The church of Corinth was in the throes of an illness with two symptoms: one member was involved in an incestuous relationship and the other members were politely looking the other way. Paul didn't have to summon his great diagnostic powers here. The sickness of the church was plain to everybody except its own members.

It is one thing, however, to see the problem; it is quite another to know what to do about it. In these verses, Paul turns from diagnosis to treatment (5:3-8) and a possible side-effect (5:9-13). The treatment, of course, addresses both symptoms. First, Paul proposes a treatment for the incestuous member (5:3-7) and then one for the indifferent members (5:8).

## The treatment for the incestuous member

What do we find Paul proposing for the incestuous member? He says, **'Deliver such a one to Satan for the destruction of the flesh'** (5:5). There has been a good deal of contention over the meaning of these words. Some believe they are Paul's way of describing excommunication from the church. The church, they argue, is Christ's domain, while the world is Satan's domain. To be delivered to Satan, then, is to be placed outside the church.

Others take the much stronger view that this was, in the words of Henry Alford, 'a special power ... of inflicting corporeal death or disease as a punishment for sin'.[24] Those who take this position cite the case of Ananias and Sapphira (Acts 5:1-11) and the words of the apostle John that there is a sin unto death (1 John 5:16).

Which of these two interpretations should we adopt? Many recoil from the thought of God inflicting sickness or death because of sin and quickly opt for the former. I am convinced Paul has both actions in mind. A careful study of this passage will show he is discussing two distinct actions. One is his own apostolic action and the other is church action.

### Apostolic action

The apostolic action is described in verses 3 and 4. Even though Paul was absent from the church, he had already pronounced sentence upon this man, and he was simply calling upon the church to announce his sentence.

An apostle delivering someone to sickness or death because of sin — how can such a thing be? Those who have difficulty with this have never really come to grips with the unique position of the apostle in the early church. The apostle was not the equivalent of today's pastor or preacher. The apostle was a special envoy of Christ. As such, he received direct revelation from Christ and was given special authority over the church. In handing down this sentence, Paul was not acting in a high-handed, dictatorial fashion, but was acting **'in the name of our Lord Jesus Christ'** and **'with the power of our Lord Jesus Christ'** (5:4). In other words, he was acting upon the command and authority of Christ and for the honour of Christ.

There is a great irony here. Some who profess to be most horrified at Paul handing over a guilty man to sickness or death are quick to defend our society handing over innocent babies to the abortion mill and the elderly to euthanasia.

### The church's action

If this handing over to destruction was Paul's action, what was to be the church's action? Paul tells them to **'purge out the old leaven'** (5:7).

This was something all Paul's readers would have readily understood. The Passover Feast celebrated the deliverance of the Jewish people from their bondage in the land of Egypt. The Jews were required before the Passover Feast began to thoroughly search their homes and to remove all leaven. Part of the celebration of this feast consisted of mixing a fresh lump of dough. This new lump was to have absolutely no yeast or leaven in it. The Passover signalled a new beginning and, therefore, none of the old leaven was to be left around to contaminate the new lump. The leaven represented the life they were leaving behind in Egypt, and the new lump represented their new life of freedom.

Paul applies all of this to the Christian. The Christian is not just someone who has turned over a new leaf, or an old relic who has been painted and patched up. He is completely new. He is not just reformed but transformed. And make no mistake here, this newness is all due to the work of Jesus Christ on the cross. The Israelites were spared from the sentence of death on the land of Egypt by placing the blood of a lamb on their doors. The angel of death passed over all the houses marked by that blood. So the Christian is saved from God's sentence of eternal death through Jesus Christ, who is the Passover Lamb. Because of Christ, the Christian is freed from slavery to sin and Satan and is made new.

The Christian's responsibility is to demonstrate this newness by the way he lives. Because he is a new 'lump' in Christ, he is to leave behind the remnants of the old life. The sins of the old life are not to be reintroduced into the new life.

This is precisely what the church of Corinth was in danger of doing. By tolerating the sin of this incestuous member they were allowing leaven from their old lives to exist in their church. Just as a little leaven soon leavens a whole lump of dough, so the sin of one soon influences and corrupts the whole church.

When Paul tells them to purge the leaven from their midst, then, he is telling them to remove this incestuous member from their church! The church was to follow Paul's apostolic sentence with excommunication!

All of this seems very harsh and cruel to many. They regard both the apostolic action and the church action as mean and vindictive. In prescribing these actions, however, Paul makes it clear his concern was that the incestuous member and the testimony of the church be restored. The motive for his own action of handing this

man over to Satan was **'that his spirit may be saved in the day of
the Lord Jesus'** (5:5). In other words, Paul wanted this man to be
renewed in his spirit so he could again be useful to the Lord.
Evidently, this is what happened. In 2 Corinthians 2:5-11, Paul
urges the church to forgive and comfort the one upon whom they had
to inflict punishment.


## The treatment for the indifferent members

Two forms of discipline were to be employed against this incestuous
member. One was apostolic action, while the other was church
action. But what of the indifference of the members themselves?
How does Paul doctor this? He does so by continuing to use the
Passover theme. He implores them to **'keep the feast'** (5:8). In other
words, they were to rejoice in their deliverance from sin, just as the
Jewish people rejoiced in their deliverance from Egypt. The Jewish
Passover lasted for seven days, but Paul is calling upon the church
to continually celebrate their deliverance from sin through Christ
who is our Passover. A certain poster puts it like this: 'We are an
Easter people, and "Hallelujah!" is our song!'[25]

What does this have to do with indifference? Simply put, praise
always kills off indifference. Indifference cannot coexist with
celebration. It is impossible to come into worship and praise the
Lord for salvation, then walk out into the world to ignore his
commands. The greatest safeguard against sin is regular, frequent
praise for salvation.

That is why pastors are always urging people not to be mere
spectators in worship. It is not that they want to badger you, but
simply that they want you to reap the fullest possible benefits from
worship. If you enter wholeheartedly into worship, you will be
strengthened in your personal battle against sin and Satan.

If the church of Corinth had been adequately celebrating the
salvation provided by Christ, they could not possibly have tolerated
the sin that was besmirching the name of Christ in the eyes of the
whole city. If they had been properly worshipping Christ, they
might have seen this incestuous member repent before church
discipline was needed. May God help us to see the power of continual praise. It has a cleansing effect on the Christian and a convicting
effect on the sinner. And may God help us to repent of nonchalant,
casual worship and begin to worship him in 'sincerity and truth'.

# 17.
# The boat and the water

*Please read 1 Corinthians 5:9-13*

Paul, the spiritual doctor, has given the church of Corinth his diagnosis of a serious problem in their midst and the treatment for it. What was his diagnosis? One incestuous member and a great number of indifferent members! And what treatment did he prescribe? The incestuous member was to be handed over to Satan (5:5) and dismissed from the church (5:7), and the indifferent members were to kill off their indifference through continual celebration of their salvation (5:8).

In this passage, Paul turns his attention to discussing a side-effect that could easily arise from employing this treatment. He could see some of the church members falling into the pendulum syndrome and reasoning like this: 'If it's wrong for us to associate with another Christian who has fallen into sin, it must be more wrong to associate with those who have never professed faith in Christ at all.'

This kind of thinking already existed to some degree in the church because of something Paul had previously written, namely, that they were not to **'keep company with sexually immoral people'** (5:9). Paul simply meant they were not to be socially intimate with this type of people, but some of the Corinthians took his words to mean they were to have absolutely no contact at all with them. So in this passage Paul kills the proverbial two birds with one stone. He prevents the treatment he has proposed for the incestuous member from being wrongly applied, and he sets the record straight on what he wrote in the previous letter.

What, then, is Paul's teaching in this passage? What it amounts to is this: maintain purity in the church and contact with the world. A good way to understand this teaching is to think of the church as a boat and the world as water. It is fine for the boat to be in the water, but it is disastrous for the water to be in the boat! That sounds simple enough, but Christians have had a difficult time maintaining this balance.

## Maintaining contact with the world

Some Christians want to take the boat out of the water. They are aware of the many and varied dangers as long as the boat is in the water. They know the water conceals treacherous reefs that can easily rip open the hull of the boat and let the water in. They conclude, therefore, that the best thing to do is get the boat away from the water.

It is easy to see how appealing this idea would have been to the Christians in Corinth. Their city was a very intimidating place to practise the Christian faith. They were just a handful of people, and as they went out each day to do their work, they found people who had descended into the vilest, most detestable lifestyles imaginable swarming all around. The city was overrun with the sexually immoral, the covetous, extortioners and idolaters (5:10). Don't think for a moment these were the only things going on in Corinth! Paul just mentions these to indicate what type of city it was.

Other generations of early Christians found society to be equally intimidating, and they actually retreated from it by spending their lives in monasteries. There they could nurture the spiritual life and be completely away from all the temptations and pressures of society. This was such a common practice that church historians actually refer to the age of 'monasticism'.

We know all about how intimidating society can be. Ours doesn't take a back seat to Corinth or to any other when it comes to debauchery and corruption. In fact, it seems as if the vices of Corinth have been bequeathed to us. But many Christians seem to think we are doing a fairly good job of confronting our society. After all, we haven't built any monasteries lately and hidden ourselves from the world. Or have we? You see, one doesn't have to go to the mountains or the woods to become monastic. It is possible to make monasteries out of our own churches and not really have any substantial contact with the world. We can easily fall into the pattern of putting on our Christianity when we come to church, taking it off when we leave, remaining incognito during the week and then dashing back into our churches to do our Christianity again. If this is not monasticism, it is certainly very close to it.

The grand assumption behind all forms of monasticism is that Christianity cannot prosper in the rough and tumble of the godless world; it is so delicate it will perish when it comes into contact with wickedness. Perhaps the most urgent need of our day is for those of us who are Christians to become so utterly convinced of the truth of our message that we no longer fear having to take it out into the marketplace. We must learn to place our focus on the right point. The issue is not how bad our society is, but how good and strong Christianity is.

Jesus himself made it clear, in both example and teaching, how he would have us relate to this world. Thank God, he did not respond to the evil of this world by staying at a safe distance in heaven, but plunged right into the midst of it. And he has made it plain that his followers are to follow his example by comparing them to salt and light. Salt, to do its work, must be in contact with food; light, to do its work, must confront darkness.

So we are to do exactly what Jesus prayed for us to do: be in the world, but not of it (John 17:14-15). Paul observes that there is really only one way to be completely away from sin and that is to leave this world! (5:10).

## Maintaining the purity of the church

Others in the church, of course, had no trouble with this point at all. They completely understood Paul's teaching. To them, the very thought of absolute separation from the world was ludicrous! Christians must simply learn to put up with the paganism swirling all around.

But being in contact with paganism every day — working with nice pagans, seeing how they act, and hearing how they think — has a way of dulling spiritual senses. Gradually, the inner protest against paganism grows feebler and feebler, and 'Joe Christian' finds he is not as disturbed by it as he once was. In fact, Joe finds it easier and easier to think paganism is not so bad after all, and he begins thinking, saying and doing things that would never even have crossed his mind a few months back. Oh, he still loves the Lord and goes to church, but he doesn't feel as if he is really slipping because he finds other church members are becoming less 'rigid' and more tolerant of 'Corinthianism'. His house group even discussed the matter, and the conclusion seemed to be that times were changing and the church must change along with them or get left behind!

Does this all sound familiar? It is the old story: let the camel get his nose in the tent, and you will soon find you have a whole camel in the tent! The camel was definitely in the tent of the church of Corinth. They had learned to accept sin in the church as readily as they did in their community. In avoiding the ditch on the one side of the road (separation from the world), they drove off into the ditch on the other side (contamination by the world). Instead of keeping the boat in the water, they brought the water into the boat and were about to sink! So Paul essentially says that, while they could not expect to eliminate the immorality in the world, they could and should eliminate it in the church. He further says they must not think excommunicating one incestuous member would guarantee the purity of the church. Each individual Christian must adopt and maintain a lifestyle of purity. What would such a lifestyle mean? For one thing, they would not associate with any professing Christian who had a worldly lifestyle. Paul urges them not to **'keep company with anyone named a brother, who is a fornicator, or covetous, or an idolater, or a reviler, or a drunkard, or an extortioner — not even to eat with such a person'** (5:11).

Many would argue Paul was going off the deep end here. They agree the Christian should maintain contact with sinners, but they also believe there is nothing wrong with maintaining contact with professing Christians who are living worldly lives. What possessed Paul to make this distinction? Simply this: Paul wanted the church to be living proof that Christianity makes a radical difference. If someone professed faith in Christ and didn't demonstrate this radical difference, Paul wanted the world at least to see that the other members of the church didn't approve. In other words, Paul wanted to make it clear Christianity is not some nebulous, vague blob that each man defines and practises as it suits him. Christianity is a distinct and definable reality, and when someone takes the name of Christ but refuses to live up to the standards, he should not be treated as a brother in Christ. If we were to put this approach into practice, we would not only show the world Christianity makes a difference, but would also bring many a backslider to repentance.

## Getting it the right way round

The church of Corinth was failing on this vital matter. She was quick to condemn the sins of those outside the church but unwilling to deal with the sins of those within her own ranks. Paul's words in verses 12 and 13 make it clear that this was back to front. The church is not to judge those who are on the outside. God himself will take care of that in due time. The church is, however, to discipline those who fail to walk in a manner worthy of, and consistent with, the faith they profess to hold.

Today's church seems to be as guilty of this inversion as the Corinthians. She is quick and eager to denounce the sins of society without realizing that such denunciations really amount to a denial of her gospel. If unregenerate people are capable of living righteous lives they don't need the life-changing power of the gospel. In other words, we shouldn't expect Christian living from those who are not Christians. But we should expect it from those who claim to be Christians.

Sin always constitutes a great crisis for the Christian, and it thrives not only in society but also in the church. What is the Christian to do about the sin he sees in society? Paul calls for a balancing act. The Christian is certainly not to condone sin in society, but he must maintain contact with society. The Christian himself is, however, to be so committed to holiness and purity that he refuses to maintain contact with any professing Christian who is not living a pure life. The Christian, then, is to keep the boat in the water without letting the water into the boat.

# 18.
# Christians in court

*Please read 1 Corinthians 6:1-8*

The first eleven verses of this chapter seem to be strangely out of place. Paul has been calling for the church to take disciplinary action against a particularly disgusting case of sexual immorality in their midst (5:1-13). He is about to launch an impassioned plea for each Christian to maintain sexual purity (6:12-20). Between these two sections, however, we have this passage which deals with Christians taking each other to court. It almost seems as though Paul, in the middle of dealing with the problem of sexual immorality, says, 'And, by the way, don't sue each other either.' Literary critics would hasten to say Paul was mistaken to bring in this new theme without completing his discussion on sexual immorality.

Why did Paul, at this particular point, give instruction on this issue of Christians taking each other to court? The truth is that he has been dealing simultaneously with the themes of sexual immorality and church discipline. In chapter 6, he simply follows each theme to its logical end.

## Is it right for Christians to judge?

What he said in chapter 5 about church discipline required the church to pass judgement, and many of the church members were, as we can well imagine, extremely reluctant to do so. Some were, no doubt, ready to suggest this matter of the incestuous member should not be handled by the church at all, but simply be handed over to the secular courts. Any talk of Christians judging made them extremely nervous. Should Christians ever judge another Christian? If any Christian has a grievance against another Christian, why create turmoil in the church over it? Why not just let the secular courts handle it, so the church doesn't have to dirty its hands? In the church of Corinth, there was a deep reluctance to pass judgement and yet an eager willingness to go to secular courts.

So we have two questions before us. What about the first? Is it right for Christians to judge? Everything Paul says in chapter 5 makes it quite clear he assumes it is. In fact, he closes chapter 5 by asking, 'Do you not judge those who are inside?' (5:12). But most Christians today seem to think Paul was on the wrong track here. They read his words and quickly say, 'We're not supposed to judge.' I sometimes think the favourite quote of Christians is, 'Judge not, that you be not judged.' Many who are at an utter loss on how to begin quoting John 3:16 find the words of Matthew 7:1 coming easily to mind.

Suffice it to say, Jesus was directing his words about judging to self-righteous individuals who have a hypercritical spirit. He forbade such people from pronouncing on matters that were none of their business and from expressing their opinion without knowledge of the facts. Paul, on the other hand, was talking about the whole church passing judgement on a clear-cut violation of biblical doctrine and conduct.

## Christians and the courts

But what about the second problem — the readiness to take Christian disputes to secular courts? This was, of course, just another indication of their most fundamental problem, which was contamination with the world. Their church was honeycombed with division. Where did that problem come from? From copying their society! Sexual immorality seemed to be ready to engulf them completely. One member had already fallen into terrible sin and others, we may assume from what Paul says in the last half of this chapter, seemed to be teetering on the brink of it. Where did all this come from? From copying their society! On top of all that, they were eager to submit a church problem to secular litigation! Why? Because that was how problems were handled in their society! The Greeks were famous for their love of legal action. They cultivated the intellect and loved argumentation and debate. What better place to show one's intellectual prowess than in court?

The Greeks of that day would feel right at home in America

today. Legal action abounds on every hand. The thinking of our day seems to be if you haven't had any success playing the lottery or winning in Las Vegas, then you might as well try your luck in court! You might just come away with the jackpot! You don't even have to worry about finding a legitimate grievance; any frivolous, petty thing will do.

Paul didn't write these words simply to bemoan the litigation mania of his day. He firmly believed one should not expect unredeemed people to act as if they were redeemed. On the other hand, however, he insisted that redeemed people ought to act like redeemed people. So he wrote to forbid Christians to take each other to court.

Let's make sure we understand what he is saying. He is not forbidding Christians all recourse to legal action. There are many legitimate reasons for a Christian to seek legal advice: making a will, drafting business contracts, etc. Paul is not even forbidding the Christian to go to court to settle a dispute with an unbeliever. Paul himself found it necessary to take advantage of the Roman judicial system when he was arrested for preaching the gospel. What, then, is his teaching here? Simply this: a Christian should not go to court to settle a dispute with another Christian.

Why did Paul take such a dim view of this? Were the secular courts so corrupt that Christians couldn't get justice there? Not at all. It was rather that believers taking each other to court constituted a denial of the Christian's distinctiveness and his destiny. As soon as Christians walk through the doors of the courtroom they have, according to Paul, suffered defeat (6:7, NASB) because they have denied their whole standing as Christians.

## The Christian's distinctiveness

Let's think about the Christian's distinctiveness (6:1,4-8). Just who is a Christian? Is he someone who walked down an aisle, nodded agreement to some assertions and got his name on the church book? No! The Christian is one who has undergone a complete and radical change. This change is captured for us by two words: **'unrighteous'** and **'saints'** (6:1). Those who are not Christians are unrighteous. Every single child of God was in that category at one time, but he or she is no longer there. He has been placed in a completely different realm. He is now among the saints. Who are the saints? They are those who have been called, by the grace of God, out of their unrighteousness and set apart as God's own people and for his own purposes.

As a saint, the Christian bears certain distinguishing marks. For one thing, he is concerned in all he says and does about the honour of Jesus Christ. He realizes he owes this radical change to what Christ did for him, and he is very anxious not to do anything to bring reproach upon the name of Christ. He is also deeply concerned about all his brothers and sisters in Christ. He knows Christ loves them, and he loves them too. He also fully subscribes to the teachings of the Bible. He knows the Bible is God's Word and that it gives him instruction in how to live for the Christ he loves.

One thing the Christian learns as he studies his Bible is that it is better to suffer wrong than to do wrong (Matt. 5:38-40). The Christian would rather waive his rights than inflict one iota of damage upon the name of Christ. When the Christian has a dispute with another Christian, he will — out of concern for the honour of Christ, love for his brother in Christ and obedience to the Word of God — seek to resolve the dispute. If the two of them are unable to iron out the dispute, they will take it to the church and the church will help them sort it out. The one thing they will not do is give the unbelieving world the opportunity to say, 'If there was anything to Christianity, these Christians would be able to work out their own difficulties.'

Two Christians, who love the same Lord and each other and bow to the same authority, can work out any problem! In fact, Paul seems to suggest Christians have so much common ground that the least gifted member of the church should be able to handle any disputes that might arise (6:4).

## The Christian's destiny

Taking a brother to court, then, constitutes a denial of the Christian's distinctiveness. But Paul doesn't stop with that. He goes on to suggest Christian lawsuits deny the Christian's destiny (6:2-3). What is that destiny? Paul says Christians are going to judge both the world and angels! This is not something Paul dreamed up on his own. The Lord Jesus himself said his twelve disciples would be associated with him in judging (Matt. 19:28). Other scriptures extend this judging to include all Christians. Jude writes, 'Behold, the Lord comes with ten thousands of His saints, to execute judgment on all...' (Jude 14-15). And Paul says to Timothy, 'If we endure, we shall also reign with Him' (2 Tim. 2:12). If we are going to be involved in judging on this scale, we most certainly should be able to handle trivial disputes that pertain to this life.

Everything Paul says in this passage is built on this grand assumption: redemption is the mainspring of the Christian's life. It is not something he merely keeps in a box and takes out on Sunday. It colours every aspect of his life, it controls his thinking, it governs his living and it guarantees a glorious future. May God help us to always avoid anything that denies such a glorious redemption.

# 19.
# Who goes to heaven?

*Please read 1 Corinthians 6:9-11*

The church of Corinth was contaminated by the world. Division, sexual immorality and love for litigation were all prominent features of their society, and it looked as if they were well on the way to becoming prominent features in the church.

The church members themselves seemed to be taking all this contamination with a grain of salt. What if they were living like the world? As long as they were saved, it didn't really matter! If they were doing things that were wrong, what need was there for worry? They could always count on a loving God to forgive them! If God always forgives sin, why forsake it?

Paul, on the other hand, has been insisting throughout this letter that there is a radical difference between the child of God and the unbeliever. In the first half of this chapter alone, we can see a great divide running through his words. On one side are those he terms the 'unrighteous' (6:1) and 'unbelievers' (6:6). On the other side are those he terms 'saints' (6:1-2) and 'brethren'.

## The unrighteous will not go to heaven

Some of those who claimed to be on the Christian side of the divide were maintaining they could keep one foot on each side. In the verses before us, Paul drops a bombshell on all such thinking. He flatly asserts that people who continue in sin are not going to make it to heaven. **'Do you not know'**, he writes, **'that the unrighteous will not inherit the kingdom of God?'** (6:9). And he goes on to assert that anybody who believes otherwise is deceived.

So there could be absolutely no mistake about what he was saying, Paul proceeds to catalogue some lifestyles that are incompatible with the kingdom of God. The first half of the list is primarily devoted to sexual sins. **'Fornicators'** are those who are guilty of all forms of sexual sin. **'Adulterers'** are the married who engage in sex outside of marriage. **'Homosexuals'** and **'sodomites'** are those who engage in sexual acts with persons of the same sex. The word translated 'homosexual' literally means 'soft' or 'effeminate' and probably refers to the passive partner in a same-sex affair; the word translated 'sodomite' probably designates the more active partner.

Only the word **'idolaters'** doesn't seem to belong in the first half of this list. It could be that Paul included it because sexual acts played such a prominent rôle in the worship of idols in Corinth. Or perhaps he included it to suggest that those who practise these sins are guilty of making sexual pleasure their god.

The second half of Paul's list deals primarily with sins against one's fellow man. **'Thieves'** and the **'covetous'** are those who are in the grip of greed. The only difference is that the covetous desire the possessions of others, while the thief actually appropriates them. **'Drunkards'** may seem, at first glance, to be only abusing themselves, not their fellow man. The fact is, families in particular and society in general have had to pay a heavy toll for this sin. **'Revilers'** are those who destroy with their words. **'Extortioners'** are those who secure financial gain by taking unfair advantage of others.

Perhaps you are wondering why Paul selected these particular sins. He could easily have mentioned others. Why these? We must keep a couple of things in mind. First, Paul undoubtedly intended only to compile a representative list, not an exhaustive one. Secondly, these were probably the most prominent sins in the city of Corinth.

Please don't misunderstand what Paul is saying. He is not suggesting that Christians are perfect and they never fall into any of these sins or others. There are plenty of examples in the Bible of great men of God falling into terrible sin, but that is not what Paul is talking about. He is referring to continuing in these sins. The Christian has his lapses into sin, but his basic bent is towards righteousness, and he hates the sin he falls into. The unbeliever is just the opposite. His basic bent is towards unrighteousness, and he hates righteousness.

The reason why people who live in sin cannot enter heaven is plain to see. It is 'the kingdom of God'. And what is God's fundamental characteristic? It is righteousness, or holiness! David Prior puts it in these words: 'Because God's kingdom reflects his own character of righteousness and compassion, those who insist on living by different standards will not be there.'[26] And Geoffrey Wilson adds: 'For as righteousness is the fundamental characteristic of God's kingdom, so those whose lives are still characterized by unrighteousness cannot hope to acquire an interest in that kingdom.'[27]

This is a very sobering truth indeed, but thank God it is not the only truth in these verses. We can go on to conclude no one is too unrighteous to be cleansed.

## No one is too unrighteous to be cleansed

'Such were some of you,' Paul says. Some of the members of the church had been among Corinth's vilest sinners. All the Corinthians were sinners, but Paul specifically calls attention to those who at one time practised the lifestyles he mentions. Why did Paul want to single out these? It was to make the point that even the vilest sinner can be cleansed and made fit for the kingdom of God!

Paul says a great change had taken place in the lives of those who once practised these lifestyles. They had been washed, sanctified and justified. The word **'washed'** probably refers to regeneration. Paul, in his letter to Titus, makes mention of the 'washing of regeneration' (Titus 3:5). What is regeneration? It is God planting new life within the sinner, giving him a new nature. The word **'sanctified'** means 'set apart'. When the sinner receives life from God, he is set apart for the purposes of God. The word **'justified'** means the sinner is declared guiltless before God. He is no longer under the condemnation of God's law, but stands clean and uncondemned before God.

In the Greek, all three of these words are verbs in the aorist tense, which indicates the action is completed. These people had undergone a once-for-all, unrepeatable transformation. They were changed and would never be the same again! Yes, they could still slip into acts of sin, but they were no longer dominated and controlled by it.

**Cleansing is only through the work of Christ**

How can this happen? How can one be washed, sanctified and justified? Our text gives the answer. The third truth Paul lays before us in these verses is that no one is cleansed except through the work of Jesus Christ.

Paul says the Corinthians had experienced this great change **'in the name of the Lord Jesus and by the Spirit of our God'**. It is apparent from these words that cleansing from sin is the result of the work of the triune God. Each person of the Trinity plays a vital rôle in the work of salvation. God the Father is the originating cause of redemption. It was he who planned the work of salvation even before the world began. God the Son is the mediating cause of redemption. He is the one who actually paid the price for us by receiving on the cross the penalty due to sinners. And the Holy Spirit is the effecting cause of redemption. He is the one who actually does the work in our hearts and applies the work of salvation to us.

If the whole Trinity is involved in the work of salvation, is it correct to say no one is cleansed except through the work of Christ? Yes, because the work of Christ is the centrepiece of the whole plan of redemption. It was the plan of God the Father to send Christ to purchase redemption, and it is the work of Christ that the Holy Spirit applies to our hearts when we are saved. Because the work of salvation is centred on Christ, Scripture tells us there is salvation in no other (John 14:6; Acts 4:12; 1 Tim. 2:5-6).

Just what did Christ do to make it possible for us to be cleansed from even the vilest sin? First, he left the glories of heaven to become one of us. As one of us, he did what we have utterly failed to do. He lived a perfect life and, in so doing, provided the righteousness God demands. Then he went to the cross and bore in his own body the penalty we so richly deserve.

Does God, then, demand perfect righteousness to get into heaven? Jesus Christ has provided that righteousness! Does God say no sin will enter there? Jesus has paid for my sin. Do you see it? He took my sin, and I take his righteousness!

If you want to get to heaven, then flee to Jesus Christ! You may think your sins are too great, but they are not. The redemptive work of Jesus Christ is sufficient to save the greatest sinner. Paul himself was a vile sinner but was still saved by Christ! You can be too. Simply come to Christ confessing your guilt and your sin. Cast yourself upon what he did for sinners, and you will discover what it means to be washed, sanctified and justified.

# 20.
# Slack saints and slick slogans

*Please read 1 Corinthians 6:12*

'If it feels good, do it!' 'It's all right as long as no one gets hurt!' 'You can't legislate morality!'

Our society is awash with slogans. What is a slogan? It is a form of intellectual shorthand. The slogan bypasses the intellectual process and announces only the conclusion. You have probably heard the story about the fellows who told the same jokes so many times they finally decided to number them. When they wanted to tell a particular joke they would simply call out the number and everybody would laugh. Slogans are to the thinking process what those numbers were to the jokes.

Some slogans are good because the reasoning behind them is sound. Other slogans are not so good. They are inherently flawed because the reasoning behind them is defective. Some slogans are both good and not so good. They are good if applied in the right way, but not so good if applied in the wrong way.

The Corinthians were fond of a couple of slogans. One was good; the way they were applying it was not good. The other slogan was not good at all.

## A good slogan misused

The good slogan came from the apostle Paul himself. He was constantly saying, **'All things are lawful for me.'** Some versions translate it: 'All things are permissible to me.'

This slogan was Paul's way of emphasizing the freedom Christians enjoy in Christ. Nothing thrilled Paul more than this freedom.

Prior to his conversion, he was a strict Pharisee who based his hope of salvation solely on his ability to keep the law of Moses. He was scrupulously cautious about the most minute details of his life. But the harder he tried to keep the law, the more miserable he became. Finally, by the grace of God, he came to see he could never produce enough righteousness on his own to qualify for heaven. At the same time, he came to understand that Jesus Christ is the only one who has the kind of righteousness that is pleasing to God, and that the righteousness of Christ counts for those who renounce their own righteousness and trust Christ's. When Paul came to understand this, the shackles fell off his soul and he was made free! He no longer had to monitor the minutiae of life to see if he was meticulously keeping the law. Some of the things he had been trying to avoid he now saw as completely harmless!

This is what Paul made reference to when he used his slogan: 'All things are permissible for me.' Instead of going through the long explanation of his experience, he would just capture it all with this slogan. It was a good slogan, and it had good reasoning behind it.

But some in the church of Corinth had seized Paul's slogan and were using it in a way he never intended. In fact, the way they were using it nauseated him. They were actually maintaining that the freedom Paul emphasized included the freedom to sin! Specifically, they were using Paul's slogan as a theological excuse to plunge headlong into their society's sea of sexual immorality. They were equating Christian liberty with carnal licence! When we really want to do something, it is not hard to find some way to justify it.

## A thoroughly bad slogan

They weren't content, however, merely to twist Paul's good slogan so it was beyond recognition. They added to it a slogan of their own which was thoroughly bad: 'Foods for the stomach and the stomach for foods' (6:13). They probably picked up this slogan from their society. Corinth, as we have noted, was a city of philosophy. The common response of many of these philosophers to any sexual relationship was to say it was no more right or wrong than the act of eating. Sexual acts are merely gratifying a bodily appetite, nothing more. Just as the stomach was made for food and food was made for the stomach, so sex was made for the body and the body for sex!

It is not hard to see the significance of all this for our own time. Sexual immorality is as common and culturally acceptable today as it was then. The pressure to do what everyone else is doing is immense. Many Christians are finding it so difficult to remain sexually pure that they are ready to welcome any kind of new theological thinking that would excuse them for indulging in immorality. And theologians, anxious to oblige, scour their Bibles to see if they can find the Achilles' heel of old-fashioned morality. In the last few years, for instance, some of these theologians have arrived breathlessly upon the scene to proudly announce that the Bible does not forbid homosexuality *per se* but only promiscuous homosexuality.

Surrounded with faltering Christians and faddish theologians, we urgently need a clarion call to sexual morality, and we have it in two parts in this passage. First, the apostle rescues his good slogan from the distortion it had suffered at their hands (6:12). Secondly, he shows the absurdity of their other slogan (6:13-20).


## Boundaries to freedom

Paul doesn't in the least retract his slogan and thus retreat from championing Christian liberty. Instead he makes it clear his slogan was never meant to justify sexual immorality or any other sin. How does he do this? Look back to verses 9 and 10. There the apostle solemnly affirms that those who continue in sexual sin will not enter the kingdom of God at all!

In saying all things were lawful or permissible for him, Paul quite obviously did not include sexual immorality! That is not permissible for the Christian! In other words, when Paul said 'all things', he did not literally mean all things without exception are permissible to the Christian. We often say 'everybody' is going to a party, but we quite obviously don't mean that everybody in the whole world without a single exception is going to be there. We should grant Paul the right to use words in the same way we do.

What, then, did Paul mean by his slogan? He intended it to apply only to indifferent matters. There are certain issues that are not clearly defined. Some Christians think they are right while other Christians think they are wrong. Such issues are often described as 'grey areas'. They are morally neutral, and Christians can legitimately disagree with each other on such matters.

How does one go about settling such a dispute? It is at this point Paul's slogan comes into play. Paul says the Christian is free to do anything not inherently wrong, but even then he needs to keep a couple of boundaries in mind.

Setting boundaries around freedom sounds strange to us. Our generation has taken freedom to mean the absence of all boundaries, but a little reflection reveals there is no such thing as absolute freedom in this fallen world. Americans prize their freedom of speech, but that freedom is not absolute. Justice Oliver Wendell Holmes, in a classic ruling of the Supreme Court, said freedom of speech doesn't give one the right to shout 'Fire!' in a crowded theatre unless, of course, there is a fire. Freedom of speech also doesn't give Americans the right to threaten the president. There are boundaries to this fundamental right.

## Edification

What are the boundaries Paul places around Christian freedom? First, there is the boundary of edification. Paul says, **'All things are lawful for me, but all things are not helpful.'** Even though a particular act might not be inherently wrong, it doesn't necessarily mean the Christian should engage in it. Is it profitable to him? Will it build him up in his faith? Someone has observed that a dog can lick a skunk at any time but it just isn't worth it! So the Christian can give his time and energy to things that are not wrong in themselves but are also not necessarily helpful to his Christian walk.

There is nothing wrong, for example, with the Christian playing golf. But if he finds himself becoming so occupied with it that he has no time to read the Scriptures, to pray, to spend time with his family, or to go to church, it is wrong! In such a case, something innocent has become harmful because the Christian has let his liberty to do this thing cross the boundary of edification.

## Enslavement

The second boundary Paul places on Christian liberty is the principle of enslavement. Paul says, **'All things are lawful for me, but I will not be brought under the power of any.'** The question each Christian must ask about anything he is legitimately free to do is whether he is in control of it, or it is in control of him. If any innocent diversion controls and dominates my life, it is no longer a freedom but a slavery, and I must say 'No' to it. Freedoms are only freedoms as long as we are free to say 'No' to them.

There is much here for us to ponder. Sexual temptation abounds on every hand, and Christians find themselves pressured to breaking-point. How are we to respond? Are we to try to find some theological excuse for indulging in sin? Are we to pretend that the freedom we have in Christ includes freedom to sin? Or are we to recognize that we have been called to holiness? That call, instead of being given a licence to sin, means that we do not even engage in innocent things that do not edify. Do we see the far-reaching implications of Christianity? It is literally to determine how we approach every facet of life. May God give us the grace to face the sexual torrent of this time by applying our Christianity.

# 21.
# Surprise —
# It's not your body after all!

*Please read 1 Corinthians 6:13-20*

No slogan is more popular today than 'A woman has the right to decide what happens to her body.' This is considered by many to be the final word on the abortion issue. Register opposition to abortion and someone will recite this slogan and smile triumphantly as though that clinched the argument. Neither the government nor the church, the argument goes, has the smallest right to say anything about what women decide to do with their bodies.

Of course, many state governments do demand that both women and men keep their bodies 'belted up' when driving a car. And the government forbids the taking of certain drugs into our bodies. But the abortion merchants like to sweep these disconcerting facts under the carpet.

I am not surprised by such muddleheaded thinking in society, but I do get perturbed when I find it cropping up in the church. As a matter of fact, many Christians are content to slide by the issue of abortion by merely repeating this same lame slogan, and they respond to the other moral and social issues of the day by mindlessly mouthing other popular slogans.

The Christians of Corinth were doing the same thing in response to their society's massive amount of sexual immorality. They could have demonstrated the power of the gospel by standing boldly against the tide, but they locked step with their culture and meekly shuffled along saying, **'Foods for the stomach and the stomach for foods.'**

What did that slogan mean? Simply this: gratifying sexual appetite was no different from strolling to the fridge for a snack! According to this slogan, it made as much sense to debate the morality of eating a salami on rye as to debate the morality of any sex act one was inclined to engage in.

This slogan was particularly appealing to the Christians of Corinth because it enabled them to enjoy the best of both worlds. They could have Christ and the forgiveness of sins while still hanging on to their sexual immorality.

All was well until Paul burst into their peaceful little arrangement with sin and announced the shattering word that the slogan would not work for Christians. He uses six arguments to show them why their pet slogan was defective and sexual immorality was wrong.

### The purpose of the body

His first argument has to do with the purpose of the body. He says the body was not made for immorality but for the Lord (6:13). 'You like slogans so much,' Paul seems to say, 'try this one: "The body is for the Lord and the Lord is for the body."' In other words, their equating of sex and eating wouldn't hold because sex is not to the body what food is to the stomach. God did design the stomach for food and food for the stomach, but the day will come when both will be destroyed. The relationship of food and stomach is purely biological and will have no place in heaven.

What did Paul mean by his new slogan? What does it mean to say the body is for the Lord and the Lord is for the body? The body is for the Lord in that he designed it as an instrument through which we can serve him. The Lord is for the body in that the body cannot function without him. What a close connection there is between the body and the Lord! What a terrible thing, then, to take the body out of service to him and use it in a way that is displeasing to him!

### The destiny of the body

Paul's second point has to do with the destiny of the body (6:14). Since food and the stomach are so closely connected, they will share the same destiny: destruction. By the same token, since the body and the Lord are so closely intertwined, they also share the same destiny! Just as the Lord Jesus was raised from the dead, so our bodies will be raised from the dead and given eternal glory.

Thank God, when the body dies, the soul goes immediately into his presence. But that, as wonderful as it is, is not the Christian's great hope. The Christian looks forward to that day when his body will be raised from the grave and will be transformed into the likeness of Jesus Christ himself. With such a high and holy destiny awaiting our bodies, how can we use them for low and ignoble things now?

### The church as the body of Christ

Paul's third argument has to do with the corporate implications of sexual immorality (6:15). Notice how he shifts the focus away from 'the body' to **'your bodies'**. He is talking now about the church as a whole. Later in this letter, Paul says all Christians are members of the body of Christ (12:12-27).

What does this have to do with the individual Christian committing sexual immorality? Simply this: when a Christian commits immorality, he involves the whole body of Christ in his sin! The enormity of this thought causes Paul to register his personal revulsion: 'God forbid' (AV).

### The nature of the sexual act

For his fourth argument, Paul moves back to the individual Christian and the nature of the sexual act itself (6:16-17). From the very beginning, when God made Eve for Adam, the sexual act was designed to be far more than a mere joining of bodies. It is a coming together as one body. In the sexual relationship, two people become 'one flesh'.

Warren Wiersbe writes, 'When a man and woman join their bodies, the entire personality is involved. There is a much deeper experience, a "oneness" that brings with it deep and lasting consequences... Sex is not just a part of the body. Being "male" and "female" involves the total person. Therefore, sexual experience affects the total personality.'[28] We may not understand all that means, but it should be as clear as the noonday sun that there is no such thing as 'casual sex'.

This is true of the sexual relationship, no matter who engages in it. But the Christian brings something else to the sexual relationship that makes it even more serious, and that is the spirit of Christ. When he was saved he became **'one spirit'** with Christ (6:17). What does it mean to be one spirit with Christ? Doesn't it mean we have the same purposes and priorities? If we are one spirit with him and his spirit is opposed to sexual immorality, doesn't that mean that we must also be opposed to it? John MacArthur writes, 'All sex outside of marriage is sin, but when it is committed by believers it is especially reprehensible, because it profanes Jesus Christ, with whom the believer is one...'[29]

## A sin against one's own body

Paul's next point is that sexual sin amounts to a sin against one's own body (6:18). It is not just a sin with the body, or in the body, but a sin *against* the body. If you have a beautiful car and break the speed limit with it, you have sinned in the car but not against it. If you used your beautiful car to haul garbage in, you would be sinning against the car. That would be a desecration of the car because it would violate the purpose for which the car was made. That is exactly what sexual sin does to the body since the body belongs to the Lord.

## The body as the dwelling-place of the Holy Spirit

Paul brings his discussion of this matter to a powerful close with his sixth contention, namely, the body of the Christian is inhabited by the Holy Spirit of God (6:19-20). The Holy Spirit himself has taken up residence in the Christian and made the Christian's body his own sanctuary or dwelling-place. And the Holy Spirit indwells the Christian's body because the Christian is nothing less than the purchased possession of the Lord Jesus Christ. Christ purchased the Christian when he died on the cross, and as a result, the old tenant has been evicted and the Holy Spirit has moved in!

The Christian is so grateful to be the purchased possession of Christ and the dwelling-place of the Holy Spirit that he desires nothing more than to live for the honour and praise of God, who made it all possible. The Christian is not just satisfied not to defile his body; he wants actively to use his body to serve the Lord who purchased him.

Let those who do not know Christ talk all they want about being free to do with their bodies as they please. The Christian gladly acknowledges that his body doesn't belong to him but to the Lord Jesus. And in being the purchased possession of the Lord Jesus, the Christian finds true freedom!

# 22.
# Marital questions: Marriage or celibacy?

*Please read 1 Corinthians 7:1-9*

With these verses we come to a major transition in Paul's letter. Up to this point he has been dealing with two major manifestations of the Corinthians' contamination with worldly thinking and doing: lack of unity (chs 1-4) and lack of sexual purity (chs 5-6).

But now Paul turns from the contamination of the church by the world to the confusion of the church about their faith. This confusion was apparent in that they had written to Paul and asked for his guidance on several important aspects of the Christian life. They had questions about marriage (ch. 7), food offered to idols (chs 8-10), worship and the Lord's Supper (ch. 11), spiritual gifts (chs 12-14), the resurrection of the dead (ch. 15) and the giving of their money (ch. 16).

## Satan's tactics

Before rushing off into this section of the letter, it is important for us to stop and reflect on this deadly combination of contamination and confusion. Satan has effectively employed this devastating one-two punch down through the centuries. He is quite happy if he can land either, but he had scored with both in Corinth and the church was reeling! They were both contaminated and confused! They had swallowed their society's message and had failed to understand their own!

Are we faring any better in our match against Satan? Or have we taken this same combination on the chin and gone down for the count? Are we contaminated by our world? Do we accept uncritically and at face value the belief system served up by our society? Are the practices of society constantly surfacing in the church? What about confusion? Are we muddled in our thinking about the Christian message? Do we understand the basic meaning of the Christian faith and the broad ramifications of it? Or are we so confused about our faith that we cannot even see what is or isn't consistent with it?

It is important to realize Satan, like any good fighter, uses these two punches together. One always sets up the other. He uses contamination to confuse us and he uses confusion to contaminate us. So even though this letter falls into two discernible parts, both contamination and confusion are apparent on every page. It is no surprise, then, to find Paul alluding to their confusion while he was still dealing with their contamination. In chapter 6 alone, we find him asking six times, 'Do you not know?'

## The danger of confusion

Even though Satan uses both punches effectively, confusion is the deadlier of the two. In other words, the more confused we are about the Christian faith, the more apt we are to be contaminated with the world. In the book of Hosea, God pronounces this fearful indictment upon his people: 'My people are destroyed for lack of knowledge' (Hosea 4:6).

I fear the same could be said of us. Former generations of Christians grew robust in their faith by feeding it from several sources. They not only attended all the regular and special services of the church, but they made it a point to read good books with solid doctrinal content and to engage in conversation about the meaning of their faith. How times have changed! Now most Christians are content to gather their 'manna' only on Sunday morning, and their biblical knowledge consists only of what they hear then. If that isn't bad enough, the possibility of picking up solid biblical content from sermons is becoming scant indeed. This is the day of 'lite' preaching. It consists largely of dispensing advice on how to be happy, healthy and successful, and that light fare is served up with generous portions of jokes and illustrations.

Paul told Timothy to watch for those who would have itching ears and would 'not endure sound doctrine' (1 Tim. 4:3-4). Timothy undoubtedly saw plenty of them, and we are seeing multitudes again today.

## Confusion over marriage

One of the subjects about which the Corinthians were muddled and confused was marriage. It appears there were two extreme view-points on Christianity in general and on marriage in particular. Some in the church were 'libertines' while others were 'legalists'. The libertines subscribed to the notion that the body and all its activities are morally neutral. These people had a tendency to play fast and loose with marriage. They downplayed the sacredness of it and took a casual view of the sexual immorality swirling around them in Corinth. The legalists, on the other hand, were acutely aware of the sexual licence of the city, and they responded to it by suggesting the Christian should avoid sex altogether. This view, of course, inevitably led them to draw two conclusions: single life is superior to the married life, and Christians who are married should abstain from sexual relations.

With both the libertines and the legalists, marriage was the loser. So Paul seeks to steer a middle course between these extremes. The amazing thing is that Paul has suffered much abuse because of what he says. He is regularly kicked around as a mean, crotchety fellow who hated women and was violently opposed to marriage.

A little study quickly reveals that nothing could be further from the truth. Paul had a very high view of marriage. First, as a Jew, he was steeped in the Old Testament. From Genesis 2:18 (where God said it was not good for man to be alone) all the way to Malachi 2:14-16 (where the Lord denounces divorce), the Old Testament presents marriage as good and honourable. Secondly, in Ephesians 5:22-33 Paul penned one of the most beautiful descriptions of marriage ever written. Finally, Paul warned Timothy to be on guard against those who forbid marriage (1 Tim. 4:3). These facts should make it clear that Paul has been much misrepresented on this matter.

So what does Paul teach in this passage? Two things: the single life is good, but the married life is natural!

## The single life is good

He begins by saying, **'It is good for a man not to touch a woman.'** This is the phrase that stirs the wrath of multitudes who see it as proof that Paul regarded women as substandard beings. But this phrase was simply the standard way for Jews to refer to sexual intercourse. All Paul is saying is that if a man chooses to remain unmarried, it is good and right for him to do so. The statement has absolutely nothing to do with the worth of women *per se*. It's merely Paul's way of saying there should be no stigma attached to any man who doesn't marry.

In fact, Paul later admits the single life does afford one some distinct advantages in seeking to serve the Lord (7:7), but he hastens to say no one is capable of living this kind of life unless he has been given the ability to do so. Paul had this gift and was glad for it, but he recognized others didn't have it. We don't decide what our gifts are — God does. Our part is simply to discern our gifts and to use them for God's honour. Those who have the gift of singleness should recognize it as such and not feel superior to those who are married. Those who don't have the gift of singleness shouldn't seek to remain unmarried.

## The married life is natural

But if the single life is good, the married life is natural. Paul says, **'Nevertheless, because of sexual immorality, let each man have his own wife, and let each woman have her own husband'** (7:2). In other words, the legalists who reacted to the flood of immorality around them by refraining from marriage or sex within marriage were wrong. They were countering one evil by endorsing another. Marriage was not part of the immorality problem; it was the solution! It is the God-given safeguard against sexual immorality in that it gives a channel for sexual release. That is why Paul says it is better to marry than to burn with sexual passion (7:9).

## Guidelines for married Christians

Paul couldn't be content, however, merely to say marriage is natural. He proceeds to give three guidelines for Christians who decide to marry.

First, they are to practise monogamy. Each man is to have a wife and each woman is to have a husband. (By the way, these words also clearly rule out all homosexual marriages.)

Secondly, husbands and wives are to satisfy each other's sexual needs. Marriage cannot be a hedge against immorality if either partner deprives the other in this area. Like us, the Corinthians were great ones for insisting on their individual rights, but that mentality provides a shaky ground for marriage. Marriage only works if each partner concerns him or herself with the other. Marriage partners exist for each other. That is why Paul says neither has authority over his or her own body (7:4).

Thirdly, husbands and wives may abstain from sexual relations for a short, special period of fasting and praying. A couple of things should be noted here. This is not a situation in which one partner devotes him or herself to fasting and prayer, but where the two do so together. Also, the fasting and prayer mentioned here are of a special kind. Paul assumes husbands and wives will pray together regularly, but he recognizes there will be times when they will want to so give themselves to prayer that they will want to abstain from sex.

Paul, then, is making a plea here for balance. There should be no stigma attached to either the single or the married life. Much of Satan's success against us comes from his ability to take us from one extreme to another. The way to foil his strategy is to drink so deeply from the Word of God that we understand God's will. Having done that, we must earnestly pray for the Holy Spirit to help us live according to that will.

# 23.
# Marital questions:
# Divorce

*Please read 1 Corinthians 7:10-16*

The rampant sexual immorality of Corinth was putting a lot of pressure on the Christians there. How were they to respond to it? Were they simply to ignore it? It was far too pervasive for that. Were they to adopt the 'If you can't beat them, join them' approach and throw sexual purity to the wind? Some apparently thought so, but most realized the Christian faith demanded a holiness that excluded such an idea. Were they to conclude the Christian's best hope for avoiding sexual immorality was to avoid sex altogether? Many seemed to think so.

Those who opted for the latter view soon found themselves led to draw a couple of conclusions. One was that the single life was morally superior to married life. If sex is always wrong, the single life could no longer be considered merely as an alternative; it was an imperative. Paul himself was single and appeared to be the perfect model each Christian should seek to emulate in determining his or her marital status. A second conclusion the 'anti-sex' people had to draw was that those who had already 'messed things up' by getting married should either abstain from sexual relations or get a divorce.

Paul was compelled to respond to both these conclusions. He tackled the first by saying that the single life, although it does afford certain advantages in serving the Lord, is not the type of life one could live without a special gift or calling from the Lord. In saying this, Paul was essentially repeating what the Lord Jesus himself taught in Matthew 19:11-12.

The second idea had two parts: the married should either abstain from sex or get a divorce. Paul tackled the abstinence part by insisting one of the main purposes of marriage is to serve as an outlet for sexual passion and thus provide shelter from the temptation to fall into sexual immorality. Abstinence from sexual relations, therefore, is to be only for a short time, by mutual consent and for a spiritual purpose.

In the passage before us Paul focuses on the divorce issue. Few topics are more difficult and distasteful than this. As soon as it is mentioned, Christians begin to get ill at ease and edgy. They fear any discussion of the subject is bound to embarrass divorced people. Ironically, those who have gone through the trauma of divorce are often most eager to help others to avoid it.

Paul's discussion of this touchy matter falls into two sections. First, he discusses marriages in which both partners are Christians (7:10-11). Then he turns his attention to mixed marriages — those in which a Christian is married to an unbeliever (7:12-16).

## Christian couples

We can understand how Christians married to unbelievers might consider divorce, but it is surprising to find Christian couples entertaining the idea. This indicates how forcefully the anti-sex advocates had stated their position. Some couples had begun to wonder if their marriage should be ended in order for them to be more spiritual.

Paul responds to this situation by repeating the teachings of Jesus on divorce. That is what his phrase, **'yet not I but the Lord'**, means (7:10). What was the teaching of Jesus? Essentially this: marriage was instituted by God himself, and it should be considered so sacred and permanent that those who enter it will not seek a divorce except where one partner becomes involved in adultery. Even in that case, divorce is allowed but not commanded (Matt. 5:31-32; 19:3-9; Mark 10:2-12; Luke 16:18).

So to Christian couples, Paul says, 'Stay married.' They were not to allow themselves to be hoodwinked into thinking marriage consigned them to a life of second-class spirituality. They could be married and still be pleasing to the Lord. After all, marriage was instituted by God himself.

But what about those who had already been deceived into getting a divorce? It was too late for them to prevent it. So what were they to do? Paul answers by saying they must stay single or be reconciled to their former partners.

## Mixed marriages

What counsel does Paul offer those Christians who are married to an unbeliever? Let's make sure we understand the situation Paul is dealing with. He is not talking about whether a believer should marry an unbeliever. It was unthinkable to him that a Christian should ever entertain the notion. A little later, he explicitly says the Christian is free to marry 'only in the Lord' (7:39).

The situation Paul is addressing is where two unbelievers had married and one subsequently became a Christian. This was happening with great frequency in Corinth and other cities where the gospel was being preached. We can well understand how the unbeliever in this situation might contemplate initiating divorce. When asked what he found to be so difficult about his wife becoming a Christian, one man explained it like this: first, she was no longer the person with whom he had fallen in love; and, secondly, there was now another man around the house, and she was constantly talking about him and seeking his guidance. Such is the change that true conversion makes![30]

But the thing troubling Paul was that many of the Christian spouses were the ones contemplating divorce. In chapter 6 we found Paul himself teaching that the one who engages in sex with a harlot becomes one flesh with her (6:16). Some in the church were eager to use such reasoning as justification for divorcing their unbelieving partners. If sexual relations make the two partners one flesh, the Christian married to an unbeliever would be one flesh with an unbeliever. Could such a union ever be considered right? Wouldn't divorce be the best solution in such a case?

## The Christian married to a 'willing unbeliever'

Paul divides his guidance on this matter into two parts. First, he offers guidance to the Christian who is married to a willing unbeliever, that is, an unbeliever who wants to see the marriage continue (7:12-14). The Christian in this situation is to be content to maintain the marriage. He or she is not to separate from or divorce the unbelieving partner.

But what about the defilement issue? Is the believer defiled by being married to an unbeliever and in being one flesh with him or her? Far from it! Instead of the believer being defiled by the unbeliever, Paul says the unbeliever is **'sanctified'** by the believer, and the children of such a marriage are **'holy'** (7:14).

This certainly should not be construed to mean that the presence of a Christian in the home automatically saves his or her spouse and children. This is foreign to everything Paul and the other biblical authors taught about the nature of salvation, namely, that each individual must repent of his or her sins and embrace the Lord Jesus Christ as Lord and Saviour. The meaning is rather, in the words of Charles Eerdman, 'The acceptance of Christ by either a husband or wife brings into the family circle a holy atmosphere and the possibilities of a Christian home.'[31]

Is Paul suggesting that the Christian who orders his conduct according to the Word of God can expect his faith to be contagious? If so, there is much for us to ponder. Are we living in such a way that those unbelievers most closely associated with us are likely to become Christians?

### The Christian with an unwilling partner

That leads us to the other possibility in a 'mixed' marriage — the one in which the Christian is married to an unwilling unbeliever. What is to be done here? Paul stresses that the initiative rests with the unbelieving partner. If he or she desires a divorce, the believer really has no choice in the matter. Paul gives this explanation: **'God has called us to peace'** (7:15). In other words, God wants the believer to live in peace. If the unbeliever is set on divorce, it is better for the believer to let him or her go than to engage in bickering and fighting that defames the name of Christ. Some, of course, would like to use Paul's words as a blanket justification for any and every divorce, but Paul isn't advising divorce any time our personal peace is disturbed in marriage. He makes this statement only in the context of the unbeliever initiating divorce.

But wait a minute. Paul has just said the believing partner exerts a sanctifying influence on the unbelieving partner. Shouldn't the believer, then, contest divorce initiated by the unbeliever with the hope of maintaining the marriage and winning the unbeliever to the Lord? Paul's response is that even though the believer has faith that the unbeliever may be won, there is still no absolute guarantee it will happen. So Paul writes, **'For how do you know, O wife, whether you will save your husband? Or how do you know, O husband, whether you will save your wife?'** (7:16).

Suppose the unbeliever does initiate a divorce? Does the believer have the right to remarry? Most biblical scholars agree the phrase, **'A brother or a sister is not under bondage in such cases'** (7:15) means the believer is free to remarry.

Many dislike what Paul says in this passage and try to find some way to get around it. A popular approach has been to say that Paul was not writing as an inspired apostle here but was just giving his personal opinion. To substantiate this, they appeal to the phrase, **'To the rest I, not the Lord, say'** (7:12). However, this phrase is not a disclaimer of inspiration on Paul's part. To understand it we need to go back to verse 10 where he used the phrase, 'not I, but the Lord'. There, he was referring to a matter on which the Lord Jesus Christ gave explicit teaching during his earthly ministry. In verse 12, Paul is dealing with a matter the Lord had not specifically dealt with. The contrast, then, is not between inspired and uninspired teaching but between what Jesus spoke about and what he didn't speak about.

If not handled carefully, Paul's teachings on this controversial topic can generate a sense of guilt in those who are divorced and a sense of smugness in those who are not. Those who have gone through the trauma of divorce need to be reminded it is not the unpardonable sin. Even though Scripture never encourages divorce, it does permit it in the case of adultery, or in the case of the unbeliever who doesn't want to continue being married to a believer. Those who happen to be divorced for other reasons need to reflect long and hard on the fact that there is forgiveness with God.

Those who have never been divorced need to be careful they don't fall into the trap of assuming their marriage is a success just because they have been able to avoid divorce. We have a tendency to pride ourselves on just staying married, but the truth is that God isn't interested only in couples staying together. Yes, he wants that, but he also wants the staying to be out of true love and unity, not just out of dogged determination. Some of those who have gone through divorce are now more committed to having a healthy marriage than those who have never divorced.

We, like the Corinthians, live in a society where immorality threatens to engulf us. May God help us to realize the answer is not to develop an anti-sex mentality. If God gives the gift of singleness, let's use it for his glory. If God wants us to be married, let's use marriage for his glory. The best thing we can do in this sex-soaked society is not to reject sex but to demonstrate to the world the happiness that comes when it is used in the way God intended.

# 24.
# Curing the 'If only...' syndrome

*Please read 1 Corinthians 7:17-24*

Have you ever wondered what you would do differently if you could go back and live your life again? Would you select the same career? Would you marry the same person? Would you marry at all? Would you settle in the same community? Would you buy the same house? Would you choose the same friends? Would you have children?

For some, this little mind-game is nothing more than an innocent diversion. They play it for a while and then come happily back to the way their lives really are. For others, however, this is no game. They are unable to break life's monotony by toying with this question for a few minutes before dismissing it and returning to reality. This is their reality. They are completely consumed and driven by what their lives might have been had it not been for a slip in their judgement, or some turn of events beyond their control.

The fact is, many people are perfectly miserable because they realize they only get one crack at this life and their chance to enjoy it has passed them by. They suffer from the 'If only...' syndrome, and go around moaning, 'If only I had married someone else...,' or 'If only I had gone to college...,' or 'If only I had chosen another career...,' or even 'If only I didn't have such a big nose...' The list of possibilities never ends.

Some in the church of Corinth were caught in this deadly trap. They wanted to serve the Lord, but they had been deceived into believing they had forfeited any opportunity to do so. Some were in the grip of vain regrets because they were married. A popular view in the church, as we have noticed, insisted that one had to be single to be truly spiritual. So married Christians rued the day they decided to get married and wondered if they should get a divorce.

The passage before us reveals that others were also feeling the razor-sharp edge of vain regrets. The Jewish believers in the church had vain regrets about the circumcision prescribed by their former religion of Judaism. Now that they were saved and had broken with Judaism, their circumcision was a source of embarrassment to them. Should they seek to have the operation reversed?

Ironically, while some were regretting circumcision, others were regretting the absence of it. They knew it was commanded in the Old Testament as a sign and seal of God's special covenant with the Jews, and they found themselves wondering if special blessing accrued to those who had received it. Should they now seek circumcision?

Another group battling with the 'If only...' syndrome was composed of the slaves in the church. How could a slave ever serve the Lord? He had hardly any control over his own life. His time was not his own and he had little or no money. Wouldn't the slave be better off to gain his freedom, even if he had to resort to 'hook or crook' to do so?

Paul's response to all of this is to state one principle three times. Someone has said if you want to get something across to people, you have to tell them what you are going to tell them, then tell them, then tell them what you told them! Paul practises that procedure here. What is the one principle stated three times? We can put it in two simple words: 'Be content!' That is the essence of what Paul says in verses 17, 20 and 24.

Paul, of course, knew it wasn't sufficient for him merely to say, 'Be content.' As he wrote this principle, he probably could hear the rejoinder: 'Easier said than done.' So he puts in this passage three truths to help his readers achieve this elusive goal of contentment, truths like rich veins of gold that glitter in the ore.


### God's sovereignty

First, he urges them to keep in mind the truth of God's sovereign distribution (7:17-18). He says, **'But as God has distributed to each one, ... so let him walk.'** We talk a lot about luck, accidents and chance, but Scripture consistently teaches that God is in control of all things and nothing happens apart from his decreeing or permitting it.

So as far as the Corinthians' world was concerned, it didn't just happen by chance that Jews were Jews, Gentiles were Gentiles and slaves were slaves. All of this was under the sovereign control of God. God didn't suddenly look down on Corinth one day and shriek in panic, 'We're making too many Jews again!' The same is true today. God knows that nose of yours is too big to suit you. He gave it to you!

Some always respond to any talk of God's sovereign allocation by saying his distribution isn't fair. The assumption behind this objection is that somewhere in the world's archives is a guarantee that life will be minutely fair, with all receiving the same measure of weal and woe. Those who hold this view think no one should have to shed one tear more or one tear less than all of the other men and women who have tramped across the stage of history.

The reason so many think this way is that they believe this life is all there is; if someone doesn't get justice here, he will never get it. I don't want to disappoint you, but Scripture reveals that God is more concerned about preparing us for eternity than in making sure we all get through life with the same fair share of everything.

The sovereignty of God is a great mystery and our minds are very limited. We aren't able to parcel it all out and explain how it all works, but the fact that we cannot understand something doesn't make it false. Don't try to explain the sovereignty of God, but learn to rest in it. When you do you will find contentment. The most difficult and unpleasant situation is transformed by the realization that God, in his sovereign wisdom, has placed us there. If you have trouble accepting the sovereignty of God, think for a while about this: if God isn't in control of every detail, it is sheer folly to talk about trusting him.

## What really matters

Secondly, Paul urges his readers to ponder life's supreme priority. He says, **'But keeping the commandments of God is what matters'** (7:19).

In terms of receiving special blessing in the service of God, there was no virtue in either circumcision or uncircumcision. Neither was there virtue in not being a slave. God's blessing rests on those who obey him, whether they be circumcised or uncircumcised, slave or free.

Take the slavery issue. As miserable as it was to be a slave, there was nothing about slavery that prevented one from obeying the commands of God. Paul says if the slave received the opportunity to be free, he should certainly seize it; however, if the opportunity never came, he could still serve God. There are some ways of life that are inconsistent with the commands of God. The prostitute who is converted, for instance, cannot continue being a prostitute. Obedience to God would require her to make a complete break with her former way of life, but there was nothing about slavery that made obedience to God impossible.

In fact, Paul argues that the nature of the Christian faith is such that there really is no difference between the slave and the free. The Christian slave has been freed from the very same things as all other Christians — sin, Satan and eternal death — and the free Christian has himself become a slave of Jesus Christ (7:22). So, as far as Christianity is concerned, all Christians (slave or free) are in exactly the same position.

So Paul urges the slave not to spend all his time pining away over his situation, but to use that condition for the glory of God (7:21). What could a slave do? He could refuse to show the sullen, resentful attitude that was common among slaves and could work happily and willingly for his master. The master would immediately know something profound had happened to his slave and thus the way would be prepared for the master to become a Christian too. And when enough people were saved by the power of the gospel, they would rise up against slavery and abolish it. History reveals that is how slavery was eventually abolished.

Do you want to be blessed of God? Quit worrying about your circumstances and start obeying him! Isn't it ironic that we often use our circumstances as an excuse for not obeying God when God is the one who gave us those very circumstances so we could obey him?

### In our circumstances 'with God'

The final truth that inevitably produces contentment almost escapes notice. Paul wraps up his discussion of contentment by saying, **'Let each one remain with God in that calling in which he was called'** (7:24).

Have you ever noticed those two words, 'with God'? Could Paul be suggesting that the very same God who gave the difficult situation is there in the midst of it to help us bear it? How different that makes our circumstances! Then our situation is not the result of an unfeeling tyrant callously dumping difficulty on us and then walking away! After giving the burden, our loving Father steps in and helps us shoulder it! That makes the burden much lighter. No, we still don't understand all his purposes, but the fact that he is with us in the difficulty surely makes us realize that, whatever his purposes, they are right and good!

Thanks to Paul, we now have a cure for the 'If only...' syndrome. We don't have to go around with vain regrets. If anyone says such and such a circumstance in our life is a shame, we can confidently say with Paul that every circumstance is from God's will, for God's service and with God's presence!

# 25.
# Things to think about before you marry

*Please read 1 Corinthians 7:25-40*

So far in this chapter we have found Paul dealing with the problems of those who were already married. These people had evidently been victimized by a group within their church who claimed to enjoy special revelations from the Lord. The truth is that their special insights resulted, not from special revelations, but from the desire to exercise authority over others by dictating to them how they should live.

One of these so-called 'revelations' of the spiritual aristocrats was that the single state is spiritually superior to the married state. The advocates of this view had been so successful in propagating it that some of the married in the church had even begun to wonder if they should get a divorce, and some who were contemplating marriage found themselves wondering if they should give up the idea.

In the first half of this chapter, Paul addresses the concerns of those who were already married. In addition to his other instructions and exhortations, he reproaches the married for allowing themselves to be taken in by the group claiming special insights from the Lord. He says, 'You were bought at a price; do not become slaves of men' (7:24). The Christian is to live on the basis of what the Lord has clearly revealed through his appointed channels, not on what others claim to have received privately from the Lord.

In the second half of the chapter, Paul turns his attention to those who were contemplating marriage. He opens and closes this section by taking a couple of potshots at the spiritual snobs who had created all this confusion. In verse 25 he says, **'I have no commandment from the Lord, yet I give judgment as one whom the Lord in His**

**mercy has made trustworthy.'** In verse 40 he says, **'I think I also have the Spirit of God.'**

The point he makes with the first phrase is that he, unlike the spiritual snobs, would claim no special revelation in deciding between alternatives when neither one is sinful. The closing phrase is heavy with sarcasm. Paul suggests the self-appointed receivers of special revelations allow the possibility that others might also have the Spirit of God. This amounted to a crushing word in the light of the fact that it came from one of the hand-picked apostles of the Lord Jesus Christ himself! In effect, he charges them with setting themselves above the apostles of the Lord Jesus Christ.

Between these withering phrases, Paul takes up the concerns of three groups of people associated with the question of whether those contemplating marriage should follow through. In verses 25-35, he addresses the 'virgins', or those who had never married. In verses 36-38, he addresses the fathers who were responsible for arranging marriages. In verses 39-40 he addresses widows.

### The unmarried

The first of these sections is by far the longest. The reason is that Paul packs into this section what all three groups should think about in making their respective decisions concerning marriage. In other words, Paul intended the fathers and the widows to make their decisions with his instructions to the unmarried in mind. He had to add only a word or two for their special situations.

### Special crises

What, then, is the essence of Paul's teaching in this passage? It is that those who are contemplating marriage should carefully think about certain realities before proceeding. What is there to think about? One thing all should ask themselves is whether there are any special crises that would put an unusual strain upon the marriage. Paul refers in verse 26 to **'the present distress'**, and in the light of it, urges the unmarried to stay that way.

Paul was probably referring to the cloud of persecution of Christians that was already building on the horizon and that finally broke in all its fury during the reign of Nero. During that time,

Christians were subjected to all kinds of unbelievable torture. Some were fed to lions, while others were covered with wax and used as human torches. Still others were thrown into vats of boiling oil. It is easy, in the light of these things, to see why Paul would advise as he did. The only thing that could make the sufferings of a Christian worse was to know he was leaving a wife and children in the midst of such distress or, worse still, to see them tortured.

Talk about persecution and most Christians simply heave a sigh of relief, wipe the perspiration from their brow and say, 'Thank God, we don't have to worry about that.' It is not too far-fetched to say, however, that another storm of persecution is brewing. Increasingly, Christians are finding themselves the only minority that can safely be held up as objects of scorn and ridicule. If that were not bad enough, Christians also find the threat of legal action growing each day. Incredibly, some are suggesting Christians who seek to evangelize should be held liable for invading the privacy of those they seek to convert, and pastors who preach anything to cause their listeners emotional distress should be held liable. If the situation continues to deteriorate, we shall find Paul's words have a peculiar relevance to our own day and age.

### The general cares of life

Even if there is no special crisis to consider, there are certain general cares that always have to be considered by those contemplating marriage. The special crisis only occurs from time to time, but the general cares of life are with us at all times.

First among these is what Paul calls **'trouble in the flesh'** (7:28). Marriage is one of God's most precious gifts. As such, it brings great joys and delights, but that doesn't mean it is easy. The single life is a much simpler life because the single person doesn't have to adjust to, or sacrifice for another person. As wonderful as marriage is, it is still a matter of two sinners living together, which always creates a certain amount of misunderstanding and conflict.

### The shortness of life

Another item on the list of the general cares of life is the shortness of life. Paul uses two phrases to convey this. First, he bluntly asserts,

'**The time is short**' (7:29) and, secondly, he declares, '**The form of this world is passing away**' (7:31).

For the young newly-married couple, life seems to be one vast, endless expanse, but those who have been married for a while marvel at how quickly the time passes. As the married see life swiftly receding from them and death steadily advancing, a degree of sadness sets in. The more a person has invested in this life, the harder it is to see the 'form' of this life ebb away. Part of the form of this life is marriage. When this life passes, marriage goes with it. This is not to say the Christian shouldn't marry, but only that he should realize when he marries he is in a sense making himself a hostage to future sorrows.

The brevity of this life is an important consideration for every aspect of life, not just for marriage only. It should really colour the Christian's approach to, and outlook on, everything.

First, it should sweeten his *sorrows*. When his heart is broken with a keen loss, the Christian shouldn't think it is nothing, but in the light of eternity, he should be able to see it is less than what it appears to be.

The shortness of life should also temper the Christian's *joys*. Thank God, there is much for the Christian to enjoy in this life, but the knowledge that life is brief prevents him from living excessively for these joys.

The impermanence of this life should also colour the Christian's view of *possessions*. The Christian is free to use the things of this world, but he is not to become so engrossed in them that he forgets he is a pilgrim here and his real treasure is elsewhere. Remembering the shortness of life gives the Christian a true perspective on material things.

Finally, the swiftness of life should colour the Christian's view of *pleasures*. The Christian, according to Paul, should use the world without abusing it (7:31). Some Christians have opted for a very narrow view of pleasure and essentially said all pleasure is wrong. Others have imbibed so deeply from the well of the world's thinking that they uncritically condone any and all pleasures. Neither extreme is correct. The Christian can legitimately engage in pleasures, but he must not be mastered by them. Thinking often about the temporary condition of this life and the pleasures it offers will keep the Christian from becoming unbalanced at this point.

*The demands of marriage*

There is one more general concern that should be considered before
embarking on the sea of matrimony: the demands marriage makes
upon one's time and energy (7:32-35). Marriage, by its very nature,
divides one's attention. In addition to serving the Lord, the married
Christian has the responsibility of pleasing his or her spouse. The
single person, on the other hand, is free to devote him or herself
entirely to the Lord.

Nothing was dearer to Paul than the gospel of Christ and he
wanted to see it advance as rapidly as possible. So he urges the single
state for as many as can accept it; however, he recognized all could
not be single and he didn't want to put these on 'a leash' or in a
straitjacket (7:35).

## The rôle of the fathers

Having laid these two considerations — special crises and general
cares — before those who had never married, Paul turns to say a
brief word to the fathers of unmarried daughters (7:36-38) and to the
widows.

In that culture, fathers had the primary rôle in arranging the
marriages of their daughters. It appears some of the fathers in
Corinth had become so thoroughly convinced of the superiority of
singleness that they had determined their young daughters would
remain single. Some of these daughters had now reached marriage-
able age and those fathers were evidently wondering whether they
should stand by their decision or proceed to arrange marriages for
their daughters.

Paul responds by saying these fathers would not be committing
sin if they provided for their daughters' marriage (7:36). The idea
that marriage is inherently evil is not to be tolerated for a single
moment. On the other hand, those fathers who had no hesitation or
fluctuation about this matter, who were unmoved by the stigma of
an unmarried daughter, and by the thought of a daughter not finding
the fulfilment of marriage, should stay with their original determination (7:37).

Paul's stance is consistent throughout his discussion of marriage.
Singleness is good if one has the gift of singleness, but if someone
doesn't have that gift he should feel free to marry.

## Widows

To the widows, Paul says essentially the same thing: if they feel the calling to remain single they will find there is a definite happiness there. If they do not have that calling, they are entirely free to marry with one condition: they must marry another believer!

There is absolutely nothing wrong with being married, and Paul wanted the Corinthians to stop being intimidated by those who, claiming to have a hotline to heaven, were attaching a stigma to marriage. At the same time, he wanted those who were thinking about marriage not to be naïve about what it involves. Marriage is good, but it isn't easy. Special crises can make marriage unwise, and general cares always make marriage challenging.

## The relevance of Paul's teaching for today

The current crop of Christians is in desperate need of Paul's teaching on marriage. Our confusion about this vital matter appears to be just as great as that of the Corinthians. We have those with their own hotline to heaven who claim marriage is wrong. We also have multitudes who think they are free to indulge in sexual relations outside the bonds of marriage. We usually associate this practice with young people, but it is also becoming extremely common among senior citizens. Furthermore, we have those who think they may marry anyone they want without regard to whether that person is a Christian. And, of course, we have no shortage of Christians who are divorced.

Paul's instructions give us the details we need for dealing with all of these problems. More importantly, his words show us our marriages are not independent little domains in which we are free to work our wills, but they also come under the lordship of Jesus Christ. Once we begin to approach marriage from that perspective, the confusion begins to melt away. As the confusion melts away, we are enabled to demonstrate the beauty of Christianity in our homes.

# 26.
# Black, white and the murky middle

*Please read 1 Corinthians 8:1-3*

Some things are clearly right. Scripture tells us so. It is right to pray. It is right to gather with other believers for worship. It is right to speak the truth. It is right to praise God. And on and on we could go. Other things are clearly wrong, and no amount of hedging and dodging can make them otherwise. It is wrong to lie, steal, commit adultery, murder, and so on.

But not all moral issues fall neatly into one of these two distinct categories. Some issues fall into that murky middle class of things which are neither black nor white but a dingy grey. The Christian is always obligated to do what Scripture commands and to refrain from doing what it forbids. But so far as we can tell, on these murky middle issues, God has not clearly revealed his will.

How, then, is a Christian to go about determining whether to practise, or refrain from participating in, things that fall into this grey area? Christians tend to answer that question in one of two ways. Some look at the absence of God's revelation on a certain practice and say, 'It must be right!' Other Christians look at the absence of God's revelation on the same practice and say, 'It might be wrong!'

## The debate about food sacrificed to idols

The church in Corinth was engaged in fierce debate on an issue that fell into this murky middle area. Unable to come to agreement on it, they finally wrote to Paul and asked for his guidance. The issue they were debating was meat that had been sacrificed to idols. Two questions were involved. First, should the Christian ever eat meat when he knew part of it had been used to make a sacrifice to an idol? Secondly, should the Christian ever attend a banquet in which sacrifices were made to idols? Paul deals with the first question at great length (8:1 - 10:13), the second question in a much briefer fashion (10:14-22) and then gives a brief summary of the whole matter (10:23 - 11:1).

It is very hard for us to appreciate the significance of these questions for the early Christians. Their culture was simply overrun with idols. For a good description of how pervasive idolatry was in the major Greek cities of that day, we have only to read Luke's account of Paul's visit to Athens. That city was so given over to idols that they even had an altar with the inscription 'To the Unknown God' (Acts 17:23). The impression we get is that the Athenians had made altars to every god they could think of, yet they were still afraid they had offended one god by leaving him out; therefore, they made this altar.

Food sacrifices were an essential part of the worship of all these gods for two reasons: the gods had to be kept happy, and the food had to be cleansed or purified. The common belief of that day was that demons were constantly trying to invade humans and the easiest way for them to do so was by attaching themselves to food. By being sacrificed to a god, the food was purified and could be eaten safely.

Each food sacrifice consisted of three parts: the first part was consumed in the offering itself; the second part was given as a payment to the priests; and the third part was kept by the offerer.

The Christians, of course, were not making sacrifices to idols, so what was the problem? Two things. First, the priests for the idols could not possibly use all the meat they received, so they sold most of it to the butchers of the day who put it on the market. Secondly, when a Christian was invited to someone's home for a meal, there was a good chance that the meat served had been used in idol-worship.

## The 'strong' and the 'weak'

I have already mentioned the two schools of thought among Christians when any issue in the grey area comes up. These two schools had both weighed in for this debate in Corinth. One school consisted of those Paul calls the **'weak'** Christians. These were the ones who were afraid to do anything not explicitly permitted by God for fear that it might be wrong. If they attempted to do so, they found themselves conscience-stricken and miserable.

On the other hand were the **'strong'** Christians, those who were able to practise anything not strictly forbidden and not feel any guilt at all. The problem was that these 'strong' Christians had very little patience with their weaker brothers and sisters and, when the issue of eating meat arose, they rather enjoyed flaunting their ability to eat this meat and causing the weaker Christians to squirm. When any of these weaker Christians raised an objection, the stronger Christians would chide them: 'Don't you know anything? There is only one God. All these idols are nothing. And besides, food doesn't mean anything to God.'

So these stronger Christians were framing the issue in terms of knowledge; that is, they were saying they were able to do these things because they were more knowledgeable than their weaker brothers and sisters. In putting the issue in this way, they were probably suggesting that although God had not given his will on this grey area to everyone, he had given it privately to them. There have always been those in the church who seek to give the impression that they are so close to the Lord that he gives them special revelation and withholds it from the church in general. From what Paul has said in this letter about other issues, it is apparent that Corinth had a good number of people who suffered from this spiritual élitism.

## Warnings about knowledge

So before ever taking up the issue of meat sacrificed to idols, Paul deals with the arrogant attitude of these stronger Christians. In fact, his whole discussion of this issue is addressed to the stronger Christians. He talks to them about the weaker Christians. Essentially, Paul says that even if these stronger Christians did possess great knowledge, they had no reason to be proud and boastful about it.

First, he declares that *knowledge was not their private domain*. They were going around saying of their little group, 'We all have knowledge.' Paul responded by saying, **'We know that we all have knowledge'** (8:1). They were evidently reserving the phrase exclusively for themselves, but Paul expands it to include all Christians.

They were putting the emphasis on 'we', but Paul put it on 'all'. Christians don't all know everything and they don't all know the same things, but they all know some things. Therefore, no Christian should look down on his brother or sister in Christ.

Secondly, Paul says those who possess knowledge still have not arrived because *knowledge is inferior to love.* While knowledge puffs up, love edifies, or builds up. No one believed more in the importance of knowledge than Paul. Wherever we turn in his writings, we find him insisting time and time again on the need for knowledge. One can make absolutely no progress in the Christian life without knowledge. But just as Paul was second to none in emphasizing the need for knowledge, so he was second to none in emphasizing that knowledge alone is not sufficient. So we find Paul firmly declaring we must always hold the truth with love (Eph. 4:15). Truth straightens us but love sweetens us.

Thirdly, Paul punctures their pride of knowledge by saying *knowledge is limited.* No one knows as much as he needs to know and most of us don't know nearly as much as we think we know. Paul says, **'And if anyone thinks that he knows anything, he knows nothing yet as he ought to know'** (8:2). The more a person knows, the more he realizes how much there is yet to know and the more he is humbled by it all.

Finally, Paul says *the purpose of knowledge* is not so we can brag about how much we know, but so we can love God more perfectly (8:3). The person who is truly knowledgeable in the things of God doesn't even think about how much he knows. He is simply lost in the desire to love God and to serve him. Scripture tells us that when Moses was so filled with the Spirit of God that his face actually glowed, he was unconscious of the glow. In like manner, we may rest assured that the more we really know about God, the less conscious we shall be of our knowledge.

The real question, as far as Paul was concerned, is not how much we know but whether we love God. If we truly know God, we will love him; if we love him, it is because he knew us and loved us first (Gal. 4:8-9; 1 John 4:19). Ultimately, all our knowledge is a matter of God's grace, so there is absolutely nothing for us to boast about.

So Paul begins to answer the question about this murky issue of eating meats sacrificed to idols by taking direct aim at the Corinthians' pride. They thought their problem was whether to eat meat or to refrain from it, but Paul says the real problem was their attitude.

Are you suffering from spiritual élitism? Do you look down on your brothers and sisters in Christ? Do you feel you are so advanced in knowledge that you are on a plateau by yourself? Heed Paul's words! Forget about how much you know and concentrate on loving God!

# 27.
# The weakness in the strong Christians' knowledge

*Please read 1 Corinthians 8:4-13*

The 'strong' Christians in Corinth were claiming that their freedom to eat meat sacrificed to idols and to attend banquets where such sacrifices were made was due to a superior degree of enlightenment. They enjoyed flaunting this enlightenment and belittling those who didn't possess it. As far as they were concerned, the real problem in their church was not meat at all, but rather the ignorance of the 'weak' Christians. And they probably thought the whole dispute would be quickly resolved by writing to Paul. He undoubtedly would congratulate them on their knowledge and freedom, deliver a resounding rebuke to the weak Christians, and the controversy would be over.

Paul's opening words must have come as a severe shock to them. He began, not by rebuking the weak Christians for having such fragile consciences, but by reprimanding the strong Christians for being so proud of their knowledge (8:1-3).

Has it ever occurred to you that only the humble can learn? As long as we think we already know, we cannot learn. So before taking up their question, Paul deflates the ego of these strong Christians and, by so doing, opens the door for them to learn.

After reading Paul's sharp words about the danger of taking pride in knowledge, we would expect him to begin demolishing the arguments of the strong Christians. Surprisingly enough, he doesn't. Instead, he proceeds to point out the essential correctness of their thinking.

**One true God**

Their justification for eating this meat consisted of two arguments.
First, because idols are not really gods at all, there could be no harm
in eating meat sacrificed to them. Secondly, food doesn't make one
acceptable to the only true God. Paul was very happy to set his seal
of approval on both arguments. In fact, he not only heartily endorsed
the first argument but even enlarged upon it (8:4-6). He began by
acknowledging the many things men were calling 'god' and 'lord'.
The term 'god' was anything to which deity was ascribed. The term
'lord', on the other hand, was probably reserved for secondary
mediators, that is, the channels through whom the gods could be
approached.

But calling something 'god' or 'lord' doesn't make it either of
these things, and Paul quickly affirms that there is in reality only one
true God and only one mediator (8:6). The true God is the one whom
Christians worship and serve. He is known to them as the 'Father'.
That means they have an intimate, personal relationship with him in
which they find warm love and acceptance as well as protection and
care. But as wonderful as the image of fatherhood is, it alone cannot
express all God is to the Christian. The Christian also freely
acknowledges God as the Creator and sovereign Ruler. Paul says
God is the one **'of whom are all things'**, and the Christian exists
**'for Him'** (8:7).

Let's pause a moment to consider these two phrases. Paul doesn't
merely say most Christians feel, or should feel, this way about God.
This is the way God is as far as the Christian is concerned. Yes, he
is the Father who loves us, but he is also the Sovereign who rules us.
I dare say most professing Christians are far more fond of the idea
of God as Father than they are of God as Sovereign. Those who do
get around to acknowledging God as Sovereign usually find it easier
to agree that he made everything than to admit we exist for him. It
is very easy for us to get so twisted in our thinking that we have God
existing for us and our comfort rather than ourselves existing for his
purposes.

**Only one mediator**

That brings us to Paul's next emphasis. The only way we can know
this one true God is through the one true Mediator — the Lord Jesus

Christ himself. He is the one **'through whom are all things, and through whom we live'** (8:7).

Paul's words about the Mediator are extremely important. It is not enough for the Christian merely to claim there is only one true God. Many in Corinth would probably have been quick to assert they were worshipping this God with their idols. Many today suggest God is actually present in the idol-worship of the heathen. Some even go so far as to say it is immoral for churches to send missionaries to pagan nations because they are already worshipping God in their own way.

By adding these words about the Mediator, Paul blows all such notions out of the water. He not only makes clear that there is only one true God, but also shows there is only one way to know and worship him, and that is through the Lord Jesus Christ.

### Food does not affect our standing before God

The second argument the strong Christians were using also received approval from Paul. He adds no words of amplification on this point, but that doesn't lessen the fact that he did wholeheartedly agree with it. What was this argument? Simply this: food doesn't have anything to do with our standing before God (8:8).

The reason this issue of eating meat sacrificed to idols had arisen was because God hadn't revealed his will about it. And the reason he hadn't revealed his will is because neither eating nor refraining from eating affected one's relationship with God. Those who ate this meat were not one bit closer to God than those who refrained from eating, and vice versa.

### The effect of our actions on others

The fact that Paul agreed the strong Christians were essentially correct in their thinking should not be construed to mean they were totally correct. So Paul, after having endorsed their two major arguments, turns their attention to the crucial omission in their thinking. The strong Christians thought it was enough simply to be convinced of the rightness of their position and then to go ahead and do what they felt inclined to do. If another Christian disagreed with them, they simply produced their arguments and went right on enjoying their freedom in Christ. Their attitude tended to be, 'If these weaker Christians can't eat this meat, it's their problem, not mine. I've got the right to do whatever I want.' Nothing could have been further from the truth. The Christian life is not a solo flight and, therefore, the Christian can never say he doesn't care how his actions affect his fellow Christians.

So, having said the strong Christians were right to realize idols are nothing, Paul proceeds to say, **'There is not in everyone that knowledge'** (8:7). Paul was probably referring to those who had recently been converted to Christianity from a life of paganism. They were so steeped in idol-worship and all it involved that it was exceedingly difficult for them now to think of the idol differently. John MacArthur explains: 'They knew that there is only one right God but perhaps they had not yet fully grasped the truth that there is only one real God.'[32]

No matter how persuasively the strong Christians marshalled their arguments, the weak Christians were simply not able to eat meat sacrificed to these idols without being conscience-stricken. To the strong, it was simply meat, but to the weak, it was still meat offered to an idol.

Furthermore, having said the strong Christians were right to understand that food doesn't commend us to God, Paul goes on to say they still should not regard themselves as totally free to eat this meat (8:9-13). Why not? Paul responds with a hypothetical situation. Just suppose, he argues, that a Christian whose conscience is opposed to eating this meat sees a fellow Christian go into one of these idol temples and eat. What kind of effect would this have on this weak Christian? In all likelihood, it would encourage him to do the same thing. What would be so bad about that? He would be violating his conscience about this matter. He would be doing something he really believed to be wrong, and that would be a sin for him. Are we clear at this point? If we do anything our conscience condemns on an issue on which God has not revealed his will, we have sinned.

But there is more to it than that. I may feel free in my conscience to do a particular thing. But if my doing this thing causes a Christian who is conscientiously opposed to do the same thing, I too have sinned! I have sinned against my brother or sister in Christ and, therefore, I have sinned against Christ himself (8:12).

So the question for the Christian is not simply whether he can defend a particular course of action intellectually, or whether he can engage in it without guilt. The question is rather how this particular action will affect his brothers and sisters in Christ. Yes, knowledge is important! Yes, liberty is important! But love for my fellow Christians is more important! Why? Because Christ valued my brothers and sisters so highly that he died for them (8:11). And I, as his follower, cannot treat lightly what he has paid so dear a price for.

For the Christian, then, freedom doesn't just mean doing whatever he wants. It also means not doing those things that will harm others. We are not truly free until we are free to say 'No' to our desires and wants. So Paul concludes this section by saying, **'Therefore, if food makes my brother stumble, I will never again eat meat, lest I make my brother stumble'** (8:13).

# 28.
# Saying 'No' to personal rights

*Please read 1 Corinthians 9:1-18*

The Corinthians were embroiled in a great debate on whether they should eat meat sacrificed to idols. This was an issue on which God had not clearly revealed his will, and some had concluded they were free to eat this meat, while others had concluded the opposite. Paul responded to their plea for guidance by laying down a fundamental principle: the Christian must be willing to forego doing anything in a grey area that causes a fellow Christian to stumble. Or we can put it in this way: the Christian must always give love priority over both his knowledge and his liberty in these matters on which God has not pronounced. When knowledge and liberty cry, 'Indulge!', love will often cry, 'Abstain!'

It seems, when we come to chapter 9, that Paul has finished dealing with the matter of eating meat and has gone on to a completely different matter. Some even argue this chapter is an abrupt digression in which Paul completely forsakes the matter at hand and begins to defend his apostleship. Only after ranging far afield, the argument goes, does Paul realize he hasn't fully answered the question put to him by the church and returns to it in chapter 10.

But chapter 9 is not an interruption in Paul's argument at all. Actually Paul is here illustrating from his own life the very principle he laid down in chapter 8. One of the great criticisms levelled at preachers is that they fail to practise what they preach. Paul doesn't give the Corinthians a chance even to raise this objection. He seeks to prove beyond any shadow of doubt that he was practising the very same principle he urged upon them.

**Four questions**

The first part of this passage consists of Paul showing that he had actually gone above and beyond what his principle required (9:1-15). The first thing he does is ask four rhetorical questions in rapid-fire succession.

'**Am I not an apostle?**' he asks. The apostles possessed a unique authority in the church. If anyone could legitimately claim to be exempt from the duty of foregoing personal rights and privileges, it was an apostle.

Next, Paul asks, '**Am I not free?**' He knew some would protest against the principle he had laid down. The Christian is supposed to be free in Christ, but how can he be considered free if he has to give up his freedom for the sake of another Christian? Essentially, Paul is saying, 'I have practised this principle and retained my freedom.'

Paul's third question is, '**Have I not seen Jesus Christ our Lord?**' Some of the strong Christians in the church were always quick to claim special revelations from the Lord. They might even have been claiming that God had privately revealed to them his will on some of these grey areas. By asking this question, Paul was saying he had received the greatest revelation God had to give. The implication is that the Corinthians should be willing to submit to his authority when he laid down any principle.

We know from what Paul says in 2 Corinthians that there were those in the church who disputed his apostleship and claimed to be apostles themselves. One of the qualifications for apostleship was being an eyewitness of the resurrected Christ. By reminding them that he had seen the risen Christ, Paul was at the same time validating his own claim to apostleship and invalidating the false claims of others.

Finally, Paul asks, '**Are you not my work in the Lord?**' Essentially, Paul says the Corinthians had more reason to accept his apostleship than anyone else because they had experienced the power of it in their conversion.

**What Paul gave up**

Do you see the point Paul is making? If he, an apostle, was willing for the sake of other Christians to forego his rights, how much more the Corinthians should be! But the length to which Paul was willing to go to practise the principle of foregoing personal rights becomes even clearer when we look at what he had given up. It wasn't something in the grey area at all! It was rather something of an undebatable nature! What was it? It was his right to receive payment from those to whom he ministered. He specifically says he had the right to expect them to pay enough for him to have his needs met (9:4), to have a Christian wife to travel with him (9:5) and not to have to work with his own hands (9:6). Before telling them why he had given up his right to their financial support, Paul goes to great lengths to prove that remuneration for the preacher is indeed beyond debate.

He first argues that this is *a universally recognized principle* in every realm of human endeavour (9:6-7). A soldier fighting for his country does not pay his own way. The farmer who plants a vineyard expects to eat of its fruit. A shepherd is entitled to use the milk from his flock. All of these are commonly accepted, with no one even raising so much as an objection. So it should be with paying the preacher.

Then Paul shows that remuneration for the preacher is *clearly taught in Scripture* (9:8-10). He quotes Deuteronomy 25:4. This verse says that even oxen are entitled to eat the very grain they are threshing. God didn't give this command out of some unusual concern for oxen, but to teach his people that in taking care of his oxen a man was taking care of himself. If the labourer expected to receive the fruit of the oxen's labour, he must take care of them. The same is true with God's people. By giving the minister the support he needs, they are helping themselves. When a minister knows God's people love and support him, he works even harder for their good.

Paul also appeals to *their sense of values* (9:11-12). He had imparted spiritual things to them. Did they now regard it as too much to share their material things with him? A very serious question is at stake here: which is greater — the spiritual or the material? How we answer that tells us a lot about ourselves. On top of that, Paul enjoyed a unique relationship with them. He was their spiritual father. If others were entitled to share their material things, he was even more so (9:12).

Finally, Paul appeals to something his readers were already familiar with. *Those who served in the temple* in Jerusalem received their living from the temple (9:13). The priests were supported by the worshippers. No one disputed this, nor should anyone dispute the principle of a Christian congregation paying their minister. In fact, Paul says the Lord has distinctly commanded that the pattern that prevailed in the temple should prevail in the church (Luke 10:7).

In asking the Corinthians to be willing to give up personal rights, Paul was only asking them to do what he himself had done. As an apostle, he could have claimed their financial support, but he had refused to do so. And, again, their financial support was a matter on which God had clearly pronounced. It wasn't even in the grey area. So Paul had the right to expect the Corinthians to be willing to give up the eating of meat sacrificed to idols for the sake of those conscientiously opposed to it.

## The passion that drove Paul

But having revealed his own practice of this principle, Paul turns to say why he did it. The second emphasis in this passage, then, is the passion that drove Paul (9:16-18).

Some people have secret passions. They are able to keep hidden from others the one thing that drives and motivates them. Paul's passion was no secret. After the Lord Jesus Christ confronted him and converted him on the Damascus Road, it became the supreme passion of his life to preach the gospel of Jesus Christ. Instead of trying to hide that passion, Paul spent the rest of his life flying it high.

Some are not even conscious of the passion that masters and controls them. Paul, however, was profoundly conscious of the gospel, and it was the touchstone for everything he did. Here we have him saying he had forfeited his right to the financial support of the Corinthians. What was the explanation for such an action? Paul says it was all for the sake of the gospel!

Some preachers give the impression that they can be just as happy not preaching as they are preaching; however, Paul knew what it was to have a compulsion to preach. **'Woe is me,'** he says, **'if I do not preach the gospel!'** (9:16). He literally says he had no choice in this matter of preaching; he was 'drafted' into it. His position was rather like that of the slave whose master gives him a 'stewardship', or trust to fulfil (9:17). The slave is not given any choice in the matter; he is simply told what he must do. While he had no choice about whether to preach, Paul did have a choice regarding the remuneration for it, and this he willingly gave up. It became his reward to have no reward (9:18).

Does this mean all preachers should preach without pay? No. Paul went to great lengths to prove the preacher is entitled to financial support. But it does mean we all should ask ourselves some very searching questions. Is the gospel as important to us as it was to Paul? Are we giving anything up for the sake of the gospel? No, we don't share Paul's calling to be an apostle, but all who are saved share his gospel. Shouldn't we too feel something of the loyalty to the gospel he felt?

# 29.
# The gospel-dominated Christian

*Please read 1 Corinthians 9:19-27*

The 'strong' Christians in Corinth were in the habit of deciding issues with one thing in mind: themselves! Their rights, their freedom, their comfort, their enjoyment — these were the concerns that dominated and governed their decision-making. As far as Paul was concerned, their whole orientation was wrong. Instead of thinking only about themselves, they should have been considering the impact of their actions on their fellow believers (8:9).

In saying this, Paul wasn't merely handing down an edict from an ivory tower; he was talking about a principle he had been practising himself. While these strong Christians debated whether they should give up the questionable practice of eating meat sacrificed to idols, Paul had been living for years without something to which he was clearly entitled, namely, wages for his preaching!

Why had Paul given up his right to receive payment for preaching? He says he didn't want to do anything to hinder the progress of the gospel (9:12). He doesn't go into detail about how his receiving money would hinder the gospel. He just says it became his reward to preach the gospel free of charge (9:18). Perhaps Paul refused money because he didn't want to leave the impression that his preaching was financially motivated. He knew his hearers would never embrace the gospel if they ever got the idea that his allegiance to the gospel was due only to the desire to make money. So he wanted to make clear that his preaching was due solely to necessity being laid upon him. Only then would people judge the gospel on its own merits.

Whatever the precise reason Paul had for thinking remuneration would hinder the gospel, one thing is as clear as day: he was sold out to the gospel. He was a gospel-dominated man! For him no sacrifice was too great if it aided the gospel.

It seems, then, that Paul has added another item for the strong Christians to consider in determining the proper course of action on a questionable matter. In chapter 8, he said they should make their decisions with the conscience of their weaker brother in mind. In chapter 9, he seems to suggest they should emulate his example and make all their decisions in the light of how the gospel would be affected. In reality, of course, the two things cannot be separated. The gospel made them all brothers in Christ. Therefore, when Paul tells them to consider their brothers, he is saying they should consider the gospel.

The question for us to consider is whether we know anything of Paul's burning passion of allegiance to the gospel. Can we be fairly characterized as gospel-dominated? Do people around us get the impression that the gospel must be the most wonderful and glorious thing there is? Or do they get the impression that it is pretty much a dull, drab thing?

How does one go about determining whether one is gospel-dominated or not? Let's look at the two pictures Paul uses for himself in the verses before us. If we can see something of ourselves in these two pictures, we can conclude that we share his allegiance to the gospel.

## Paul: the slave

Consider first the slave (9:19-23). Is there any lower level of living than this: no rights or privileges; unable to freely come and go; no holidays, fringe benefits, or retirement — only toil, hardships, deprivation and abuse? All of that and more was the lot of the slave. No one in his right mind would ever choose to be a slave, but Paul says that is exactly what he had done. Through the gospel of Christ, he had been freed from all forms of tyranny and oppression, but he turned right around and volunteered for slavery!

What possible incentive could be powerful enough to compel him to do such a thing? Paul simply answers, **'That I might win the more'** (9:19). Five times in four verses (9:19-23) he uses that word 'win'. Then he changes to the word **'save'** in verse 22. Winning, saving — what is he talking about? Paul is registering his intense desire to see others come to know the Lord Jesus Christ as Saviour and Lord, and, at the same time, his desire to see them grow into mature Christians. So great was this desire that he says, **'I have made myself a servant to all'** (9:19).

Are we concerned about this winning and saving? Many are not. Some think all will automatically be saved so there is no point in our doing anything. Others think if God wants people saved, he will do it without any help from us. But if Paul, this great apostle, didn't excuse himself from winning and saving people, how can we?

Just how far was Paul willing to take this winning and saving business? For one thing, he says he had become as a Jew to the Jews. And because the Jews were those under the law of Moses, he adds, by way of amplification, that he had come under the law.

Paul was, of course, a Jew by birth. Prior to his conversion, his Jewish heritage was the very essence of his life. After he was saved, he didn't think of himself primarily as a Jew, but rather as a Christian. He still, however, had an intense yearning to see his own people saved (Rom. 9:1-5), and to that end, he was still willing to comply with certain Jewish regulations and ceremonies. This is why he compelled Timothy to be circumcised (Acts 16:3) and why he himself kept a Nazirite vow when he went to the temple in Jerusalem (Acts 21:23-26). We shouldn't construe this to mean Paul was willing to compromise the essential truths of the gospel. Geoffrey B. Wilson says of him, 'But if he was always ready to respect Jewish scruples..., he was never prepared to sacrifice gospel principles to Jewish prejudice.'[33]

In addition to all of this, Paul says he had become **'to those who are without law, as without law'** (9:21). He is referring to the Gentiles who were not under the law of Moses. Paul, of course, spent most of his ministry carrying the gospel to the Gentiles. The very customs that opened the door for him to gain a hearing among the Jews closed the door among the Gentiles. So Paul, as if these customs were a mere garment, removed them and put them aside when he was with the Gentiles. In saying to the Gentiles he was without law, Paul didn't mean he was under no law at all, but quickly adds that he was under the law of Christ (9:21).

Paul closes out this section by saying he had become weak to the weak. Here, he comes to grips specifically with the issue at Corinth. It is obvious that he is going beyond evangelism here. He has been talking about winning Jews and Gentiles to Christ, but those he calls 'weak' were already Christians (8:11). So we must understand his term **'win'** to mean, as indicated earlier, not only bringing people to know Christ, but also bringing them to Christian maturity.

There really is nothing more to be said about what Paul meant by becoming weak for the sake of the weak. He said it all when he vowed to eat no meat if it caused a brother in Christ to stumble (8:13).

Some might be inclined to think, in the light of what Paul has said, that he was nothing but a compromiser. Nothing could be further from the truth. What he is talking about here is simply common sense in evangelism and in maintaining sound Christian relationships. It is what some call the 'principle of incarnation' in evangelism. Christ, in order to save us, had to become one of us, and if we are to win others, we must be willing to identify with them.

## Paul: the athlete

The second picture we have of this gospel-dominated man is the athlete (9:24-27). Actually, Paul uses two athletes to convey the devotion he felt to the gospel. The first is the runner (9:24-26a), and the second is the boxer (9:26b-27). These athletes have much in common. They both compete for a prize, they both must train diligently, and they both must guard against distraction.

Both are, therefore, appropriate emblems for the Christian. As far as competing for a prize is concerned, the only difference between these athletes and the Christian is that the latter competes for a prize of far greater value. The runner, for instance, runs for what Paul calls a **'perishable'** crown — probably a crown made of pinewood. The Christian, however, is running for an 'imperishable' crown (9:25). If the runner is willing to work so hard for something of such little value, how much more should the Christian be willing to work hard! And, whereas only one runner could win a race, every single Christian can receive the imperishable crown! So Paul urges the Corinthians to **'run in such a way that you may obtain it'** (9:24).

If the Christian is to gain the prize, he must, like both the runner and boxer, train diligently. The runner is **'temperate'** in all things (9:5). That means he exercises self-control. For example, he cannot expect to win if he grows careless about his diet. And the boxer also has to **'discipline'** himself if he expects to win (9:27). Paul portrays this as punching himself black and blue in order to serve the Lord effectively. We shouldn't take him to mean that we ought to abuse our bodies. That is not his point. He is simply stating the fact that the body and its various appetites are the weapons sin tries to use against us, and we must, therefore, keep our bodies under control.

The alternative to this kind of discipline is to be **'disqualified'** (9:27). No, Paul is not saying he is afraid of losing his salvation. He is simply recognizing that his failure to discipline himself would result in being placed on the shelf as far as any usefulness to God is concerned.

Finally, if the runner and the boxer expect to succeed, they must be focused on the goal. If the runner runs aimlessly, wandering first to one side of the track and then the other, he is guaranteed not only to finish last, but to be the laughing-stock of the race. If he is to win, he must, without wasted motion or effort, drive straight towards the finishing-line (9:26).

It is the same for the boxer. If he steps into the ring and turns away from his opponent and simply flails at the air, he will find himself flat on his back counting the stars. If he is to win his match, he must focus all his attention on his opponent and hit him hard and often (9:26).

We see immediately the absurdity of the runner and the boxer going about their business aimlessly. We wouldn't hesitate to say that the runner who runs aimlessly deserves to finish last of the field, and the boxer who boxes aimlessly deserves to get knocked out. But are we going about the Christian life in an aimless way? Are we guilty of approaching Christian living in a manner that we would scorn and ridicule in other walks of life? Doesn't honesty drive us to admit that many of us are not nearly as serious about our Christian living as we are about our other endeavours?

These pictures of the slave and the athletes make it easy for us to see how Paul viewed the Christian life. As far as he was concerned, it was such a serious business that it required hard work and concentrated effort. And this is how we shall view it if we are gospel-dominated.

How do we measure up against Paul, the slave and the athlete? Is the gospel important enough to us that we are willing to waive our freedom and our comfort to carry it to others? Is the gospel important enough to us that we are willing to discipline ourselves and avoid all other distractions? Each of us must answer for him or herself! But as we search our hearts for the answer, let us be aware that lost men and women around us are waiting to see how important the gospel is to us. We cannot expect to win them to something that has not won our highest allegiance and our most diligent efforts.

# 30.
# The mentality for running the race

*Please read 1 Corinthians 10:1-11*

The Corinthians were fumbling their way through the dark maze of what to do regarding meat sacrificed to idols. Some members of the church were strong in their view of Christian liberty and felt entirely at ease in eating this meat; other members didn't have this strong sense of liberty and were conscience-stricken at the mere thought of partaking of it. Something had to be done to break the impasse in the church. So Paul stepped into the fray by offering this guiding principle: those Christians with a strong sense of personal liberty must be willing to give up their liberty if the practice of it causes another Christian to stumble (8:9-13).

Paul knew his principle would solve the problem if the so-called strong Christians would only adhere to it. But there was the rub! The principle required a certain disposition of mind — a disposition these Christians gave no evidence of possessing. The principle required diligence and drive, determination and discipline, but these words weren't even in the vocabulary of these strong Christians. Their favourite words were desire, privilege, gratification and enjoyment.

Paul knew, therefore, that just laying this principle on the table wasn't sufficient. He had to supply some motivation if he were to expect these strong Christians to pick up this principle and put it into practice. But what would it take to motivate these people? Paul decided to rely on a couple of examples. The first was positive in nature. Paul showed how he had gone above and beyond the call of duty in practising this principle himself and how he had been blessed in the process (9:1-27).

## The example of Israel

In the passage before us, Paul uses a negative example, the example of Israel under Moses. Here was a group of people who were extremely free with the same words as the Corinthians, and they lost everything!

The bridge between Paul's positive example and Israel's negative example is the metaphor of the runner preparing for a race (9:24-27). As far as Paul was concerned, the Christian life is a great race. It requires all those qualities that were in short supply among the strong Christian. Paul wanted to make sure he ran his own race well and that he didn't end up as a 'castaway'. No, he wasn't afraid he might lose his salvation at the end of it all, but he was acutely aware of the possibility of losing the Lord's approval of his ministry and being set aside by the Lord.

Was Paul overdoing it a bit? Not at all. The Israelites of old also had a race set before them. They had been called to show to others the glory and knowledge of God. It was certainly a great privilege, but they somehow got so occupied with the privilege that they forgot the responsibility. They took their calling to mean they had already won the race and didn't apply themselves to it, and God cast them away! They were disqualified from the race. Yes, being cast away is a very real and terrible danger!

If the Corinthians were to avoid being disqualified from the race, they had to pay careful heed to the example of the Israelites.

## Great privileges

First, they needed to reflect on the similarity between their privileges and those enjoyed by Israel. They were very proud of their privileges and they thought the fact they had been given these privileges meant they didn't need to make any effort.

Hadn't they been gloriously saved? Hadn't God delivered them from the kingdom of sin and darkness? And hadn't they been publicly identified with Christ through baptism? And weren't they regularly coming to the Lord's Table to enjoy fellowship with him and with other believers?

Deliverance from the old life, identification with a new life, communion with Christ and other believers — these are certainly not insignificant! And, fortified with these wonderful blessings, the so-called strong Christians were ready to dismiss any talk of sacrifice, commitment, or discipline, whether it came from Paul or someone else. Can't you hear them now? 'Wait just a minute. We've been saved and baptized. We participate in the church. What else is there?'

Does this kind of talk sound vaguely familiar? It should. It is the same kind of talk we hear from many professing Christians today. Talk to them about doing something for Christ and they say, 'Now wait a minute. I've been saved and baptized. I go to church when I can. As far as I'm concerned, that's enough.'

But now it is Paul's turn to say, 'Wait just a minute.' The Israelites, he points out, also had a remarkable deliverance to look back on. God had miraculously delivered them from their bondage in Egypt and from the tyranny of Pharaoh.

And they also had a kind of baptism. Paul says, **'All our fathers were under the cloud, all passed through the sea'** (10:1). That cloud under which they walked out of Egypt and that sea through which they passed effectively separated them from their old life and identified them with a new leader, Moses, and a new life.

The Israelites even had their own kind of communion (10:3-4). Their equivalent to the bread of communion was the manna God showered upon them in the wilderness. And their equivalent to the wine was the water which God supernaturally provided from a rock. Paul sees that rock as a type of Christ, who was continually present with them. Just as Christ was present with the Corinthians to sustain and nurture them, so he was present with the Israelites throughout their wilderness journeying.

What was Paul's point in discussing these privileges? Why was he so intent on likening the Corinthians and their privileges to the Israelites and their privileges? Paul lets the other foot fall in verse 5: **'But with most of them God was not well pleased...'**

## Severe judgement

Yes, the Israelites enjoyed great privileges, but they still came under severe judgement. **'Their bodies'**, Paul says, **'were scattered in the wilderness.'** Of the multitude who left Egypt only Joshua and Caleb actually lived to enter the land God had promised to give to the nation. That is how great God's judgement was upon them!

What did they do to bring such devastating judgement upon themselves? Paul lists five sins of which they were guilty.

First, *they craved evil things* (10:6). Paul probably had in mind the time, described in Numbers 11, when the people were yearning for the foods they had enjoyed in Egypt. So great was this yearning that God had to send a great plague upon them to bring them out of it. Many perished in that plague.

These people were also guilty of *idolatry* (10:7). Paul cites the time they built the golden calf (Exod. 32). While Moses was on Mt Sinai receiving instructions about how to worship God, they were down below worshipping another god altogether.

Then Paul mentions their *sexual immorality* (10:8). This was often part of idol-worship, but Paul alludes to one specific episode in the life of Israel, when the men committed immorality with the daughters of Moab at one of their idol feasts (Num. 25:1-9). God's judgement on that occasion caused the loss of over 23,000 lives.

The fourth sin Paul mentions is *testing the Lord* (10: 9). This sin amounts to pushing God to the limit by seeing how much we can get away with. The Israelites did this in another episode described in Numbers. Tired of God's provisions for them, they accused him of bringing them to the wilderness to die. God responded to this test by sending poisonous snakes into their camp. These snakes bit many and caused them to die (Num. 21:4-9).

Finally, Paul mentions the sin of *murmuring or grumbling*. This sin continually cropped up among the Israelites, but the greatest instance of it was when Korah and others began to complain about the leadership of Moses and Aaron. God's response was to send **'the destroyer'**, an angel of death, into the camp. Again, many died (Num. 16).

## A warning for us

Great privileges and great judgement — what a strange combination! We want to say it has to be either one or the other, but Israel proved it can be both. And that is what Paul wanted the strong Corinthians to see. He had asked them to give up a personal liberty for the sake of the race that had been set before them. But they were reluctant to do so. They loved this meat from their former way of life. So great was their yearning for it that they were even willing to flirt with the idolatry and sexual immorality that surrounded it. They were stretching the grace of God to breaking-point to justify their love for it, and they grumbled at any suggestion that they should change their position. So we have Paul saying to these Corinthians, 'Look out! You are acting very much like the Israelites of old. If you don't change, you can only expect God's judgement to fall!'

We shall be terribly mistaken if we think this passage of Scripture is just about Corinthians and Israelites. It is about them, but it is also about us. Paul says, **'Now all these things happened to them as examples, and they were written for our admonition'** (10:11).

So we must ask ourselves how we are doing in our race for the Lord. Are we going about it with diligence and discipline, or are we as complacent and casual about it as the Israelites and Corinthians were? Here is one way to check how you are running the Christian race. Think about your favourite sports team for a moment. Would you want that team to go about their sport the way you go about your Christianity? How many games would they win if they did?

# 31.
# Coping with temptation

*Please read 1 Corinthians 10:13*

I have two dogs. Blackie is a very sweet, gentle dog with an extremely delicate disposition. Toby, on the other hand, is boisterous, quarrelsome and generally arrogant. Needless to say, Toby stands in dire need of frequent stern warnings. But correcting Toby is not as easy as it sounds. I have observed over the years that I can't correct him too sternly without having a profound effect on Blackie. Invariably, I find at the end of my fiery denunciations of Toby that Blackie is quivering in a corner. Guilty Toby takes my warnings with a grain of salt, while innocent Blackie is immediately smitten with guilt and terror.

Paul had a similar problem on his hands with the Corinthians. Many in the church of Corinth needed the stern warning he delivered in the first twelve verses of this chapter. Because they were so intent on gratifying their own desires and so reluctant to discipline themselves, they were running the risk of being cast aside from further usefulness in the Lord's work. They had to be brought to their senses before it was too late. But Paul knew it was possible, in our anxiousness to solve one problem, to create another. In his mind's eye, he could see the effect his strong words of warning would have on some of the weak Christians. He knew they would feel it was all just too much for them. The responsibilities were so great. The opportunities for failure were so numerous. How could they possibly succeed in the Christian race? To help these delicate, timid Christians, Paul wrote the words of the verse before us.

It is, of course, one of the most beloved of all Bible verses. Many weary, worn Christians have come to it and found sweet solace and consolation. It is not hard to see why this verse yields such great benefits. It deals with a matter every Christian is concerned about — temptation. We always tend to associate that word with enticement to sin, but the word Paul uses here *(peirasmos)* carries no negative connotation. It simply means to test or prove. Sometimes we are tempted to sin, but this type of temptation never comes from God (James 1:14-15). When God 'tempts' us it is always in the sense of testing or trying our faith in order to bring us to a greater reliance upon him.

Because Paul uses this general term, we may conclude he has in mind any kind of trial that comes upon the Christian, whether it is a solicitation to sin or a testing of faith. The Corinthians were, of course, facing both of these. The solicitation to repeat the sins of Israel was strong, but God's call to discipline was also strong.

This verse is loved, not just because it deals with an intensely vital subject, but because of what it says about this theme. It contains both a general affirmation about the nature of God and some specific teachings about coping with temptation.

## The faithfulness of God

Regarding the nature of God, Paul simply says, **'God is faithful.'** Were some of the Corinthians about to wilt under the pressure? Were they ready to throw up their hands in despair? If so it was because they had somehow slipped into the notion that the Christian life was solely their responsibility, that it all depended upon them. To all of these, Paul seems to say, 'I'm not surprised you are discouraged. You are forgetting about God's faithfulness!'

In other words, Paul wanted them to understand that the work of salvation is all God's work and, therefore, it cannot fail. God started the work of salvation in them and they could rest assured he would continue it until they were safely at home in heaven. Paul says to the Philippians, 'He who has begun a good work in you will complete it until the day of Jesus Christ' (Phil. 1:6).

And Paul was not the only one who believed this. The apostle Peter wrote, 'His divine power has given to us all things that pertain to life and godliness, through the knowledge of Him who called us by glory and virtue...' (2 Peter 1:3).

These verses must not be taken to mean we can be entirely passive in the Christian life, as though there was nothing for us to do.

Some always interpret these verses to mean that if God does the work there is nothing for us to do. They forget that even though God does the work, he does it in and through us. In another statement to the Philippians, Paul says, 'It is God who works in you both to will and to do for His good pleasure' (Phil. 2:13).

In asking the Corinthians to be committed to the Christian race and to avoid the sins of the Israelites, then, Paul was not asking them to do the impossible. He was only asking them to do what God's grace enabled them to do. They were not alone with the large responsibilities of the Christian life. The God of their salvation was at work in them to empower and enable them to bear those responsibilities.

Those three words, 'God is faithful', ought to come as an encouragement to any Christian who is beleaguered by doubt, weariness, or discouragement. Does the Christian life seem to be too much for you? Think about this: God is faithful! Do the responsibilities seem to be too numerous and too great? Find shelter here: God is faithful! Does your growth in grace seem small? Take courage from this: God is faithful! Does your power to stand firm against sin seem meagre? Take your stand on this truth: God is faithful! The Christian life becomes an intolerable burden when we fall into the trap of thinking it all depends on us, but it becomes a delightful journey when we live it in consciousness of God's enabling power!

That reminder about God's character should have been sufficient in and of itself to pick up any timid Christians who were staggering under the load of responsibility; however, Paul was not content to leave it there. He proceeded to give two provisions this faithful God makes for those who are facing temptations.

## God provides a hedge

First, he says God provides a hedge for the tempted. In other words, he filters some temptations out before they ever have a chance to get to us. For one thing, he filters out all uncommon or extraordinary temptations. Nothing is allowed to come through the hedge that is not characteristic or typical for mankind. Sometimes we think our burdens are unique, but they are not. No matter how great our burden, we may rest assured others either have carried, or are carrying, burdens just as great.

God also uses his hedge to filter out any temptation that is too hard for us to bear. This is the unpopular part of the verse. Some object to it because it demolishes a favourite excuse for sin, namely, that the temptation was just too great. 'Situation ethics' is a moral system built on the premise that we are sometimes placed in circumstances in which we have no choice except to sin. But this verse teaches that God never places the Christian in a situation where sin is unavoidable.

Others dislike this teaching because they are sure the trials and burdens they are carrying are indeed far too much to bear and that God has failed to keep his promise. There is not much one can do to convince these people otherwise. They are the type who would regard any kind of trial as too severe. They think God exists just to smooth their pathway, and any bump in the road is proof he has failed them. The sad thing is that these people miss the comfort of simply resting on God's promise. It is much easier to face a trial when one is able to say, 'I don't know why this trial has come, but I know the Lord will give me strength to bear it.' Where does a person get comfort if he considers his trials to be proof that God cannot be trusted? Better to trust, with the hope that you will someday understand, than to have neither understanding nor trust!

No one in human history has suffered more than Job. But even though his trials were terrible and severe, God's protecting hedge was still around him. How thankful we should be that God's filtering hedge still exists for us!

## God provides a bridge

The second provision God makes for the tempted is the bridge. Paul says, when God allows a temptation to come through the hedge to test and try us, he also provides a **'way of escape'**. What is this way of escape? Is it the sudden appearance of an angel to snatch us away at the last split second? Or is it a sudden burst of spiritual energy that surges through us and enables us to say a resounding 'No!' to temptation? Check a Greek New Testament, and you will find the definite article 'the' used with the singular noun 'escape'. That means Paul really was talking about only one way of escape, not a different way of escape for each temptation.

To discover this way of escape, we have to do nothing more than look at Jesus himself. Before beginning his public ministry, Jesus escaped the temptations of Satan by confronting them in his Father's power. And that power was available to him because he was a man of intense, fervent prayer (Matt. 4:1-11). At the end of his ministry, Jesus told his disciples the way of escape from temptations: 'Watch and pray, lest you enter into temptation' (Mark 14:38).

The way of escape from temptation, then, is not God dashing in at the last minute to pick us up and carry us out of the situation. It is facing the temptation and going through it with the power God supplies to those who walk with him in prayer and discipline.

# 32.
# Fleeing from idols

*Please read 1 Corinthians 10:14-22*

The Corinthians were embroiled in a fierce debate on meat that had been sacrificed to idols. Paul responded to this debate by dividing the question into two parts. First, should the Christian ever eat this meat? Secondly, should the Christian attend banquets where meat is sacrificed to idols?

Paul's response to the first question is, 'It depends.' If someone felt free to eat of this meat, he should not hesitate to do so except when his eating caused another Christian to stumble. In other words, he should be willing to refrain from eating in the presence of another Christian who might be troubled by it (8:9-13).

Paul knew this principle was not easy to put into practice. He knew it called for a certain kind of mentality, one which was willing to discipline itself and sacrifice personal rights. So Paul went to great lengths to encourage the Corinthians to develop this mentality. He used his own willingness to sacrifice as a positive example of this attitude (9:1-27); he used the nation of Israel as a negative example of it (10:1-13).

In this passage, Paul turns to deal with the second part of this issue: should a Christian attend banquets or ceremonies where these idol sacrifices were made? To this, he issues a resounding 'No!' There was no room for debate or discussion on this matter. When it comes to idolatry the only appropriate response for a Christian is to flee.

We can be sure Paul's 'No!' had a shattering effect on the Corinthians. These idol feasts were a popular and prominent part of their culture. They were one of the primary social outlets of the day, and any suggestion that they should be given up was bound to meet with much disfavour. Had we been lingering around the Corinthians' assembly room when they received Paul's letter we could have heard the muttering and murmuring: 'Paul has gone too far this time. As long as we don't actually worship the idols themselves, what harm is there in going to these feasts?'

Some have depicted Paul as something of an ogre who just enjoyed churning out dos and don'ts for other people to follow. They know he was an apostle and apostles had special authority over the churches, but they have the impression that Paul got carried away with his authority and more or less made rules just for the sake of making them. The truth is that Paul did not make rules arbitrarily. When he did establish certain guidelines for behaviour he invariably explained why they were necessary. So we should not be surprised to find Paul following up his flat warning, **'Flee from idolatry,'** with some solid and sensible reasons. He considered these reasons to be so inescapable that the Corinthians themselves would be forced to side with him (10:15).

### Participation leads to fellowship

What, then, were Paul's reasons? First, he points out that participation leads to fellowship. Paul uses a form of the word *'koinonia'* a total of four times in this passage. *'Koinonia'* itself appears twice in verse 16 and is translated each time as 'communion'. Another form of the word appears in verse 18 and is translated 'partakers'. A third form of the word appears in verse 20 and is translated 'fellowship'.

The word *'koinonia'* refers to the fellowship of those who have things in common. A prime example of Christian fellowship is the Lord's Supper. Christians observe this supper because they have certain things in common. All Christians have been delivered from sin and made part of God's family by Jesus Christ's sacrificial death on the cross. The Lord's Supper celebrates and commemorates this. The cup represents the blood that Jesus Christ shed for us; the bread represents the body in which he bore the penalty for our sins.

While the Lord's Supper is clearly symbolical in nature, the drinking and eating are not merely mechanical experiences for the Christian. As he drinks the cup and eats the bread, he is made aware again of what a great price the Lord Jesus paid for him, and his heart goes out in love and adoration to Christ. So while the Christian is engaged in the Lord's Supper, he is enjoying fellowship or communion with Christ, and he is also enjoying fellowship or communion with his brothers and sisters who share his love for Christ. In other words, there is a spiritual reality behind the Lord's Supper. While partaking of the elements, the believer is, at the same time, fellowshipping with that spiritual reality — Jesus Christ himself.

Paul brought up the subject of the Lord's Supper because it perfectly parallels what takes place in the worship of idols. Even though idols are not really gods (10:19), there is still a spiritual reality at work in idolatry: the reality of demons. These demons are at work in that they both instigate the idolatry and influence the worshippers. So anyone who participates in idol worship is flinging open the door and inviting demonic influence into his life.

Paul's emphasis has a particular significance for our own time. Our society is overrun with renewed interest in Satan, witchcraft and demons. Some dismiss all of this as nothing more than innocent fun, but it is far more sinister than that. Those who become involved in these activities are opening themselves up to demonic influence and possession.

This ought to show us that worship is not something to be taken lightly. There are only two kinds of worship: true and false. True worship brings us into contact with the reality of God; false worship brings us into the realm of Satan.

## Participation leads to identification

That brings us to consider Paul's second reason for urging the Corinthians to stay away from these idol feasts. We may summarize it in these words: participation leads to identification.

Think about the Lord's Supper again for a moment. What does it mean when a group of people drink from that cup and eat that bread? Doesn't their drinking and eating identify them as followers of Christ? Paul says it does. Those who participate in the Lord's Supper, even though they be many in number, become **'one bread and one body'** (10:17). Our participation in the Lord's Supper clearly marks us out as belonging to the Christian realm, and anyone who sees our participation would be justified in assuming we are followers of Jesus Christ.

Paul makes the same point from the Old Testament sacrificial system (10:18). The priests who offered the sacrifices were allowed to take a portion of the meat for their own use. Anyone who saw some men taking a portion of the sacrifices for their own use would quite naturally assume they were priests and were, therefore, entitled to this meat.

Paul's application is abundantly clear. If people are identified by what they participate in, the Corinthians would certainly be assumed to be idolaters if they put in an appearance at an idol temple.

Do we have the courage to look Paul's point squarely in the face? Many of us have grown exceedingly careless at this point. We want to be identified with Christ, but we also want to go to places and do things that automatically identify us with the world. David tried the same fence-straddling technique in his day. Even though he was one of the people of God, he led his men into the land of their sworn enemies, the Philistines. The response of some of the Philistine leaders was the cryptic question: 'What are these Hebrews doing here?' (1 Sam. 29:3).

In like manner, we may think we are getting away with our participation in sinful practices, but the people of the world are not fooled. They see our inconsistency and ask, 'What are these Christians doing here?'

### The danger of provoking God

Paul has one more reason for the Corinthians to stay away from idol worship. He has argued that participation opens the door to fellowship with demons and also leads to identification with idolaters. Now he concludes by saying fellowship and identification lead to provocation.

The Christian is one who belongs to God. Through Christ's death on the cross, God purchased each and every believer to be his own prized possession and to live for his purposes. Just as a husband or wife is entitled to a spouse's affection and will not tolerate him or her sharing that affection with anyone else, so it is with our relationship to God. He is entitled to our affection, and he will not tolerate us sharing with another what belongs exclusively to him.

If we truly belong to the Lord and try to give our allegiance to another god, we are, in effect, entering into a state of war with God.

The only one in a position to risk war with God is the person who is stronger than God. Since none of us is in that category, we are wise to avoid provoking him by staying away from all things that compete with him for our loyalty.

# 33.
# Crucial considerations in decision-making

*Please read 1 Corinthians 10:23 - 11:1*

How does the Christian go about making a decision on a questionable matter? Keep in mind that a questionable matter for the Christian is one in which God has not revealed his will. If God has spoken on an issue, then it is settled for the Christian. When God says something is wrong, it is wrong; when God says something is right, it is right. The Christian does not always refrain from the wrong and do the right, but he knows God's revealed will is right and good and desires to obey it.

But there are some issues on which God has not spoken. What is the Christian to do when he comes up against one of these issues? Some say all that is necessary is simply to pray until you get a sense of inner peace about what you are to do. Once you have this inner peace, they argue, you are justified in taking any course of action you want, and you shouldn't worry about what anyone else says or thinks. If someone is troubled or hurt by your decision, you simply tell him you have peace about it and he should mind his own business.

Prayer is certainly a vital element in the Christian's decision-making and should never be minimized. But we would do well to be suspicious about some of the answers to our prayers as well as our inner peace. The truth is that we all have the tendency to hear the voice of our own desires and to conclude we have heard God's voice. And sometimes we can have inner peace about things we shouldn't. Even though he was running from the explicit will of God, Jonah found enough inner peace to fall asleep in the middle of a storm.

Is there some firmer ground on which we may take our stand in this business of deciding questionable matters? Paul says there is. In wrapping up his discussion of how Christians should respond to meat that had been sacrificed to idols, he focuses on the two supreme priorities of the Christian and how to apply them.

What are the Christian's priorities? There is no room for debate here. The Lord Jesus himself said the greatest command is to love God, and the second greatest command is to love our neighbour (Matt. 22:34-40). Paul must have had the words of Jesus in mind when he wrote this passage because he tells the Corinthians to **'do all to the glory of God'** (10:31) and to seek the other's **'well-being'** (10:24).

## The glory of God

What does it mean to do everything for God's glory? It means to live in such a way that God receives the credit. It means to live so those around us will have to explain our lives in terms of God. It is to live in such a way that there will be no other logical explanation for us except to say our lives have been touched by God. The apostle Peter urged his readers to live with integrity so those around them would glorify God (1 Peter 2:12).

Unbelievers govern their lives solely in terms of what will please and gratify them, but the Christian is different. While he is not opposed to legitimate pleasure and comfort, he doesn't make his decisions with only those things in view. He consults the glory of God. He asks himself if a particular action will bring honour to God, or if it will bring reproach upon his name. In other words, the Christian lives with a consciousness of God.

## The good of others

In addition to keeping God's glory in mind, the Christian must also keep the good of others in mind (10:23-32,33). As far as the Bible is concerned, there are only two groups of people in all the world: those who know God and those who don't. If we are to keep the good of others in mind, then, we must take into account the needs of both groups.

What is the pressing need of those who already know God? Paul says it is to be edified. And what does it mean to be edified? It means to be built up in the faith, to grow up into Christian maturity and stability. There certainly can be no question about what is the pressing need of those who do not know God. They need to be evangelized! They need to hear the gospel of Christ declared and to see it demonstrated.

The mentality of this age is totally opposed to this teaching. This is the day and age of the individual and his or her rights. The banners under which the current generation marches are 'self-esteem' and 'self-fulfilment'. Even Christians have not been immune to being swept along by the tide of self. Many don't hesitate to excuse themselves from church attendance by saying, 'Sunday is the only day I have for myself.' It is not at all unusual to hear Christians say things like, 'I'm tired of living for others; I'm going to live for myself for a while.'

## A practical example

Paul was an extremely practical man and he couldn't be content merely to affirm the Christian's priorities. He goes on to include in this passage specific details on how these priorities were to be worked out in terms of specific practices. First, he takes up the question of the Christian eating in his own home (10:25-26), then he turns to consider the Christian eating in another's home (10:27-30).

Regarding the former, Paul says the Christian should feel free to buy and eat any meat available in the market. Even though some of this meat may have been used for idol sacrifices, the Christian need not feel any moral compunction about eating it. Instead, he should simply look upon this meat as part of the bounty provided by the Lord and should thankfully receive it (10:26).

But what about eating with someone else? Paul supposes a Christian who feels free to eat this meat has been invited to the home of an unbeliever (10:27-30). What was this Christian to do in this situation? Paul says he shouldn't even bring up the issue of the meat's origin (10:27). But what if someone else brought it up? It is conceivable another Christian attending the same meal might mention that a portion of this meat had been sacrificed to idols. Or the unbelieving host himself might, as a test of the Christian's convictions, mention the meat's origin. In either case, the Christian who felt free to eat this meat should simply refrain from doing so in this situation. Why? To avoid throwing a stumbling-block in the path of the other Christian or the unbelieving host.

Paul elaborates on this teaching by imagining himself in this situation. 'Here I am,' he says, 'in this unbeliever's home. Someone mentions that part of this meat has been used in idol sacrifice. What am I going to do? It is the same meat I eat privately without any pangs of conscience, but I'm not going to eat it in this situation. Why not? I am not going to let my liberty to eat this meat become a topic of conversation and condemnation! I'm not going to allow the liberty I appreciate and enjoy to be reproached and condemned!' (10:29-30).

Does this make sense to you? Can you see how a Christian can feel free to do a particular thing but would refrain from it in the presence of others? Can you see how he wouldn't want his liberty on this issue to be a stumbling-block or a debating-point? If so, you have understood the point Paul is making.

Now look at both of these cases again. What do you see? Do you see Paul saying the Christian is free to eat this meat privately because **'The earth is the Lord's, and all its fullness'**? (10:26). Those are not his own words. He is quoting Psalm 24:1. Now here is the interesting part. When he forbids the Christian to eat this meat in the unbeliever's home he quotes the same verse! Does that surprise you? Why does he quote the same verse to defend eating and then to defend not eating? In the first case, the Christian should feel free to eat of this meat because it was part of the Lord's full bounty. But in the second case, the Christian was to abstain from eating because the Lord's bounty is so great the believer would not be under any hardship by not eating of this particular meat in this particular situation.

## Getting our priorities right

Why had this question of eating meat sacrificed to idols become such a controversial issue in the church of Corinth? Isn't it obvious that some of them had begun to lose their bearings? They had lost sight of their twin priorities — the glory of God and the good of others — and could only see their right to gratify their own desires by partaking of this meat. Others insisted just as strongly that this meat should not be eaten. The church was at an impasse. Was there any way out? Yes! Paul says the way out was for each one to start thinking again in terms of God and others!

How is it with us? When we stand before a questionable issue, how do we go about deciding what to do? Do we remember God and others and make our decision in those terms? Or have our priorities become lost amidst the world's clamour for self-centred living? And another question comes to mind: what might God do in this dark world if his people began to take their priorities seriously?

# 34.
# Women and worship

*Please read 1 Corinthians 11:2-16*

Paul has answered the Corinthians' questions on marriage and meat sacrificed to idols. In these verses, he turns his attention to the area of public worship. Evidently, the Corinthians had three major concerns relating to this vital area: the conduct of women in worship (11:2-16), the administration of the Lord's Supper (11:17-34) and the use of spiritual gifts (12:1 - 14:40).

Paul's instructions on the first of these issues pose many difficulties. This passage is considered by many to be not only the most difficult passage in this letter but the most difficult in the entire New Testament. Must a woman wear a head-covering to church? Is a woman allowed to pray and prophesy in church? If so, how do we reconcile this with what Paul says in the fourteenth chapter about women being silent in the church?

The difficulty of interpreting this passage is compounded by the fact that this topic is one of the most hotly debated in society in general. It is very easy for the Christian to pick up certain ideas from society, then carry these to the Bible with the expectation of having them confirmed. It should be quite obvious that many of the things troubling the church today would not be problems at all if they were not problems in society. The church has to be sensitive to the trends of society and address itself to those concerns, but that doesn't mean she should simply parrot what her society happens to be saying at a given moment. Today's church seems to be doing exactly that. There wasn't a gay rights movement in the church until there was one in the world! There wasn't an abortion rights movement in the church until there was one in the world! And there wasn't a militant feminism in the church until there was one in the world! Don't these things indicate that the world just has to name a song and Christians start humming the tune? Let society sneeze just once and half the church seems to come down with a cold!

## The problem at Corinth

Before we immerse ourselves in the details of this passage, we need to try to grasp something of what was going on in the church of Corinth. If you and I could climb into one of those imaginary time-capsules and take ourselves back to Corinth in the days when Paul was writing, one of the first things we would probably note was the similarity of the dress of the men and women. The main difference in the dress was that the women wore a head-covering. This article was just what the name indicates — something to cover the head, not a veil to hide the face. It should be pointed out that almost all the women of Corinth wore this head-covering. The only women who didn't were the mistresses and prostitutes.

Evidently, the thing that was causing problems in the church was that some of the women were either not wearing the head-covering to church, or they were removing it during the service. Those who argue the former speculate that there was something of a feminist movement going on in Corinth at the time and that the women of the church were leaving their head-coverings at home in order to declare their liberation. Those who argue the latter suggest that the women were getting caught up and carried away by the excitement of worship and were throwing the head-covering aside.

There is no need for us to make a choice between these alternatives. The result was the same in either case: Christian women were appearing in the worship services as if they were immoral women! This, of course, caused the men to be distracted, and distraction of any kind is a mortal enemy to true worship.

The prostitutes and immoral women of our day are also characterized by a certain kind of dress. We may rest assured that if one of these women should put in an appearance at one of our services it would have a disrupting effect on our worship. This isn't to say we shouldn't allow such women to come to church. If they attend, we will have to make the best of it. But the women who belong to our church and have her best interests at heart will surely try to spare us from the distraction of dressing like immoral women!

What Paul has to say about this problem, then, arose not from some dislike for women and a desire to keep them in their place, but rather from a deep concern to safeguard Christian worship from anything that would spoil or diminish it. Can we identify with the apostle at this point? Do we have a zeal for worship? Are we jealous about our worship services? Do we detest those things that disrupt worship and detract from it? Do we understand that true worship requires studied concentration from each of us?

## The question of headship

Paul has always received a lot of bad press for how he dealt with the rôle of women, but just a casual glance at this passage ought to convince one and all that he does not deserve the reputation he has received. As an apostle, he could simply have told the women of the church to wear their head-coverings and washed his hands of the whole matter. Instead, he gives himself to a detailed explanation as to why the head-covering was necessary. It is obvious from what he says that the head-covering was, in that culture, vitally related to the headship of the man. This, of course, is what so many women find infuriating. Why should the man be considered the head of the woman? Aren't women just as good as men?

The problem is that we take man's headship over the woman to mean two things: women are inferior to men, and men are entitled to treat them as inferior. Nothing could be further from the truth. First, headship doesn't mean the woman is inferior to the man. Paul needed to use only one phrase to blow that idea out of the water. He says, **'The head of Christ is God'** (11:3). Have you ever stopped to weigh that out thoroughly? The Bible clearly teaches that Jesus Christ is God himself and is, therefore, equal to God in every respect. Jesus himself made this clear when he said to Philip, 'He who has seen Me has seen the Father... Do you not believe that I am in the Father, and the Father in Me?' (John 14:9-10).

How, then, can Paul say God is the 'head' of Christ? He is not talking about headship in the sense of personal worth, but in terms of function. In order to work out the plan of redemption, Jesus, who was equal to God in every respect, voluntarily submitted himself to the Father. So Paul says in Philippians that, even though Jesus was equal to God, he didn't cling to the trappings of deity but humbled himself and became obedient even to the point of dying on the cross (Phil. 2:5-8).

In the light of this, we can conclude that the headship of the man doesn't mean that the woman is inferior to the man. The woman's submission is to be like Christ's: a voluntary subordination of an equal in order to ensure the smooth functioning of church and home.

If men and women are equal in value and worth, the man has no right to interpret his headship to mean he can run roughshod over women. Instead, he should see his headship as a rôle that God has given him and understand that he must answer to God for how he uses it. Paul says, **'The head of every man is Christ'** (11:3). The man has no right to act like a tyrant towards women, because his head, Jesus Christ, forbids it!

Some resist the idea of man's headship by saying our redemption through Christ has overturned it. They argue that man's headship came about as a result of his fall into sin. Since redemption frees us from the domain of sin, the argument goes, we are also freed from the headship that was imposed.

There is only one fly in the ointment. Man's headship was not based on man's fall into sin but on God's creative act. Man is given the rôle of headship because God designed it to be so. Paul points out that man was made first, then the woman was made from the man and for the man (11:8-9). Why did God do things in this way? To ask that is rather like asking why there are radishes. They just are there. And man's headship is there! God put this order in creation because it pleased him to do so.

### An abiding principle and a cultural expression of it

What about the head-covering then? If women are voluntarily to subordinate themselves to men, does this mean they are to still wear head-coverings? No! Why not? Because the head-covering doesn't mean in our culture what it did then. The absence of it then identified a woman as immoral and disrupted the church. The absence of a head-covering doesn't do either of these things today. In other words, we have to distinguish between what is culturally dated and what is eternally valid. The head-covering was culturally dated, but the principle of man's headship is eternally valid.

Another example of this distinction is the kiss of greeting Paul told Christians to use (2 Cor. 13:12; 1 Thess. 5:26). The kiss was that culture's way of expressing a warm welcome. In our day, a handshake suffices, but the principle of Christians showing warmth to each other remains the same!

This passage gives all Christians plenty to think about. Do we give the public worship services of the church the priority Paul gave them? Do we take care not to identify ourselves as immoral people? Are we willing to submit to the authority of Scripture? Or do we resist and resent when its teachings rub us up the wrong way? Let's make it our chief concern to honour and glorify God. When that becomes our grand pursuit, a lot of trivial concerns will melt away and the church will be moulding society instead of society moulding the church.

# 35.
# Subverting the Supper

*Please read 1 Corinthians 11:17-34*

The word 'subvert' is a nasty word. It means to cause ruin or downfall by undermining, to cause someone or something to be overthrown or destroyed. We usually think of subversion in connection with the government of a nation being overthrown. Those who bring about the downfall of a government, we call 'subversives'.

In the passage before us, Paul accuses the Corinthians of subverting the Lord's Supper. He says that when they gathered together it did more harm than good (11:17), that what they were doing could not really even be called the Lord's Supper (11:20) and that they might as well stay at home and forget the whole thing (11:22,34).

Reading such stern language might cause us to think the Corinthians didn't believe in observing the Lord's Supper and were gathering secretly and plotting ways to get it removed from the calendar of activities. Nothing could have been further from the truth. The Corinthians believed in the Lord's Supper and regularly observed it. It was the way in which they were observing it that was causing the problem. They didn't intend to subvert the communion, but that was the result of the way in which they were going about it.

Paul's discussion of this matter may be summarized under three heads: the selfishness of their observance (11:17-22), the symbolism of the ordinance (11:23-26) and the seriousness of their offence (11:27-34).

## The selfishness of their observance

First, let's consider the selfishness of their observance (11:17-22). It is quite obvious from Paul's words that the Corinthians had instituted something like a 'pot-luck dinner' prior to the actual observance of communion. This meal has come to be known as the 'agape' or 'love feast'. Evidently most of their abuses of the Lord's Supper stemmed from this meal.

The motives behind the institution of this meal were noble and sound. The whole church family, rich and poor alike, would gather at the appointed time and enjoy each other's food and fellowship. Two great benefits would follow. First, the church family would itself be strengthened. As the people got to know each other better, they could truly bear each other's burdens and be made aware of various needs for ministry. Secondly, those outside the church would surely hear about the gospel of Christ transcending social distinctions and welding diverse people together into one body. Such a phenomenon was bound to attract the interest of unbelievers.

It would seem, then, that the church could never look better than it did when it came together for the love-feast and the Lord's Supper. But all was not peace and light. What started out as a noble ideal had disintegrated into a nightmare. The divisions Paul so vigorously denounced in the opening chapter of this letter were more pro-nounced and evident during the fellowship meal than at any other time. Specifically, some of the more well-to-do members were 'jumping the gun'. Instead of waiting for the starting-time, they were arriving ahead of time. All the better, you see, to sit with your friends and to make sure you get to eat the prime rib you brought rather than the bread and cheese the poor members would bring! When the lower-class members who had to work all day finally arrived, the prime rib was gone, and it was just a hasty snack of bread and cheese or no supper at all! If this wasn't bad enough, some of the 'upper-crust' members were also going overboard sampling the wine and were getting tipsy before the Lord's Supper ever got under way.

After the poor had gobbled down their food, this charade known as the love-feast came to an end, and the church turned their attention to observing the Lord's Supper. What fine shape they were in! The rich members were stuffed to the gills and 'under the influence', while the poor members were angry and frustrated over the treat-ment they had received! They could call what they were doing an observance of the Lord's Supper, but it was really nothing more than a mockery of the sacred observance. The Lord's Supper had been subverted!

**The symbolism of the ordinance**

Suddenly, Paul turns his attention away from their abuses of communion to the symbolism of the ordinance (11:23-26). Why did he bring this up? Isn't it obvious he wanted them to put the way they were observing communion alongside that first observance and marvel at the difference?

What was our Lord's purpose in instituting this supper? It was to give his people something to commemorate his death. When Jesus broke the bread and gave it to his disciples, he told them to eat in remembrance of him (11:24). When he took the cup and passed it to his disciples he said, **'This do, as often as you drink it, in remembrance of Me'** (11:25). Every time the child of God comes to the Lord's Table and partakes of the bread and the cup, he is openly proclaiming that he remembers the death of Jesus Christ on the cross and that he will continue to do so until he is able to meet him face to face (11:26).

Why should the death of Christ be remembered? It is because of his death that Christians enjoy eternal life. On the cross, Christ took our place. He paid for our sins by receiving in his own body the judgement of God.

The central principle of the whole plan of redemption, then, is sacrifice. We could not have been delivered from our sins had Jesus not sacrificed himself on our behalf. When Jesus broke the bread for the disciples he said, **'Take, eat; this is My body which is broken for you...'** (11: 24).

'For you' — that is the heart of the gospel! Jesus didn't regard his own comfort or convenience but sacrificed it so undeserving sinners could have everlasting life. The Corinthians claimed to be his followers and, as such, should have reflected something of his character. But the principle of sacrifice that brought Jesus to the cross was nowhere to be found in their fellowship meals or in the Lord's Supper. They were not willing to give up their favourite foods so the poor members could have a good meal. They were not willing to give up an hour or two with their own special friends so they could spend a little time getting acquainted with those who were not in their clique. Irony of ironies — they gathered together to commemorate a principle they were unwilling to practise! Were they remembering Jesus when they came together? Not really!

## The seriousness of their offence

From rehearsing the meaning and purpose of the Lord's Supper, Paul turns to show the seriousness of their offence (11:27-34). We live in a day of easy-going, sentimental Christianity. We tend to think anyone who wants to can observe the Lord's Supper, and he can observe it in any fashion he pleases. Anyone who dares suggest otherwise is considered bigoted, dogmatic and narrow. Paul's words must come as a terrific shock to such people. He actually goes so far as to say that those who partake of the Lord's Supper in an unworthy manner are guilty of the body and blood of the Lord Jesus Christ.

When all is said and done there are only two classes of people in all of this world, and the death of Jesus Christ is the great dividing-line. There are those who have received the benefits of his death and there are those who are so opposed to him they would crucify him again. When a Christian comes to the Lord's Table in the wrong way, he treats the death of the Lord Jesus in a shameful way and places himself in the company of those who hate Christ and would crucify him again. No, he hasn't lost his salvation, but he is acting in such a way that it looks as if he has!

God, of course, doesn't take kindly to such treatment of his Son's death and, in the case of the Corinthians, had already visited judgement upon them. Paul says some of them were sick and some had already died because of the way they had profaned the Lord's death and trampled upon it (11:30).

Some Christians become quite terrified when they read such things and they conclude that the best thing to do is never to partake of the Lord's Supper. Two things must be said in response to this attitude.

First, the Lord's Supper is not optional for the Christian. It is commanded, and refusal to comply with such an explicit command from the Lord can also bring chastisement.

Secondly, we must keep in mind that there is a great difference between being worthy of partaking of communion and partaking worthily. No one ever has been, or ever will be, worthy to partake of the Lord's Supper, but that is not what Paul is talking about here. His concern was to get the Corinthians to start partaking of the Lord's Supper in a worthy manner.

We all know different occasions require different kinds of behaviour. We don't act the same way at a funeral as we do at a football match or a party. Paul's point is that we are to partake of the Lord's Supper in a manner that is appropriate to the occasion.

## The right way to partake of the Lord's Supper

What is the appropriate way to observe the Lord's Supper? Two things are absolutely essential.

One is *examination of the heart* (11:28). This means each child of God is to sift through his heart, confessing the sin he finds there. Is there coldness and hardness towards the Lord and his Word? Confess it and ask for God's forgiveness. Is there bitterness or resentment towards a brother or sister in Christ? Confess it. Is there a selfishness that contaminates and colours your life? Confess it. Paul says the one who judges himself doesn't have to fear God's judgement (11:31). The purpose of chastisement is to get us to face our sins and to deal with them. If we are doing this in our own hearts, there is no need for judgement. The Christian is never going to be perfect in this life, but he should be examining his heart and confessing his sins on a daily basis. This keeps him in fellowship with the Lord. If the Christian has failed to keep his accounts with the Lord current, the Lord's Supper is a good time to do some catching up.

The second part of worthily partaking of the Lord's Supper is *to discern the Lord's body in the process* (11:29). What is it to discern the Lord's body? It means we recognize that the elements symbolize the body and blood of Christ and salvation comes only from his death on the cross. It means we express our gratitude to him for his death and we worship him as we partake of those elements. Examination of ourselves and adoration of the Lord will keep us from falling into the errors of the Corinthians and will make the Lord's Supper a sheer delight.

# 36.
# Testing the spirits

*Please read 1 Corinthians 12:1-3*

This passage begins a long section in which Paul deals with the vast area of spiritual gifts. The Corinthians were having quite a bit of trouble in this area and they had asked Paul several questions. From what Paul says in chapters 12-14, we assume they had questions about spiritual gifts in general and about one gift in particular, the gift of tongues.

We certainly have no trouble identifying with their concern about the spiritual gifts. Our own day is one in which there is intense interest in this controversial subject. What are spiritual gifts? What is their purpose? Does every child of God possess a gift? Have some gifts ceased, or are all still in existence? What is the baptism of the Spirit? And what about this gift of tongues? What exactly is it? Is it still given today? If so, are all Christians meant to have it?

Some, of course, would have us believe all these questions can be answered very easily, but most of us find them quite taxing and tedious. The difficulty comes in trying to hold in tandem two clear biblical principles. On one hand, the Bible tells us, 'Do not quench the Spirit' (1 Thess. 5:19). On the other hand, it tells us to 'test all things' (1 Thess. 5:21).

### 'Do not quench the Spirit'

What is the meaning of the first of these principles? What is it to quench the Spirit? It means to deny or suppress something that is truly of God. It is obvious that many of us have driven off into this ditch. We have had a tendency to close our eyes to anything and everything that would disturb our lives and challenge our complacency.

How tragic this is when we stop to think about the conditions that prevail within the church today! Can there be any doubt that the church of Jesus Christ is in a most lamentable and deplorable state and sorely in need of a spiritual awakening? It is true that statistics are fairly good. A huge majority of Americans claim to have been born again and to have a personal relationship with the Lord Jesus Christ. But when we look past the mere profession to hard realities, what do we see? Isn't it obvious the church is having hardly any impact at all on this world? Isn't it safe to say God's people are virtually indistinguishable from people in general? Don't we hold essentially the same values and spend our time and money on the same things? Isn't it true that we often are guilty of using the same kind of language the people of the world use? Isn't it also fair to say God's people seem to have the same problems and crises as unbelievers? Don't we, for example, seem to have just as much difficulty holding our homes together as do unbelievers?

In addition to all of that, doesn't it seem to you that God's people have very little interest in serving the God they are supposed to love? Church leaders constantly remark about how hard it is to get people to commit themselves to the work of the Lord in any sort of substantial way. Take the area of church attendance, for example. Many churches have long since abandoned Sunday evening services because it is so difficult to hold attendance. Many have found pageants and musicals to be the only programmes they can offer and still expect to receive only modest support from their own members.

Thank God, there are those who see the superficial commitment, the dead orthodoxy and the worldliness of the church and carry a burden for revival. The last thing these people want to do is quench the Spirit of God. So when any movement or teaching comes along that has some depth of commitment and spiritual vitality to it, they are extremely reluctant to question it. Some who fervently desire spiritual renewal have been known to say things like, 'Anything is better than this even if it's wrong.'

### 'Test all things'

For this reason, many have forgotten all about the second principle Paul mentioned to the Thessalonians: 'Test all things' (1 Thess.

5:21). In other words, in avoiding the ditch on the one side, they have driven headlong into the one on the other side. What does it mean to 'test all things'? It simply means we are not to accept every teaching at face value. We are to be alert and discerning. Why is this necessary? The apostle John gives us the answer: 'Beloved, do not believe every spirit, but test the spirits, whether they are of God; because many false prophets have gone out into the world' (1 John 4:1).

Some people are so innocent and naïve as to think any feeling or impression they have, or any message delivered in the name of God, must be true and right. They fail to realize two basic truths. First, there are many spirits at work in this world. Paul says, 'For we do not wrestle against flesh and blood, but against principalities, against powers, against the rulers of the darkness of this age, against spiritual hosts of wickedness in the heavenly places' (Eph. 6:12). The second truth undiscerning Christians fail to see is that Satan is a great counterfeiter. He delights in taking something that is genuinely of God and copying it. In this way he not only deceives people, but also discredits the work of God.

In his second letter to these same Corinthians, Paul warns about Satan's counterfeiting work. He says false apostles are able to transform themselves into apostles of Christ because they get this power from Satan, who 'transforms himself into an angel of light' (2 Cor. 11:14).

It appears the Corinthians had fallen into the second of these traps and were naïvely accepting at face value everything that was said or done in the name of God. They seem to have been overly enamoured of the more glamorous, emotional gifts and especially the gift of speaking in tongues. They had failed to see that speaking in tongues was not a uniquely Christian phenomenon and that Satan was just as capable of counterfeiting it as he was other aspects of Christian experience. Their great need, therefore, was to test the spirits.

Only three options are available to those who are trying to discern what messengers and messages truly come from God.

First, we can say all are from God, but if we select this option, we have to find some way to explain why the messengers and messages contradict each other. Does God simply have trouble making up his mind on what he wants to say? Or does he forget what he said to this messenger over here and say something quite different to the messenger over there?

Our second option is to say none of the messengers and messages are from God. This is an attractive option to many. They hear the competing voices of our day and conclude that no one can ever say with any degree of certainty who is telling the truth, so we might as well forget the whole thing.

The third option is to say some are truly speaking for God and some are not. This is what the Bible tells us (1 John 4:1). If this is the case, we are left with the question of how we determine which is which.

The Corinthians were having much the same problem many of us are having. They tended to be rather gullible and naïve about these things and were, therefore, accepting at face value any message that claimed to be of God. In particular, they seem to have been susceptible to accepting anything that moved or stirred their emotions.

The apostle Paul didn't leave them to flounder about in their own confusion and uncertainty, but he gave them a couple of things to keep in mind when they were confronted with the question of whether a particular teaching was from God.

**Emotions are unreliable**

First, he warns them to not make the stirring of their emotions the determining factor in this business of testing the spirits. This is, of course, what many naturally tend to do. I dare say the vast majority of Christians have adopted the creed, 'I know because I feel.' For them, emotion is the final court of appeal. If a particular message has touched or moved them, they are convinced God has spoken and they will not lend countenance to the slightest hint they might be deceived.

Evidently, the Corinthians had fallen prey to this same kind of thinking. So before he ever tells them how to test the spirits, Paul tells them how *not* to do it. He does this by simply calling to their minds what their former religion of paganism was like. The emotional fervour of those religious practices was so great that Paul says they were **'carried away'** by it (12:2). The picture Paul draws with this term is of one who has fallen into a river and is swept along by the mighty, raging current. In other words, Paul says their old religion so stirred their emotions they were oblivious to everything else.

Instead of finding what was true and right in paganism, they were, according to Paul, being **'led'** (12:2) around by Satan! Even though the idols themselves were **'dumb'**, there was a sinister reality behind them, the reality of Satan himself.

So the fact we are moved by a tidal wave of emotion doesn't mean we are hearing from the true God. The truth we must always keep in mind is that Satan is able to give people great emotional experiences. If someone today goes into some kind of frenzy or ecstasy or speaks in tongues, many leap to the conclusion that they are seeing God at work. Little do they know that the pagan religions offered these very same things!

## 'Jesus is Lord'

If we are to determine what is truly of God and what isn't, we need something more stable and settled than the shifting sands of emotion. Paul gives us the fixed principle we need in three little words: **'Jesus is Lord.'**

In those three words, we have the very essence of the Christian message. The name 'Jesus' is our Lord's human name, given to him by Mary at his birth. The term 'Lord', however, is an official title and it means he has sovereign authority. So when Paul says, 'Jesus is Lord,' he is affirming that the man known as Jesus of Nazareth was and is nothing less than God himself in human flesh and is the sovereign Ruler of all things! So Paul is saying exactly the same thing as the apostle John when he says, 'By this you know the Spirit of God: Every spirit that confesses that Jesus Christ has come in the flesh is of God, and every spirit that does not confess that Jesus Christ has come in the flesh is not of God' (1 John 4:2-3).

Jesus and Lord — our whole theology must embody and revolve around these two poles. Many find it almost impossible to embrace both these truths. Some exalt the 'Jesus' part. To them, the Lord Jesus was a very fine and wonderful man, probably the best man who ever lived, but still just a man. Others exalt the 'Lord' part. To them, human flesh is inherently evil, and they end up saying Jesus' humanity wasn't real, but was like a costume he wore.

Some think Paul mentions the phrase, 'Jesus is accursed' (12:3) because someone had actually blurted this out while being caught up in a state of ecstasy in one of the worship services. The more likely explanation is that some of the Corinthians had fallen into the trap of exalting 'Lord' over 'Jesus'. A popular notion among the Greek people of that era was that everything physical was evil. It is probable that some of the church members in Corinth had imbibed this notion and carried it over into their theology. The practical outworking of it was to disparage the physical body of Jesus. Therefore, these church members could exult in Christ's deity and curse his humanity and not see they were contradicting the gospel message.

This was a contradiction Paul simply couldn't tolerate. No one who is a true child of God can ever curse Jesus. The Holy Spirit of God came into this world for the specific and express purpose of glorifying the Lord Jesus Christ (John 16:14). Therefore, we may be sure the Holy Spirit is not at work in any context in which Jesus Christ is spoken of in a disparaging fashion. On the other hand, when someone embraces Jesus Christ as Lord, we may rest assured the Holy Spirit is at work because no one can ever come to Christ unless the Holy Spirit enlightens and enables him. So Paul says, **'No one can say that Jesus is Lord except by the Holy Spirit'** (12:3).

What is it to become a child of God? No question is more important and yet has more debate and confusion swirling around it. It is much more than just believing in God or joining a church. In fact, it involves embracing what the Lord of glory did in the man Jesus! It means recognizing why he had to come (because man is a sinner and is completely helpless to do anything about his sin). It is embracing by faith what he did on the cross and submitting to him as Lord with the full intent of living under his lordship! This is what the Holy Spirit produces wherever he works, and anything less than this is not Christianity!


**Three tests we can apply**

So let's go back to our original question. How are we to discern whether a particular message is of God? Paul says we should use the 'Jesus is Lord' test. Does this message exalt Jesus Christ as Lord? How can we tell whether a message is exalting Christ? First, we need to ask ourselves if it is constantly exalting and exhibiting self. Many messages claim to exalt Jesus, but all they do in reality is parade man and his religious experiences!

Secondly, we should be very frightened of any message that is built on a new revelation. If Jesus Christ is Lord, he is the final and supreme revelation. God has said his last word in Jesus Christ (Heb. 1:1-4), and anyone who claims to have received a new word should be disregarded and avoided.

Thirdly, we should reject out of hand any message that contradicts the teaching of Scripture. The Holy Spirit came, as we noted, to glorify Jesus. We have his witness to Christ in the pages of Holy Scripture. The Bible was inspired by the Holy Spirit (2 Tim. 3:16; 2 Peter 1:19-21). What it says is what he says. Paul called the Word of God 'the sword of the Spirit' (Eph. 6:17). If the Holy Spirit produced Scripture, doesn't it stand to reason he is going to stand by it and not contradict it? In other words, we may safely assume the Holy Spirit is always going to agree with Scripture. If someone comes along with a message that contradicts the clear teaching of Scripture, we may safely conclude this person is not of God.

These are all implications that naturally evolve from Paul's fixed principle of the lordship of Jesus. We live in a time when all sorts of people with all sorts of messages claim to be from God. Many even claim to be able to prove they are from God by performing various signs and wonders. How are we to cope with such a time? Let's arm ourselves with Paul's principle ('Jesus is Lord'), work out the implications of it and adhere rigorously to it.

# 37.
# General guidelines
# for spiritual gifts

*Please read 1 Corinthians 12:4-11*

Two kinds of Christians trouble me greatly: those who are not spiritual enough and those who are too spiritual. Of course, it is impossible for any of us to be too spiritual in the true sense of the word. But when we misunderstand what true spirituality is and begin to practise a pseudo-spirituality, we are too spiritual. Any amount of a bad thing is too much. Unfortunately, a lot of modern Christians think they are spiritual, but their spirituality is in their own minds.

Many of the Corinthians were firmly in the clutches of a pseudo-spirituality, and this had caused the whole church to get entangled in debate on the question of what constitutes true spirituality. The Corinthians were so confused and divided over this matter that they finally decided to write to Paul for help.

What or who is truly spiritual? Paul begins his response to this particular question by saying, 'Now concerning spiritual gifts...' (12:1). But the word 'gifts' is not in the original language. In reality Paul begins by saying, 'Now concerning spiritualities...' So Paul's discussion of spiritual gifts is set in the larger context of what it is to have true spirituality.

## A negative approach

Paul, then, was concerned to counter a defective spirituality that had developed in the church of Corinth. From what he says in these three chapters (12-14), we can conclude that this defective spirituality had certain distinct features. First, it placed the emotions above the mind and assumed that, the more emotionally overpowering something is, the more spiritual it is. Secondly, it encouraged people to progress from Christ to the Holy Spirit. Thirdly, it assumed all truly spiritual Christians would evidence their spirituality in the same way. Fourthly, it elevated certain gifts to a special status. Fifthly, it assumed Christians could take various steps to secure for themselves certain gifts. Sixthly, it placed the edification of the individual over the edification of the congregation. Finally, it placed the gifts of the Spirit above the graces of the Spirit and created a situation in which people were exercising their gifts in an unchristian way.

In the first three verses of this section, Paul counters the first two features of this defective spirituality by reminding the Corinthians of two indisputable facts. First, the moving of emotions was part of their former religion of paganism and could not, therefore, be used as a barometer of what is right and true. Secondly, the Holy Spirit himself came to honour and magnify the Lord Jesus Christ, and, therefore, any attempt to place the Spirit above Christ is wrong and is grieving to the Spirit.

In the verses before us, Paul begins to dismantle some of the other leading features of their flawed spirituality. He does so by putting three correcting principles in place: the diversity of the Spirit's work (12:4-10), the priority of the church's good (12:7) and the sovereignty of the Spirit's will (12:11). For all who firmly grasp them, these principles will go a long way towards preventing a slide into the slough of pseudo-spirituality.


**The diversity of the Spirit's work**

In dealing with the first of these principles, Paul uses three words to indicate the various ways in which the Holy Spirit manifests himself in the life of the church: *'charismata'*, *'diakonia'* and *'energemata'*.

*'Charismata'* simply means 'varieties of gifts'. By the way, that word in and of itself counters the notion that Christians can do something to secure a certain gift. If one could earn it, it wouldn't be a gift.

*'Diakonia'* means 'varieties of service'. It is the same word that is often translated 'deacon'. This word takes a slap at those who were

using their gifts as badges of spiritual superiority. The Lord Jesus Christ came to be a servant, and those who follow him should not be found trying to dodge servanthood.

*'Energemata'* means 'varieties of energies', or 'varieties of powers'. This word indicates that the children of God are to give evidence that God is at work in them. They are not to be a people of deadness and barrenness but a people of life and energy.

Did you notice how Paul connected each of these three words with a different member of the Trinity? He mentions the Spirit in connection with the gifts, the Lord in connection with the services or ministries and God the Father in connection with the power or energies. Are we to explain this as a mere literary device Paul chose to employ, or is there a deeper meaning? I suggest Paul was pulling the Corinthians away from one of their misconceptions and pointing them in the right direction. One of the tenets of their defective spirituality was that all Christians should evidence their spirituality in the same way. Paul's words show them that they were looking for their unity in the wrong place. God's people do not all possess the same gifts. Their unity lies not in their gifts but in their God! No matter what our gifts, we may rest assured they are distributed by the Spirit for the service of the Lord as appointed and energized by the Father.

The three words Paul uses ought to be sufficient to convince us of the great diversity of the Spirit's work, but Paul goes on to mention specifically nine gifts bestowed by the Spirit. At the end of this chapter, he gives another list (some say two lists) of gifts provided by the Spirit and there includes even more gifts.

We shall return to look at these gifts in more detail later. The truth for us to latch on to at this point is the variety in the Spirit's work. Because of this variety, we should resist any temptation to put the Spirit of God in a straitjacket by suggesting all Christians should have the same gift. This brings us to consider the second principle Paul emphasizes in these verses.

## The priority of the church's good

We have all these manifestations of the Spirit at work in the life of the church. What is their purpose? Is it so Christians can call attention to themselves and receive adulation from others? Paul says the Spirit works in all these ways **'for the profit of all'** (12:7).

Ours is a day of great emphasis on the individual and his rights. However legitimate that may be for society, it has a devastating effect on the church. Christians seem to have uncritically adopted the idea that each individual is the measure of all things and have carried it right over into their practice of Christianity. Talk to one of these about missing worship services and he will say, 'I don't get anything out of church.' Ask him to take a position of responsibility and he will say, 'I don't have time.' Ask him to support the church with his tithes and offerings and he will say, 'I don't agree with how the church spends the money.' Do you see the point? Everything is considered in terms of what brings the individual the most comfort instead of what does the church the most good!

If you are an 'I' Christian, Paul's words are apt to make you squirm. He calls upon the Corinthians to be done with 'Lone Ranger' Christianity, to repudiate their own desires and convenience and to start putting the good of the church above every other consideration. We are familiar with John F. Kennedy's words: 'Ask not what your country can do for you, but what you can do for your country.' Isn't it time for all who know the Lord to stop asking what the church can do for us and start asking what we can do for the church? For the Corinthians, this meant shelving the notion that the spiritual gifts were for their personal gratification. What will working for the church's good require of you and me?

## The sovereignty of the Spirit's will

The third correcting principle Paul lays before the Corinthians has to do with the sovereignty of the Spirit. Paul says the Holy Spirit distributes to **'each one individually as He wills'** (12:11).

'As He wills'. These three words lead me to draw a couple of conclusions. First, the Corinthian idea that all Christians should have the same gift or gifts and that certain steps can be taken to receive these gifts is foolishness. It is the Holy Spirit who determines who receives what gift. Asking God for a specific gift or claiming it by faith doesn't mean we shall receive it. The Spirit of God controls these matters. Secondly, if the Holy Spirit is sovereign in giving the gifts, we have to say it is possible for him to give certain gifts for a while and then totally withdraw them!

Many Christians have made a couple of grand assumptions at this point. They assume all the gifts have to be in operation in every generation of Christians and that once a Christian has a particular gift, he will always have that gift. But the sovereignty of the Spirit would seem to mean that certain gifts will cease altogether, and that individuals may be given a gift for a particular moment in the church's life. When that moment passes, the gift could very well pass as well.

It has frequently been said in recent years that the key to the church's experiencing a new age of the Spirit is to help Christians discover and use their spiritual gifts. There is, of course, great promise and potential for the church in the area of spiritual gifts; however, the sad truth is that many churches have found the spiritual gifts to be a source of division and heartache instead of renewal and blessing. I suggest this is largely due to our being so preoccupied with the gifts themselves that we forget the general principles that govern them. Before we ever ask what this or that particular gift means, we must make sure we are conscious of these three principles: the diversity of the Spirit's work, the priority of the church's good and the sovereignty of the Spirit's will. Only then will we avoid the snare of pseudo-spirituality and realize the enormous potential the gifts offer.

# 38.
# Many gifts, one body

*Please read 1 Corinthians 12:12-27*

Many of the Corinthians had the notion that all Christians should have the same gift and that definite steps could be taken to this end. In the verses preceding these, Paul cogently and powerfully argues that the Spirit of God has placed a great diversity of gifts in the church for her good. Furthermore, the Holy Spirit has done this because it is his sovereign prerogative to do so. It is futile, therefore, to try to dictate to the Holy Spirit regarding spiritual gifts.

In this passage, Paul anticipates an objection. He knew some of the Corinthians would be anxious to seize his teaching about diversity and make it into something quite dangerous. In short, he could see them arguing that such diversity would seriously disrupt the unity of the church. In order to head off this response, Paul simply demonstrates that diversity of gifts in no way threatens the unity of the church but actually enhances and promotes it. He accomplishes this by using the example of the human body. Could there be a better example of diversity within unity? Nothing is more obvious than the fact that the body consists of many different parts. But that doesn't mean it is not united or that it is at war with itself. All the parts are necessary for the body to do what it was designed to do.

To drive home the truth that diversity doesn't threaten unity, Paul urges the Corinthians to consider the real source of their unity (12:12-13) and the real threat to their unity (12:14-27).

## The source of unity

What is it that unites Christians? Does their unity come from their all being just alike? Is the reason for it that they all resemble each other like peas in a pod? Or is it rooted in something else? Paul declares that the real source of unity for Christians is their common spiritual experience. He says, **'For by one Spirit we were all baptized into one body — whether Jews or Greeks, whether slaves or free — and have all been made to drink into one Spirit'** (12:13).

Through this common spiritual experience, diverse people had been made one. Jews and Greeks had very little in common with each other, but the church of Corinth consisted of people from both cultures. Slaves and free may have had even less in common, but the church of Corinth also had members from both groups. There is no way to explain the unity of these people in natural, cultural terms. So how did it come about? Paul says they had all been 'baptized into one body', and had all been 'made to drink into one Spirit'.

It is obvious that the baptizing and drinking are equivalent expressions; Paul is talking about the same spiritual experience. To be baptized is to be completely immersed or submerged in water, and to drink is to take water into our bodies. By using these two terms Paul was saying the Corinthians had been incorporated by the Spirit into the body of Christ and had at the same time been filled with the Spirit.

Some would have us believe the baptism of the Spirit is an experience that takes place after conversion. They argue that there are really two groups of Christians: those who have been saved but not baptized by the Spirit, and those who are not only saved but also baptized. Christians in the first group supposedly live spiritually anaemic lives and have carnal ways, while Christians in the latter group abound in spiritual power and blessing. Those who hold this view cite the example of the Samaritans (Acts 8:5-17) and the Ephesians (Acts 19:1-7). In each case, it appears that some who already knew Christ received the baptism of the Spirit subsequent to their conversion.

What about all of this? My immediate response is simply to point out that this two-tier concept completely ignores the whole point of Paul's argument in the verses before us. Paul, as we have seen, was concerned to show the Corinthians the basis of their unity. Notice how he stresses the word 'all' in talking about this baptism of the Spirit. If this baptism is an experience only a few Christians have, Paul certainly slipped up in appealing to this as the source of their unity.

But how do we explain the cases of the Samaritans and the Ephesians? These were special cases and should in no way be taken as examples of the normal Christian experience. In the case of the Samaritans, God delayed the granting of the Spirit until Peter and John arrived. Why? So the rift that had existed for centuries between Jews and Samaritans would not be carried over into the church. In the case of the Ephesians, a close study of their replies to Paul's questions reveal that they had never truly been saved in the first place. They received Christ then and there, and the Holy Spirit came upon them at the very same time.

Paul's point, then, is that there was no need for the Corinthians to worry about the diversity of gifts fracturing their unity because their unity lay elsewhere — in their common experience of being placed in the body of Christ by the Holy Spirit and in receiving the Holy Spirit. But we know from what we read in Paul's letter that the Corinthians were in fact divided over this matter of the spiritual gifts. Even though they shared this wonderful common experience of being converted, their fellowship was fragmented and fractured. The thing Paul wanted them to see was that their division was not due to the Holy Spirit placing a great diversity of gifts in their church, but to their attitudes towards that diversity (12:14-27).

**The threat to their unity**

We can easily see from Paul's words that two very damaging attitudes about the gifts were running loose in the church.

*A sense of inferiority*

The first of these attitudes was one of inferiority (12:15-20). Some in the church considered their gifts to be very modest and were essentially saying, 'They don't need me.'

Paul ridicules this notion by imagining a conversation between various members of the human body. Suppose the foot, because it doesn't possess the dexterity of the hand, concludes it really doesn't belong to the body. How ridiculous! Just because the foot cannot perform like a hand doesn't make it any less a part of the body!

If you find yourself sympathizing with the lot of the foot, think about the ear for a moment. If any part of the body would seem to have a legitimate cause for complaint it would have to be the ear! It is located in close proximity to the eye, yet no one notices or comments on the ear except when it is too big! People are always making nice remarks about the eyes, but when was the last time someone came up to you and said, 'You certainly have lovely ears!' But despite all of this, the ear is still very much a part of the body!

Suppose for a moment that every member of the body could be the part it most wanted to be and all chose to be the eye. What a fix that would put us in! If the whole body were an eye, we wouldn't be able to hear, smell, or do any of the other umpteen things our bodies do. But we would certainly see very well!

Now carry all of this over to the church, and suppose each member could choose the gift he most wanted. What would the church be like? Great numbers of people would be doing one or two things while untold numbers of tasks would be left undone. Therefore, the Holy Spirit determines who gets what gift in order to ensure the work of the church gets done. And that is why no one needs to feel inferior about his or her gift. Each person and each gift is placed in the church by God himself for a purpose; each is necessary. Although some gifts are not as important as others, all are necessary.

*An attitude of superiority*

A second harmful attitude the Corinthians had about the gifts was the attitude of superiority (12:21-27). Those with this attitude were essentially looking down at others and saying, 'I don't need them.'

Paul combats this attitude by simply staying with his analogy of the human body. He admits some members of the body **'seem to be weaker'** (12:22), and some parts need to be clothed and adorned to make them more attractive. But that doesn't change the fact that each part is necessary and plays a valuable rôle. The unattractive parts, when adorned, fit in very well with those parts which need no adornment, and the body becomes one harmonious entity.

In the human body, the more attractive, presentable parts don't look down with disdain on the less attractive, unpresentable parts. Instead, the parts function as a whole, and when one part hurts, the whole body hurts; when one part experiences pleasure, the whole body feels the pleasure.

This is the way the church should function. Even if we are granted gifts that place us in the forefront of the church's life and ministry, we have no right to take any of the other members of the church for granted. God has placed each person in the church and gifted each person, and we need each other!

Just as the body, then, has diverse members and yet is one, so it is with the church. Diversity does not threaten the church. The church needs it and thrives on it! But the attitudes of inferiority and superiority will threaten and destroy any church. So let's dispense with the 'They don't need me' and the 'I don't need them' attitudes and get on with the business of living and ministering for the Lord to whom we belong.

# 39.
# Have the gifts ceased?

*Please read 1 Corinthians 12:8-11,28-31*

When Christmas comes round, most children are so completely occupied with opening their presents they don't have time for anything else. Many Christians seem to have much the same approach to spiritual gifts. They don't want to be detained with explanations. They simply want to get down to business: 'Do I have a gift? Do I have more than one gift? How can I tell which gift is mine?'

Preachers have fed this mentality by preaching elaborate series of sermons on what the various gifts are and how Christians can go about discovering and utilizing theirs. A careful study of Paul's treatment of this vital subject makes it quite clear he was far more concerned with the principles behind the gifts than with the gifts themselves.

We have isolated the following major principles: there is great diversity in the Spirit's giving (12:4-10); all the gifts are for the good of the church (12:7); the Spirit decides who gets what gifts (12:11,18); and the fact that there is a diversity of gifts doesn't threaten the unity of the church (12:12-27).

### The lists of gifts

With these principles firmly in place, we are in a position to look at the actual gifts Paul mentions. Perhaps the one thing that leaps out and catches our attention is the lack of precision we find in what Paul says about the gifts. He gives two lists of gifts in this one chapter and the two lists are quite different. Some of the gifts he mentions in the first part of the chapter, he ignores in the last part; he mentions gifts in the last part of the chapter he didn't mention in the first part.

When we begin to compare Paul's two lists here with the other three lists of gifts in the New Testament (Rom. 12:6-8; Eph. 4:7-11; 1 Peter 4:7-11) we find much the same thing. Gifts that appear in one list are nowhere to be found in the other lists. No matter where we look, we find a casualness and almost a carelessness about listing the gifts. Why? The answer should be quite obvious. Paul and Peter, the only two men who gave lists of the gifts, wanted to avoid the very thing so many of us are guilty of: adopting a mechanical, rigid approach on this matter.

Some look at the lists of the gifts and immediately say all the gifts have ceased, that they were all temporary provisions for the early church alone. Others look at the very same lists and say none of the gifts have ceased, and the only reason we don't see them today is the church's unwillingness to claim them in faith. Those who hold this view strongly insist that Scripture nowhere says the gifts will cease, but it should also be pointed out that neither does Scripture say all the gifts will continue.

Both of these approaches seem to me to be of the rigid, mechanical sort and ultimately constitute a denial of one of the major principles Paul clearly laid down: the sovereignty of the Spirit. Both approaches essentially put the Spirit of God in a straitjacket. One says he must give all the same gifts today as he did then, while the other says he must not give any of the same gifts.

What is the true position? I suggest close adherence to the sovereignty of the Spirit will drive us to conclude some of the gifts have ceased while others have not. If the Spirit is sovereign, he has the freedom to withdraw some gifts and to continue to give others. Furthermore, if the Spirit is sovereign in the giving of the gifts, we should expect him to be giving gifts today which he didn't necessarily give in the days of the early church. The tricky part, of course, is determining which of the gifts have ceased and which haven't.

## Gifts which appear to have ceased

Perhaps we shall never be able to conclude with any degree of finality which category certain gifts fall into. There can be absolutely no doubt about others.

*Apostles and prophets*

Take the gifts of apostle and prophet, for example. Paul tells the
Ephesians the church is built on the foundation of the apostles and
prophets (Eph. 2:20). If we were to go out and start building a house,
we would lay a foundation, but there would be a definite end to it.
A builder doesn't just continue to lay the foundation; he builds on
top of a foundation that is complete and finished.

The apostles and the prophets occupied a unique place in God's
economy in that they were recipients of new revelation from God.
While the New Testament was being written, God directed and
guided the church by revealing his truth to the apostles and prophets.
When Scripture was complete, their work was done and we now
have embodied in Scripture the truth we need.

In addition to these gifts, I would say there is strong presumptive
evidence that these gifts have also ceased: discerning of spirits,
working miracles, healing, speaking in tongues and interpreting
tongues. Let's look briefly at each of these.

*Discerning of spirits*

The discerning of spirits doesn't require much comment. This gift
was tied to the gift of prophecy. When prophets declared the
revelations they had received from God, the gift of discernment
enabled those who had it to determine whether a prophet had truly
spoken the Word of God. When the gift of prophecy ceased, there
was no need for the gift of discernment to continue.

*Miracles*

Regarding the working of miracles, some would have us believe
miracles happened every single day in the lives of the Bible heroes
and that they should be happening with the same frequency to us.
The first thing we should point out to those who hold this view is that
a miracle is, by definition, something that is extraordinary. If
miracles happened every day they would be ordinary and would,
therefore, not be miracles.

A careful study of the miracles that did take place in the Bible
reveals that, far from happening all the time, they actually occurred
in four clusters: during the time of Israel's deliverance from Egypt,

during the ministries of Elijah and Elisha, during the time of Judah's captivity in Babylon and during the ministries of our Lord and the apostles. It should be noted that each of these eras was a time when God was giving new revelation. While a lot of ground is covered by those four eras, there is still a gigantic amount of time in which miracles didn't take place.

Furthermore, since the gift of miracles so closely adhered to the office of apostle (2 Cor. 12:12; Heb. 2:3-4), it is only logical to expect it to cease at the same time the office ceased.

## Healings

Healings, of course, constitute a good number of the miracles that took place in the Bible. So if we conclude the gift of miracles has ceased, we are almost bound to conclude healings have ceased as well. This is not to say, of course, that God never heals anybody today, but rather that he heals through medical processes and not through the giving of a miraculous gift to someone in the church. There are many who claim to have the gift of healing, but a quick comparison of the so-called healers of our day with the apostles will reveal some notable differences. The healings of the apostles were always complete and instantaneous and were never announced beforehand. And the apostles never failed in their attempts to heal. All of this is a far cry from what goes on with those who claim to have the gift of healing today.

## Tongues and the interpretation of tongues

What about the gifts of tongues and the interpretation of tongues? What evidence is there for saying they have ceased? We shall look more fully at these issues when we come to chapter 14. At this point, we should simply note two things: Paul always places these gifts very firmly at the end of his lists, and the later lists contain no mention of them at all. It would appear, then, that these gifts existed only in the early years of the church's life, that they gradually diminished and finally ceased. The very fact that Christians down through the years have not even been able to agree on what the gift of tongues was indicates that the gift was lost early in Christian history.

**Gifts which still exist today**

The other gifts Paul mentions in this chapter — the word of wisdom (12:8), the word of knowledge (12:8), faith (12:9), teachers (12:28), helps (12:28) and administrations (12:28) — would seem to still be existing in the church today.

The *word of wisdom* is probably the ability to see through a particular problem and to shed light on what the church is to do about it. The *word of knowledge* may very well be the capacity to grasp and communicate God's Word in a special way. The gift of *faith* should not be confused with saving faith. The latter is something all Christians have. The gift of faith is probably the ability to trust God's promises in what seems to be an impossible dilemma. The gift of *teaching* is the ability to explain the Word of God so others can understand it. The teacher, of course, is one in whom we would also expect to find the gift of knowledge. The gift of *helps* is the ability to serve and support others. Those with this gift usually serve behind the scenes and go largely unnoticed. The gift of *administrations* is the gift of leadership.

Even after we decide what gifts are still available today, we still must not let our guard down against the danger of adopting a mechanical, rigid view towards the gifts. The Spirit of God is still free to do as he pleases with these gifts. We should avoid assuming, therefore, that if we see a particular gift in some person, then this person will permanently have this gift. Assuming this has brought much sorrow to many churches. Some, for example, get the idea they have been given a permanent gift of wisdom and suddenly consider themselves to be the expert on what the church is to do in every situation. If another brother or sister in the church begs to disagree with the one who claims the gift of wisdom, he or she is accused of fighting against the Spirit of God. If the Spirit of God is sovereign in the giving of gifts, we should not be surprised to find that one brother or sister has the word of wisdom for one situation and another has the word of wisdom for another situation.

The main thing for us to carry away from Paul's discussion of the gifts is that the Spirit of God is in charge. Instead of worrying about what gifts exist today and what our gift or gifts may be, we should simply concern ourselves with serving our Lord in as many ways as we possibly can. If we faithfully do this with the right spirit, we may rest assured our Lord will be pleased and our reward will be great.

# 40.
# The more excellent way

*Please read 1 Corinthians 13:1-7*

The Corinthians were preoccupied with and enamoured of the spiritual gifts in general and the more spectacular gifts in particular. They defined spirituality in terms of the gifts and assumed those who possessed the more spectacular gifts were in a superior spiritual class and left all the others far behind.

Paul had a crushing word for all who entertained such notions. He closed his discussion of spiritual gifts in general by saying there was 'a more excellent way' (12:31). I am sure that caught their attention! I can still hear their horrified response: 'What could possibly be more excellent than the gifts?'

Paul didn't make them wait long for the answer. In simple, unadorned language he escorts them up to the very pinnacle of Christian faith and practice. What is this pinnacle? What is the Mt Everest of Christianity? Paul says it is love.

In the verses before us, Paul demonstrates the excellence of love in two ways. First, he compares it with the gifts and says they are worthless without love (13:1-3). Then he seems to look at life in general and the challenges it poses and concludes that life is unmanageable without love (13:4-7).

## The gifts are worthless without love

Look at how Paul compares love with the gifts. He selects four gifts, carries them to their most spectacular expression and concludes each time that they amount to nothing apart from love.

*Tongues*

He starts with the gift of tongues, not because he regarded it as the
most important of all the gifts, but because the Corinthians obviously did. 'Just suppose,' he says, 'that I possessed the gift of
tongues to such a degree that I not only completely outclassed the
most eloquent of men but rivalled the very angels of heaven
themselves.'

The mere suggestion of such a thing probably had the
Corinthians churning with emotion and shouting 'Hallelujah!'
Wouldn't it be wonderful to exercise the gift of tongues to such a
marvellous degree? Paul drops the other shoe by saying if he had the
gift of tongues in the superlative degree it would mean nothing apart
from love. He goes so far as to say he would, in that case, amount
to nothing more than **'sounding brass or a clanging cymbal'**
(13:1).

Several commentators point out that gongs and cymbals were
used in idol worship to arouse the gods, or to drive away false gods,
or to excite the worshippers, or all three. Whatever their purpose,
it is quite clear these gongs and cymbals were incapable of
producing a melody. They could only produce one tiring, monoto-
nous sound.

Paul's point is that the gift of tongues in its highest form would
be, apart from love, just as tiresome as these gongs and cymbals. In
our own day, much of what professes to be the zenith of spirituality
sounds terribly like a tiresome gong. Listen and you will hear the one
constant note: 'Me! Me! Me!'

*Prophecy*

Next Paul takes the gift of prophecy. As far as the apostle was
concerned this gift far outranked tongues (14:1), but it fares no better
if it is done without love. 'Take prophecy to its highest expression,'
Paul says, 'and imagine that one could actually penetrate and
understand all the mysteries and have complete and exhaustive
knowledge' (13:2). The very thought would have any prophet
licking his lips in anticipation! But Paul says it would mean nothing
apart from love.

## Faith

Then there is the gift of faith. What if we could possess that gift to such a great degree that we could be shuffling mountains around here and there! Wouldn't that be wonderful? The 'name it and claim it' crowd would dance in ecstasy at the mere prospect of mountains sailing hither and thither! But Paul's verdict is the same. Faith without love is meaningless (13:2).

## Mercy

Finally, Paul takes up the gift of showing mercy, a gift he didn't include in his list in chapter 12, but did include in his letter to the Romans (Rom. 12:8). 'Suppose,' he says, 'someone were to take the gift of mercy to the extent that he would give up every last scrap of possessions and would give himself up as a martyr' (13:3). Surely, such an act of supreme sacrifice would have great meaning. Paul says if it were done apart from love, it would all add up to nothing at all!

Have Paul's words soaked into our minds and hearts? Have we grasped their tremendous sweep? It is easy for us to mistake what he is saying. It is not simply that our service to the Lord is diminished and impaired by lack of love, but rather that there is no service to the Lord without love! No matter how highly acclaimed and applauded we may be among men, we are absolutely nothing without love!

## Life is unmanageable without love

Next, Paul says the challenges of life are unmanageable without love (13:4-7). Stop and think about what life throws at us. First, we have to contend with our own sinful nature. We are constantly told to think well of ourselves, to concentrate on our good points and to ignore our weak points, but the perceptive person cannot ignore his own heart. He knows he has more than a few weak points, and lying at the very heart of his nature is a foul swamp that constantly gurgles and bubbles up in his behaviour. Life would be challenging enough if we had only to deal with our own sinfulness, but in addition to that, we have to deal with the sinfulness of others.

The mere thought of these twin challenges is enough to make us throw up our hands in despair. How can we ever manage such demands? Paul says love is the answer for us. He gives fifteen characteristics of love, characteristics that tame the beast that lies within us and enable us to cope with the same beast crouching in others. A quick glance at these characteristics reveals each one had special relevance to the Corinthians. Paul didn't just pick these out of the air. The Corinthians were, at this particular point in their lives, exhibiting the very opposite of these traits. Let's go through Paul's list.

## The characteristics of love

First, love **'suffers long'** (13:4). That simply means love is patient, or slow to anger. It enables us to put up with all that is distasteful and trying in others.

Love **'is kind'** (13:4). It is gracious and tender. Like Jesus, it is touched and moved by the needs of the poor, sick and downtrodden.

Love **'does not envy'** (13:4). Envy is that sullen feeling of disappointment when another's success or prosperity surpasses our own. Love enables us to be happy when others are blessed.

Love **'does not parade itself'** (13:4). It doesn't allow us to put ourselves on display and to live for the notice and applause of men.

Love **'is not puffed up'** (13:4). It isn't arrogant or conceited.

Love **'does not behave rudely'** (13:5). It is too gentle and sensitive to even consider doing anything that will bring shame or embarrassment to another.

Love **'does not seek its own'** (13:5). It isn't selfish. It doesn't insist on its own way but constantly insists on seeking the well-being of others.

Love **'is not provoked'** (13:5). It isn't irritable, temperamental, touchy, thin-skinned, or easily offended.

Love **'thinks no evil'** (13:5). It doesn't keep a ledger of all the wrongs that have been done to it with a view of getting even.

Love **'does not rejoice in iniquity'** (13:6). It doesn't get any pleasure out of the failures and misfortunes of others.

Love **'rejoices in the truth'** (13:6). Love is never opposed to the truth, nor sells it out, but is always glad to see truth win out.

Love **'bears all things'** (13:7). It passes over in silence and keeps confidential all that is repugnant in others.

Love **'believes all things'** (13:7). It is always ready to see the best in others and to give them the benefit of the doubt.

Love **'hopes all things'** (13:7). It isn't pessimistic about future relationships with those who have been troublesome in the past. It is never ready to give up on others.

Love **'endures all things'** (13: 7). It has steadfast fortitude. It refuses to be conquered and dismayed.

That list of characteristics pretty well covers every area of life! If we live in love, we shall be able to meet all that life throws at us! It sounds as though all we have to do is just make up our minds to be loving, doesn't it? But many have made up their minds time and time again, only to fail time and time again. How can we ever live like this? We must realize that what we have in these fifteen characteristics is nothing less than a composite picture of the Lord Jesus Christ himself. If we want to have these characteristics in our lives, we must have him in our lives. The apostle John put it in these words: 'Beloved, let us love one another, for love is of God, and everyone who loves is born of God and knows God… In this is love, not that we loved God, but that He loved us and sent His Son to be the propitiation for our sins' (1 John 4:7,10).

Knowing Christ doesn't mean we shall love perfectly. The Corinthians proved that. Being a Christian is not the same as being perfect. Sin still resides in the Christian's nature and he has constantly to struggle against it. But we can be sure of one thing: no one who does not know Christ has the slightest hope of resembling this picture of him.

# 41.
# The permanence of love

*Please read 1 Corinthians 13:8-13*

Paul's purpose in this chapter is to demonstrate that love is far superior to the gifts. He states the proposition in the first three verses. In the remaining verses he cites the evidence to support his proposition. He first argues that love outperforms the gifts (13:4-7).

Paul opened his letter to the Corinthians by acknowledging that they possessed the spiritual gifts in great abundance (1:5,7). It is safe to say, in the light of their infatuation with the spectacular, miraculous gifts, that they claimed to possess these gifts to a greater degree than all the other gifts. But it is obvious from all we have looked at in this letter that spiritual gifts were not the only items abounding in this church. Sin was also flourishing. Spiritual gifts are, therefore, no guarantee of spiritual grace. One can have great spiritual gifts and still be unkind, critical, boastful, proud and overbearing. Love, on the other hand, safeguards us from all these things.

## Love outlasts the gifts

In the last half of this chapter, Paul moves to his second argument for the superiority of love: love outlasts the gifts. In living for the gifts and neglecting love, the Corinthians were guilty of inverting their priorities. They were guilty of living for something that would not last. This is not to say the gifts were not important. Anything given by the Holy Spirit must never be considered unimportant; however, it is possible for something to be important, yet not as important as something else. In other words, it is possible for something to be good, yet not be the best. The gifts were good, but love was the best. In focusing on the gifts, the Corinthians had placed the good above the best.

We would do well to examine ourselves at this point. Have we fallen into the error of the Corinthians? Have we got our priorities wrong? Are we living for the things that are most important? Are we living for those things that are temporary, or for those that last? The sad fact is that many spend their time and energies on concerns that are temporal and perishing and completely ignore the things that are eternal.

Paul did not tell the Corinthians to ignore the gifts, but to place love above them. Neither does the Bible tell us to forget all about every temporal concern, but to place eternal concerns above the temporal.

Let's look at what Paul says about love outlasting the gifts. His argument consists of two distinct emphases: the passing gifts (13:8-12) and the abiding graces (13:13).

## The passing gifts

We can capture what Paul says about the passing gifts in one statement. The coming of the perfect will necessarily make the gifts obsolete. But what did Paul mean by the phrase, **'when that which is perfect has come'**? (13:10). A good deal of controversy has arisen at this point. Some say the perfect represents Scripture; therefore, Paul is supposedly saying when Scripture was completely written, the gifts of prophecy, tongues and knowledge would cease. Others suggest the perfect represents the maturing of the church. Those who hold this view understand Paul to be saying these gifts were given to the church during its stage of infancy, but now the church has come to maturity and the gifts have been withdrawn.

These interpretations seem to ignore what Paul says a little later in this passage. In verse 12, he equates the perfect with seeing **'face to face'** and with full knowledge. His words there sound very much like those of the apostle John: 'Beloved, now we are children of God; and it has not yet been revealed what we shall be, but we know that when He is revealed, we shall be like Him, for we shall see Him as He is' (1 John 3:2).

It is when Jesus is revealed and we are gathered together to him that we shall 'see Him as He is' or 'see face to face'. So I contend that when Paul talks about the coming of the perfect, he is talking about the coming of the perfect age, or the coming of our life in heaven.

It is self-evident that the coming of that perfect age will make the gifts obsolete. Think about the gifts of prophecy and knowledge for a moment. What possible purpose could they serve in heaven? Paul likens them to playing with childhood toys and to looking in a mirror (13:1-12). Toys are fine for children but are unnecessary for adults. Looking in a mirror certainly doesn't give us exhaustive knowledge of ourselves, and looking into the polished metal mirrors of those days gave Paul's contemporaries even less. So it is with the gifts. They were given to fulfil a temporary purpose, but at their very best they were only partial and incomplete. When glory dawns, we shall not need the gifts any more than the adult needs the toys of his childhood. When glory dawns we shall have complete and exhaustive knowledge of heavenly things and shall no longer have any need for the dim mirrors of prophecy and knowledge.

Neither will there be any need for the gift of tongues in heaven. It is interesting that Paul uses a different word to describe tongues coming to an end. He uses the Greek word *'katargeo'* to indicate what will happen with prophecy and knowledge, but he uses the word *'pauo'* to depict what will happen with tongues. The former means 'to reduce to inactivity', and the latter simply means 'to stop or to come to an end'. In addition to that, Paul uses a different voice to describe the cessation of tongues. He uses the passive voice to describe the end of prophecy and knowledge, which indicates that something or someone will stop them. But he uses the middle voice with the gift of tongues. The middle voice indicates a voluntary action one performs upon oneself, or a self-causing action. Why did Paul use a different word and a different voice to describe the ending of tongues? John MacArthur writes, 'God gave the gift of tongues a built-in stopping place... When its limits were reached, its activity automatically ended.'[34]

A further interesting feature of Paul's discussion is that, after simply saying tongues will cease, he doesn't mention the gift again in this passage. He goes on specifically to connect prophecy and knowledge with the coming of the perfect age, but nowhere does he mention the cessation of tongues in connection with the coming of the perfect. This could very well be Paul's way of saying the gift of tongues was to cease before the coming of the perfect age. If this is true, we may legitimately ask how the gift of tongues could possibly serve any purpose in heaven when it didn't serve a lasting purpose here.

I have already argued that the gift of prophecy was one of those gifts that ceased along with tongues, but here we find Paul saying prophecy will cease when the perfect age comes. There really is no contradiction. Even though the gift of prophecy ceased, we have in Scripture the essential truths God delivered through the prophets. So the gift of prophecy can be said to continue in Scripture. When the perfect age comes, we shall no longer need the testimony of Scripture to guide us.

## The abiding graces

That brings us to the second of Paul's emphases in this passage: the abiding graces (13:13). Paul says faith, hope and love abide. They will not cease to exist when heaven's endless day dawns. Faith is, of course, the means by which we are saved. It is that precious gift of God which enables us to see Christ as the only hope for salvation and to rest completely in what he did on the cross. We are inclined to think there will be no more need for faith once we get to heaven, but that is not the case. Even in heaven we shall still depend on God and exercise confidence in him to provide for our every need.

Hope is the gift of God's grace that causes us to look eagerly forward to his promises being fulfilled. Faith makes us certain they will be fulfilled, but hope fills us with eager anticipation to see them fulfilled. How is it possible for hope to exist in heaven? We think there will be nothing more for us to look forward to after we get to heaven, but that too is a mistaken notion. God's inexhaustible treasures of glories will make heaven a place where we never get bored. There will always be some new treasure to anticipate.

Love is, of course, another of the abiding graces. We shall not only continue to love God and each other in heaven, but our love for both God and others will grow into perfect expression in heaven. Faith, hope and love will all exist in heaven, but the greatest of these graces is love. Why is this the case? I think the answer is that faith and hope are graces that are self-contained and personal. I have faith for myself and for no one else. I have hope in my own heart, but I cannot hope for anyone else. But love enables me to reach beyond myself and my own needs to be concerned about others. Love also makes me like God. God doesn't have faith or hope, but he is love.

Ours is a day in which many Christians bear strong resemblance to the Corinthians. We are more concerned about what will pass than we are about what will abide. Are we clear on the nature of the gifts? Do we understand that they are given to us as a means of serving the Lord, but that we shouldn't elevate them beyond measure and start defining spirituality in terms of them?

On the other hand, are we clear about the graces of the Spirit? Do we understand that the graces 'abide'? Many claim to be Christians today but give no indication of continuing in faith, hope and love. It is time the church got back to saying clearly that those who are saved will continue in faith, hope and love; those who do not continue in these things have never really come to know Christ. It is the nature of the graces to abide and if they are not abiding in us, it is because we have never received them.

Above all, are we clear about the need for love? Do we understand it is the supreme grace and apart from it we are nothing? May God help us to see the importance of love and to manifest it in our daily lives.

# 42.
# Tongues and edification

*Please read 1 Corinthians 14:1-19*

In his prolonged discussion of spiritual gifts, Paul has mentioned the gift of tongues several times in passing (12:10,28,30; 13:8). In this passage, he finally grapples in detail with this particular gift.

His opening words should not escape us. **'Pursue love,'** he says, **'and desire spiritual gifts.'** To pursue something is to follow doggedly after it with determination and intensity. Much of the trouble in the church of Corinth can be attributed to the members pursuing the wrong thing. Instead of making love for each other the object of determined pursuit, they were chasing after the more spectacular gifts. And why were they so interested in these gifts? Was it for the good of the church? Far from it! It was rather to gratify their own selfish desires to be known as part of the spiritual élite.

In telling the Corinthians to pursue love, Paul was not denying the legitimacy of spiritual gifts, but was simply demanding they get their priorities straight. Spiritual gifts were only to be desired, while love was to be pursued earnestly. The Corinthians quite obviously were making spiritual gifts the object of determined pursuit to the point that they didn't care who got trampled on in the process.

## The gift of tongues

The sheer amount of space the apostle Paul gives to discussing the gift of tongues makes it reasonable to conclude this was the gift they regarded as the very pinnacle of spirituality. Those who didn't possess it were probably regarded with disdain.

What are we to understand about the gift of tongues? Here the battle rages! On one side are those who assert this is the ability to speak to God (14:2) in an 'unknown' language. The speaker, they maintain, doesn't even understand what he is saying, but is speaking **'mysteries'** (14:2). His mind is suspended and he is carried beyond himself into the level of the spirit.

On the other side of the debate are those who insist that the gift of tongues was the ability to speak in a foreign language. Several arguments can be advanced in support of this view.

First of all, when the gift of tongues initially occurred, it was quite obviously the ability to speak in a foreign language. This took place on the Day of Pentecost. In describing this occasion, Luke actually names the various nationalities present in Jerusalem that day and explicitly says each individual heard the gospel in his own language (Acts 2:4-12).

Secondly, Paul uses the very same word, *'glossa,'* to describe the tongues phenomenon in Corinth as Luke used to describe what happened on Pentecost. The significance of this is pointed out by John Stott: 'One of the first rules of biblical interpretation is that identical expressions have an identical meaning.'[35]

It should be noted at this point that although the phrase 'unknown tongue' appears six times in the Authorized, or King James, Version of 1 Corinthians 14 (14:2,4,13,14,19,27), the word 'unknown' is not actually in the original Greek text. The translators of the Authorized Version added the word (indicated by italics), but the New King James Version and other modern translations omit it.

Thirdly, Paul talks in this chapter about interpreting tongues. He uses the Greek word *'hermeneuo'* which literally means 'translation'. To translate something is to put the words of a foreign language into a known language.

Finally, it is certainly noteworthy that Paul includes in his discussion of tongues two explicit references to foreign languages (14:10-11,21-22). This would seem to have only confused the issue if the gift of tongues was not the ability to speak in a foreign language.

As far as I am concerned, these are decisive and compelling arguments, and my interpretation of this chapter will be from the perspective that the gift of tongues was the ability to speak in a foreign language. I realize many others will beg to differ at this point. No matter what our understanding of this gift is, we should all be able to agree it certainly was not intended to be given the place of supremacy among the gifts. Paul's purpose in this chapter is to downplay or minimize the value of the gift of tongues and to stress the crucial importance of prophecy.

## The value of prophecy

How did Paul go about deciding that prophecy was the most valuable among the gifts? Was this merely his own personal preference that he sought to impose on others? Not at all. As far as Paul was concerned, two very vital questions must be asked in determining which of these two gifts was the more valuable: which gift edifies the saints (14:2-19) and which evangelizes sinners (14:20-25)?

Everything in the church ought to be done with these twin priorities in mind. I fear, however, that another 'e' word has been added to the list of priorities by the modern-day church: entertainment. Instead of asking if worship services edify and evangelize, many church leaders now want to know if the people 'enjoyed' the service enough to want to come again.

When we submit the gift of prophecy, along with the gift of tongues, to Paul's dual test, it is immediately clear that prophecy passes with flying colours while tongues falls far short.

Before we immerse ourselves in the details of these two tests, let's think again about the gift of prophecy. The prophet was simply one who spoke for God. He received direct revelation from God and transmitted this to the church. When Scripture was completed there was no more need for the gift of prophecy *per se*, but the preaching of the Scriptures in our day is the successor of the biblical prophet. The preacher does not receive new truth directly from God, but he takes the truth 'once delivered to the saints' and expounds and applies it.

## The test of edification

With this in mind, let's turn now to the test of edification. The word 'edify' simply means to build. If we say a service was edifying to us, we mean it was constructive and helpful, that it built up our faith. Someone said an edifying service is one in which the saints of God are built up, stirred up and cheered up.

The crucial thing to remember about edification is this: before something can be edifying, it has to make sense. People cannot be built up in their faith if they don't understand what is going on in a service. Paul uses three examples to hammer this truth home.

The first is from the world of *music* (14:7). His point is that music, to be appreciated and enjoyed, has to be intelligible. I could sit down at the piano and start playing, but no one would enjoy it because the sounds I would be producing would be indistinguishable.

Then Paul goes to *the military world* (14:8). Bugles are used by the military for giving certain commands to the soldiers. One sound from the bugle meant the soldiers were to get ready for battle. What would happen if the soldiers could not recognize that sound? Suppose the bugler just played a few random notes. No one would know what to do!

Finally, Paul actually uses the example of *foreign languages* (14:10-11). There are all kinds of languages in the world and each language makes sense if you understand it. But what happens if someone comes up to you and begins talking in a language you don't understand? The words all sound like a meaningless jumble!

It is easy to see the point in Paul's illustrations. Sounds have to make sense! We have no trouble accepting this in the world at large. We would not have it any other way! How ironic it is, then, for us to want the exact opposite in church! We cannot function in the world if sounds do not make sense. Why should we desire sounds that do not make sense in the church?

A lot of people seem to be very resentful and suspicious about the brains God gave them. They have somehow arrived at the notion that the intellect ought to be distrusted in the spiritual area and that the more spiritual something is, the more unintelligible it is. Many Christians delight in living on the basis of emotional experiences that seem to defy logic. As far as they are concerned, emotional experiences are self-authenticating — if they have experienced it, it has to be genuine and true — and any rational analysis of such experiences is of the devil.

Against all of this, we have the Bible constantly exalting the mind and urging us to use it. While there is much in Christianity that is *above* reason, there is nothing in it *contrary to* reason. So we shouldn't be surprised to find Paul saying to these Corinthians,

'Brethren, do not be children in understanding; however, in malice be babes, but in understanding be mature' (14:20).

The gift of tongues simply could not compete with the gift of prophecy on this matter of edification. For tongues to edify the church, they had to be interpreted (14:5). Evidently, a lot of speaking in tongues was going on in the church of Corinth without anyone bothering to offer an interpretation, and Paul wanted to bring this to a screeching halt. But even with interpretation, the gift of tongues is still no match for prophecy. Two stages were necessary for the church to receive edification from tongues: the tongue had to be spoken and then interpreted. Prophecy, on the other hand, was intelligible in and of itself. So even though tongues could be interpreted for the edification of the church, Paul says he would rather speak five words that could be understood than ten thousand words in a tongue (14:19).

There is much more for us to look at on this vital matter, but for now let's make sure we come away from this passage with a clear understanding of how important it is for us to strive for edification in our worship services. Anything that doesn't edify is not of God.

# 43.
# Tongues in Corinth

*Please read 1 Corinthians 14:1-2,20-26*

Although the gift of tongues is shrouded in obscurity, there are some very compelling arguments for accepting the foreign-language view. We do know, for instance, that the great cities of Paul's world were melting-pots and that people from virtually every nation and culture could be found in them. So it is safe to say every city had several language-groups represented. We also know that Jews, in particular, were already scattered throughout the Gentile world and that Paul found a sizeable Jewish community in every major city. So most of the churches Paul left behind had both Jewish and Gentile converts.

In the light of all this, it could very well have been that some of the Jewish believers prided themselves on being able to speak in the Hebrew language, and that they particularly enjoyed interjecting it into the worship services. In his commentary on 1 Corinthians, John Gill cites this as the view of the great linguist, Dr Lightfoot, and then goes on to say that even though Hebrew had become 'a dead language' it was still used by some Jews in public prayers, preaching and singing psalms.[36]

I can, therefore, picture a service just barely getting underway when a Jewish believer announces he has a 'revelation' and begins to share it in the Hebrew tongue. Or perhaps the worship leader calls upon a Jewish believer to pray and he offers his prayer in Hebrew.

We know from what we have already seen that there was a strong element of spiritual élitism in the church and a great deal of spiritual pride. This sudden use of the Hebrew language in the worship service probably caused a certain amount of admiration and a great deal of confusion — admiration because it was the language in which the Old Testament Scriptures were originally written and confusion because a good number of those present had no idea what was being said!

I can easily see this type of thing creating a couple of other problems. For one thing, those who admired this ability may have actually begun to memorize the words and phrases they were hearing in the service so they could themselves make use of them. This would explain why Paul makes mention of some who used tongues but did not have the gift of interpretation and says they should pray for that gift.

It is also easy to see how those who knew another foreign language would begin using it in the service. This would seem to explain Paul's words in verse 26: **'How is it then, brethren? Whenever you come together, each of you has a psalm, has a teaching, has a tongue, has a revelation, has an interpretation.'**

Some scholars think some of the Corinthians, in their feverish anxiety to have a 'tongue' they could use in worship, actually went so far as to bring into the church the gibberish that was routinely spoken in the pagan rituals of that day. If this scenario is reasonably close to what was actually taking place in the Corinthian worship services, it is safe to say the gift of tongues had been perverted in Corinth. No wonder Paul makes a strong plea for keeping the goals of edification and evangelism in mind and for pursuing these goals with orderliness. No saint could be edified and no sinner evangelized in the middle of mass confusion and bedlam!

**Were the tongues languages?**

Equating the gift of tongues with foreign languages does raise some difficult questions. The one that comes immediately to mind is what Paul means when he says the one with the gift of tongues **'does not speak to men but to God'** (14:2). As far as many are concerned, this is *prima facie* evidence that the gift of tongues has to be the ability to speak in an unknown tongue. The gift of tongues on the Day of Pentecost was the ability to speak to men, but this is a different kind of tongue altogether because here the speaker is addressing God, not men.

In addition to that, what does Paul's next phrase, about speaking in **'mysteries'**, mean? As far as modern-day charismatics are concerned, this can only mean the one speaking in tongues doesn't himself understand what he is saying.

For those who believe the gift of tongues is the ability to speak in an unknown, heavenly language, these two phrases prove their position conclusively and are unanswerable. A little scrutiny, however, reveals that the first phrase is nowhere near as conclusive as they would like to make us believe, and the second phrase actually contradicts them.

I say the first phrase is inconclusive because it can equally well be explained by both camps of the tongues controversy. On one hand, the 'unknown tongue' camp can say it is speaking in a language that God alone can understand. But those who hold the 'foreign language' view of tongues can equally say that, unless interpreted, the meaning of the foreign language is understandable only to God. We know from what Paul goes on to say in this chapter that his great concern was that there should not be any uninterpreted tongues in the church but that everything be done for edification. So the most natural way to understand this business of the tongue being addressed to God is to phrase it something like this: 'If you do not interpret your tongue so others can be edified, you might as well be speaking to God alone.'

But what about Paul's second phrase? What does he mean when he says the one who speaks in tongues speaks mysteries? I maintain that the word 'mysteries', instead of proving the unknown-language position, actually contradicts it. I say this because the word 'mystery' is one of the most well-defined in Scripture. Mysteries are truths which were once hidden but have now been revealed. Paul made this clear earlier in this very letter (2:6-16). If a mystery is, by definition, a truth God has revealed, the idea that speaking in tongues means speaking something one doesn't oneself understand goes right out the door! The one speaking in a foreign language, on the other hand, is speaking in that language the truths God has revealed. Those truths must be interpreted, of course, but they are still truths God has revealed.

### The purpose of tongues

Another difficult question is why, if the gift of tongues was the ability to speak in a foreign language, did God ever give it to the church? What possible purpose could it serve? The most obvious answer is that it was to be used to preach the gospel to people in foreign countries. This would explain how Paul, who claimed to know more tongues than the Corinthians (14:18), used the gift. And the gift of tongues on the Day of Pentecost clearly had an evangelistic purpose. In fact, the preaching in tongues on that day led to three thousand conversions.

Surprisingly, even though God used the tongues for evangelism on the Day of Pentecost, that was not their only purpose. The thing that so often escapes our notice is the fact that there was no inherent need for the gift of tongues even on Pentecost. Yes, there were people there from various nations, but keep in mind that these people were Jews and could in all probability still understand the Jewish language (Acts 2:5). The Jews who came to Jerusalem from other nations were, in other words, people of two languages. They could speak the language of the nation in which they were born. (Remember that many of the Jewish people had long before been scattered all over the civilized world.) These scattered Jews could still understand the Jewish language. Their national pride demanded that they keep their native tongue alive even though they were living far from their homeland.

Here, then, is the great question. Why did God enable the disciples to speak to these Jews in foreign languages? Why didn't he have the disciples preach in the one language everybody there could understand — the Jewish tongue? The answer is given by Paul. He says, **'Tongues are for a sign, not to those who believe but to unbelievers'** (14:22). To illustrate this, he quotes a couple of verses from Isaiah in which God said he would speak to the people of Israel with **'other tongues'** (14:21). The people of Isaiah's day had consistently rejected God's demand for repentance. God decided, therefore, to bring the Babylonians in to carry his people away captive. When the Jews heard the Babylonian tongue, a language they did not understand, they would know the prophets were right and God's judgement was coming upon them for their unbelief!

Sadly enough, Isaiah's day was not the last time the people of Israel rejected God's message. God spoke even more clearly and decisively to the people of Israel when he sent his Son, Jesus Christ. And what did they do? Like their forefathers, they refused to believe God's clear and distinct message. In fact, they not only refused to believe in Jesus, but they harboured so much hatred for him that they finally crucified him. Who crucified him? Not those Jews who were dispersed into the other nations, but the religious leaders right there in the capital city of Judaism — Jerusalem!

Fifty days passed and Jews from all over the world gathered in Jerusalem for Pentecost. Suddenly, the religious leaders of Jerusalem began to hear a strange sound — men speaking in foreign languages! Yes, the Jews from the various nations understood their own languages, but the Jerusalem leaders heard nothing but gibberish! What was it all about? Just like in Isaiah's day, the foreign languages they heard were the sign that God's judgement for their rejection of his Son was near! The fact that they were hearing Gentile languages right there in Jerusalem on that day was God's way of telling them he had set the nation of Israel aside and he was going to call out of the Gentiles a people for himself. A few short years after they heard these foreign languages on the Day of Pentecost, God's devastating judgement fell. In A.D. 70, the Romans attacked Jerusalem and completely demolished the city and the temple!

The gift of tongues, then, was a sign of God's judgement upon the Jewish nation. Since Israel has been set aside and the Gentiles brought in, there is no continuing purpose for the gift. The Corinthians undoubtedly knew about the foreign languages spoken on the Day of Pentecost, but, like so many in our own day, they misunderstood the nature of the gift. Instead of understanding it as God's sign of judgement upon unbelieving Israel, they saw it as a token of superior spirituality. So everyone who already knew a tongue began using it in the worship services, and those who didn't know a tongue quickly picked one up. Little did they realize they had chosen to exalt a gift that had been given as a temporary sign of judgement upon Israel, and that by using tongues, they were bringing confusion, not spirituality, into their worship services.

There was nothing wrong *per se* with speaking in a foreign language in a worship service as long as the language was interpreted. And there was still the possibility that someone from another land would walk into a service and need to hear the gospel in his own tongue. So Paul doesn't tell the Corinthians to abandon the gift. He does, however, give them certain guidelines to follow in exercising the gifts, and we shall look at these guidelines in the next chapter.

# 44.
# Guidelines for exercising the gifts

*Please read 1 Corinthians 14:26-40*

The Corinthians didn't like words like 'control' and 'orderliness'. As far as they were concerned, these were Spirit-quenching words. When they came together for worship, their purpose was to lose control and to forsake order. They wanted to become oblivious to reality and be carried away. If they could come away from a worship service saying they didn't know for a while who they were, where they were, or what they were doing, they felt they had really worshipped and that God had really been honoured.

Many current Christians have bought this view hook, line and sinker. Any sign of orderliness or planning makes them suspicious. As far as they are concerned, the Holy Spirit couldn't possibly be involved if any advance planning has taken place. They think if the Holy Spirit is in charge of a service, this brother over here will be led to 'share' something, that sister over there will feel led to sing a song, another brother over yonder will be led to offer an explanation of Scripture, and so on. In their book, orderliness equals deadness; the more enthusiasm and 'shooting from the hip' there is in a service, the more the Spirit of God is at work.

I sometimes wonder why this view of worship is so attractive to so many. Could it be that many Christians are not finding much joy and happiness in their daily lives and they want their worship to be a temporary escape from the burdens and pressures of life?

In these verses, Paul attacks the two notions inherent in the Corinthians' view of worship: the more unorganized worship is, the better it is; and unorganized worship is the supreme expression of spirituality. He attacks the first by calling for orderliness in the worship of God (14:26-35), and he attacks the latter by calling for obedience to the Word of God (14:36-40).

**Orderliness in the worship of God**

Three aspects of the Corinthians' worship appear to have been much abused and in need of regulation.

*Abuse of the gift of tongues*

The first was their exercise of the gift of tongues (14:27-28). To counter the abuse here, Paul lays down three guidelines: the number of people speaking in tongues in any given service was to be limited to two, or at the most to three; these two or three had to take turns — that is, they were not to exercise the gift simultaneously; each time someone spoke in a tongue, there had to be an interpretation so all the believers could be edified (14:5). If no one with the gift of interpretation was present, those with the gift of tongues were not to exercise it.

These guidelines take the wind out of a lot of sails today. Those who advocate speaking in tongues as a gift for our day insist it is something that is essentially uncontrollable. They maintain they are caught up by the Spirit and are irresistibly driven into ecstatic speech. Paul, however, makes it clear that those in Corinth with the gift of tongues had the ability to control it. When someone else was speaking, they could wait until he had finished, and when no interpreter was present, they could refrain from speaking in tongues!

I am convinced the answer to the current tongues controversy lies right here. Christians will never agree on whether the tongues were foreign languages or ecstatic utterances, and they will never agree on whether the gift has ceased. Even though we may be unable to agree on these points, we surely have to agree on Paul's guidelines. They are so clear as to be beyond dispute. Ironically, when we insist on following these guidelines, the interest in speaking in tongues dies immediately. In other words, when people are told they cannot run amok in the church with tongues but have to control it, they tend to lose all interest in it, or they take it to a church that doesn't insist on the guidelines.

*Abuse of the gift of prophecy*

The second area of abuse in the Corinthians' worship was the gift of prophecy (14:29-33). This gift was, as we have noted, the supreme gift as far as Paul was concerned. He recognized that its superiority didn't exempt it from abuse, so he offers three guidelines to regulate and control it: there were to be no more than two or three speaking in any given service; if one of the prophets who had not been selected in advance had a revelation during the service, the designated speaker had to give way, and in time, all the prophets would have their turn (14:31); the prophets were to be subject to one another — that is, when one prophet was speaking, the others were to judge whether his message was really inspired of God.

Here again, we see that a man could not plead an irresistible compulsion in the exercise of a gift. The gift of prophecy was to be exercised under control. Paul's concern in the exercise of both tongues and prophecy was that there be peace, not confusion, in the church of Corinth and in all the other churches as well (14:33).

## Women speaking in church

That brings us to the final area of abuse in Corinthian worship: women speaking in church (14:34-35). What debate swirls around this passage! The whole issue of women in ministry is dredged up when these verses are read. It seems to me that this issue falls outside Paul's concern at this point. Keep in mind what he is dealing with in this passage, namely, the confusion that was running rampant in the worship services of Corinth. Our interpretation of his command to the women, then, has to be consistent with the larger context of controlling this confusion.

Evidently, the women were contributing substantially to the confusion and bedlam so characteristic of Corinthian worship. Some think they were actually disrupting the services by whispering to their husbands. Others suggest they were openly and loudly challenging those who were doing the prophesying and the tongues-speaking. If either of these was the case, Paul was simply saying to the women what he would say to anyone who disrupted a service: 'Be quiet in church!' Still others think the women were the ones who were responsible for the abuse of the gift of tongues and, Paul, therefore, was forbidding them to engage in tongues-speaking at all. Whatever view we take on the precise nature of the women's abuse, Paul's point is clear: confusion has no place in worship. Unorganized bedlam is not worship!

## Obedience to the Word of God

Having made this plea for orderliness in the worship of God, Paul goes on to attack their notion that unorganized worship is the supreme expression of spirituality. That place is reserved for obedience to the Word of God (14:36-40). He writes, **'If anyone thinks himself to be a prophet or spiritual, let him acknowledge that the things which I write to you are the commandments of the Lord'** (14:37).

In other words, Paul is throwing the gauntlet down to the Corinthians. He essentially says, 'If you are so spiritual, prove it by recognizing that what I have written is the Word of God.' Paul is not only claiming he had written under the inspiration of the Holy Spirit of God, but also that any truly spiritual person will acknowledge this and submit to it. This had to be a dose of stout medicine for the Corinthians. Leon Morris writes, 'Clearly they felt free to strike out on new lines, justified only by their own understanding of things Christian.'[37]

They were acting as though the Word of God had originated with them, or as if they were the only ones who had received it (14:36). Their problem was one that has been repeated innumerable times: wanting to stand arrogantly above God's Word instead of bowing submissively before it.

We must squarely confront this issue. Like the Corinthians, we have nurtured a lust for experiences and ecstasies. It is time we nailed down Paul's fundamental principle. The Christian life is not known so much by its ecstasies as by its obedience!

Paul is not alone in making obedience to God's Word the benchmark of true spirituality. Through the prophet Isaiah, God said, 'But on this one will I look: on him who is poor and of a contrite spirit, and who trembles at My word' (Isa. 66:2). The Lord Jesus himself said, 'If you abide in My word, you are My disciples indeed' (John 8:31). On the same occasion, he said, 'He who is of God hears God's words; therefore you do not hear, because you are not of God' (John 8:47). It was also our Lord who prayed, 'Sanctify them by Your truth. Your word is truth' (John 17:17).

The apostle John added his own testimony to the importance of the Word of God: 'We are of God. He who knows God hears us; he who is not of God does not hear us. By this we know the spirit of truth and the spirit of error' (1 John 4:6).

The point is clear. The truly spiritual person is the one who listens to God's Word and obeys it. This is not to say spiritual gifts are unimportant. Paul urges the Corinthians to **'desire earnestly to prophesy, and do not forbid to speak with tongues'** (14:39). We are, then, to prize the gifts God is giving today, but we must never let them overshadow orderliness in the worship of God and obedience to the Word of God.

# 45.
# The certainty of the resurrection

*Please read 1 Corinthians 15:1-11*

Out of all the questions the Corinthians asked Paul, none surprises us more than the one he discusses in this chapter. We assume from what Paul says here that a good number of the Corinthians were in the grip of scepticism about the resurrection. They seem to have accepted the fact that Jesus himself had risen from the dead, but they refused to accept his resurrection as the guarantee of their own.

How are we to explain such a shocking thing? Some think the sceptics were simply reflecting the common Greek viewpoint of the day. The Greeks believed the body was inherently evil and that it was the prison-house of the soul. When death came, the soul was finally released from its prison. The idea of the body being raised at some later time and reunited with the soul was, to this way of thinking, the most undesirable thing imaginable. What joy could there be in the soul being placed in its 'prison' again?

Others think the scepticism in Corinth about the resurrection was due to the influence of the two men Paul mentions in 2 Timothy 2:17-18, Hymenaeus and Philetus. Because these are Greek names, it is not hard to see why some have concluded they had an influence on the church of Corinth. The essence of the teaching of these men was that the resurrection was already over for Christians. In other words, they had quite obviously 'spiritualized' the resurrection by teaching that it was something each Christian experienced in himself when he came to the knowledge of Christ. We know from what we have seen along our journey through this letter that there was a strong strain of spiritual élitism in the church of Corinth, and the teaching of Hymenaeus and Philetus certainly smacks of this.

Still others think the Corinthians' doubt about the resurrection arose from the influence of those who had been Sadducees before their conversion. One of the fundamental doctrines of the Sadducees was the impossibility of the resurrection. It could be that some of these ex-Sadducees had great difficulty in divesting themselves of this view and carried it right into the church.

We shall probably never be able to completely satisfy our curiosity about the source of this scepticism. One thing we can easily detect is that Paul considered it a calamity of the first order and attacked it with fervour. His line of attack in the first half of this chapter is neatly summarized in verse 12: **'Now if Christ is preached that He has been raised from the dead, how do some among you say that there is no resurrection of the dead?'**

First, Paul clearly demonstrates that Christ's resurrection had definitely been preached among them (15:1-11). Then he shows them that Jesus' resurrection is inseparably linked to the resurrection of his people. His resurrection is the guarantee of theirs (15:12-34). In the second half of the chapter, Paul discusses what the resurrection body will be like (15:35-49) and how the truth of the resurrection comforts and sustains all those who believe (15:50-58).

Let's turn our attention, then, to Paul's first emphasis. He shows that Christ's resurrection had been decisively and distinctly preached among them in two ways: as an indispensable part of the gospel (15:1-4) and as an indisputable fact of history (15:5-11).

## An indispensable part of the gospel

In discussing the resurrection as an indispensable part of the gospel, Paul takes the Corinthians back to the fundamental question of what it means to become a Christian. No question causes more confusion today. Many seem ready to argue that no one can say for sure what makes a person a Christian. A Christian in this day and age seems to be anyone who claims to be one. But with Paul, there was no such uncertainty or ambiguity. The Christian is one who has heard and believed a definite message. He or she subscribes wholeheartedly to a certain body of truth. What is this body of truth? It is, Paul says, that **'Christ died for our sins according to the Scriptures, and that He was buried, and that He rose again the third day according to the Scriptures'** (15:3-4).

Think about the three elements Paul mentions. First, he says

*Christ died for our sins.* Many take a very sentimental view of the cross of Christ. They understand it as nothing more than Christ showing how much he loves everybody. Of course, the cross is a mighty demonstration of the love of Christ for sinners, but it is much more than that. It was actually the site of a glorious transaction between God the Father and the Lord Jesus Christ. It was, in fact, Christ bearing in his own body the sins of his people and, in so doing, satisfying the Father's just and holy wrath against sinners. On the cross, the Father counted Christ guilty of our sins and poured out his wrath on his only Son (Rom. 5:6-8; 2 Cor. 5:21; 1 Peter 2:24). And this was, as Paul stresses, not something which just happened, or an unforeseen twist of fate, but a fulfilment of prophecy (Isa. 53:1-12).

The next part of the gospel message is that *Christ was buried.* This always catches some by surprise. The burial of Christ seems at first glance to be an almost insignificant and trivial detail. But the burial is an essential emphasis because it confirms the reality of both his death and resurrection. If Jesus was buried, he really died and there was a tomb that could actually be investigated to see if he arose!

That brings us, of course, to *the resurrection itself.* The body that died and was buried came out of the grave! Many have abandoned the idea of a bodily resurrection in favour of a spiritual resurrection. They believe Jesus' spirit continued to live and the disciples, feeling this spirit, constructed the resurrection stories. But it is obvious that Paul had no such thing in mind. It was Jesus' body that was crucified. It was Jesus' body that was buried. And it stands to reason, therefore, that it was the body of Jesus that was brought out of the grave. Jesus' resurrection, like his death, was the fulfilment of Old Testament prophecy.

This is the message the Corinthians had heard and believed. And this is the message they continued to hold fast, unless they had **'believed in vain'** (15:2). This is the same message that must be believed before anyone can become a Christian. The proof that someone really believes it is that he continues to hold fast to it. A lot of people are resting their hope of salvation on some kind of religious experience they had a long time ago while there is no present evidence of salvation in their lives. Let's nail this down once and for all: continuance is the mark of reality! If there is no present holding fast, it is because there was never a laying hold of the gospel message with a true and living faith!

**An indisputable fact of history**

Having laid down the vital elements of the gospel, Paul moves from the theological to the historical. He wanted the Corinthians to understand just how well attested the resurrection of Jesus was. It is indeed an indisputable fact of history.

To establish this, Paul first cites the witness of **'Cephas'**, better known to us as the apostle Peter (15:5). We know from what Paul said in the first part of this letter that Peter was much admired by the Corinthians (1:12). This man they admired was a powerful and unswerving advocate of Jesus' resurrection. Evidently the Lord Jesus had granted Peter a special post-resurrection appearance. This appearance is not discussed in any of the four Gospels so we assume it was something Peter told Paul about.

Secondly, Paul cites **'the twelve'** as witnesses of Jesus' resurrection. Paul is quite obviously using the general name for the original disciples. Judas hanged himself before Jesus arose from the dead. If Paul was thinking of the appearances described in Luke 24:36-48 and John 20:19-23, Thomas was also absent. What is beyond dispute is that the disciples of Jesus actually met with their risen Lord.

Perhaps the most impressive of all the witnesses of Jesus' resurrection is the one Paul mentions next: the **'five hundred brethren'** who saw the risen Christ at one time (15:6). Most of them were still living at the time of Paul's writing, and anyone who cared to do so could look them up and have the resurrection of Jesus verified!

The next witness is **'James'**, the brother of Jesus. Jesus' brothers never accepted him as the Son of God and their Lord and Saviour before he died on the cross (John 7:5). James was undoubtedly converted to Christ by this special appearance. We find him and Jesus' other brothers among the 120 disciples in Acts 1:14. James later became the leader of the Jerusalem church.

Next Paul mentions **'all the apostles'** as witnesses of the resurrection (15:7). This may be a reference to the time when Thomas was present with the others and was thus persuaded of the truth of Jesus' resurrection (John 20:20-29).

Finally, Paul uses his own encounter with the risen Lord on the road to Damascus (Acts 9:1-9) as proof positive of the resurrection of Jesus. He refers to himself as **'one born out of due time'** (15:8), that is, as one who had an untimely birth. In other words, Paul was brought into the apostolate at an unusual time, much later than the others, and in a very unusual way, suddenly and almost violently. Paul realized he was unworthy to be an apostle at all because he had so vigorously persecuted the church before he was converted. He, therefore, never grew weary of magnifying the grace of God that saved him and enabled him to labour **'more abundantly'** than the other apostles (15:9-10). If we conclude from these words that Paul was just an egotist who enjoyed bragging, we miss his point. It was the grace of God that made Paul what he was, and he talked about himself only so the grace of God could be seen and appreciated.

### The importance of the resurrection

Even though Paul was different from the other apostles in many ways, they were united in preaching the resurrection of Jesus as an indispensable part of the gospel and an indisputable fact of history (15:11). The Corinthians had believed and accepted the message of Jesus' resurrection (15:11). As I said at the outset, their difficulty was not with Jesus' resurrection but with their own. If they had no trouble believing in Jesus' resurrection, why did Paul begin by emphasizing the importance of it? It was because they had failed to see the ramifications of his resurrection. Paul wanted them to understand they couldn't hold to the bodily resurrection of Jesus without simultaneously holding to their own! The one entailed the other! So he begins at the beginning with what they were all agreed upon. From there, he moves into the area in which they were in disagreement.

There is an abundance of food for thought in what Paul says in the opening verses of this chapter, and we do ourselves a great disservice if we fail to examine ourselves seriously at several key points. Do we, in fact, understand what it is to be a Christian? Do we realize that the Christian is not simply someone who claims to be a Christian, but one who has consciously accepted the gospel message and continues to cling to that message? Do we realize that Jesus' resurrection is one of the best attested facts of ancient history and that we need not be disturbed by those who scoff at it? Finally, in the light of the certainty of Jesus' resurrection, are we living as joyfully and triumphantly as we should?

# 46.
# The consequences of denying the bodily resurrection

*Please read 1 Corinthians 15:12-19,29-34*

Have you ever had a cherished notion dashed to pieces before your eyes? Have you ever thought your viewpoint on a certain issue was unassailable, only to have someone systematically demolish it before you?

The Corinthians had such an experience. Some of them had a cherished notion about the resurrection of the body which they considered to be unassailable. They believed it was impossible for temporal, physical bodies to be raised up. When the body died, that was the end of it. The soul went to be with the Lord while the body just decayed in the grave. When preachers came to Corinth and made mention of the resurrection of the body, these Corinthians probably just smiled condescendingly and muttered a pet phrase: 'Dead men don't rise again!'

In the verses before us, Paul, one of the all-time great exploders of assorted cherished myths and notions, takes direct aim on this particular cherished notion. He starts by rehearsing the two points at which he and the Corinthians were in total agreement: the resurrection of Jesus was an indispensable part of the gospel and an indisputable fact of history. This, the Corinthians had heard and embraced (15:1-11).

## Where their denial would lead

Little did these Corinthians realize that Paul, with these opening words, had skilfully inserted a hook into their jaw and was about to draw them inexorably to see the monstrous absurdity of their position. He seems to ask, 'Are you in agreement that Jesus rose from the dead? Then you can't have it both ways! If Jesus rose, then dead men do rise! And if dead men don't rise, then not even Jesus rose!' (15:13,16). In other words, Paul says once one accepts the flat affirmation that dead men don't rise again, one is left with this syllogism: 'Dead men don't rise. Christ was a man. Therefore Christ himself didn't rise again!'

The Corinthians themselves, of course, had no intention of taking the argument that far, but Paul knew unbelievers wouldn't hesitate to do so! The resurrection of Christ is the pivotal doctrine of Christianity, and we may rest assured unbelievers will miss no opportunity to scuttle it. Give unbelievers credit for understanding that Christianity can be safely ignored if Jesus' body is still in the tomb! By saying there is no resurrection of the dead, the Corinthians were providing unbelievers with the very opportunity they were looking for, the opportunity to walk away from Christianity without giving it a second thought.

But Paul also knew their own faith would be damaged and diminished if they continued to entertain this dangerous idea. No, they weren't denying the resurrection of Jesus at this time, but Paul could see that possibility hovering menacingly on the horizon. Keep telling yourself dead men can't live again and, sooner or later, even you will begin to wonder if Jesus rose from the dead. Many a young preacher has gone into higher education convinced of Jesus' bodily resurrection and come away doubting it. Why? False doctrine has a way of wearing down our defences and worming its way into our thinking, so that we end up denying things we thought we would never even doubt!

For these reasons, Paul couldn't be content merely to point out that their scepticism inevitably led to a denial of Jesus' resurrection. He pressed on to show what a denial of Jesus' resurrection would mean for two basic groups: the bearers of the gospel message and the believing hearers of it.


## The consequences for the bearers of the message

Think about the consequences befalling the bearers of the gospel message for a moment. If Jesus did not rise from the dead, two things are undeniably true of them: their ministry is rendered meaningless (15:14) and even positively evil (15:15).

*Their ministry would be meaningless*

First, if Jesus did not rise, preaching is a vain and senseless activity (15:14). Paul was pre-eminently a preacher of the gospel of Jesus Christ, and he had suffered much in order to proclaim this message. But if Jesus did not rise from the dead, there was no message to proclaim. It was all a cruel hoax and all the time and energy he had invested, as well as the sufferings he had endured, were absolutely without meaning. A little later in this chapter, we find Paul going into more detail about the sufferings he had experienced for preaching the gospel (15:30-32). For him, life meant standing **'in jeopardy every hour'** (15:30) and experiencing death on a daily basis (15:31). He goes on to mention the suffering he endured when he was in Ephesus. That suffering was so great that Paul likened it to fighting with wild beasts!

Paul was willing to undergo all these things, and more, because he knew Jesus had risen from the grave. But he would have been a colossal fool to live like this had Jesus not risen! According to Paul, without the resurrection of Jesus, there is only one philosophy of life that makes any sense: **'Let us eat and drink, for tomorrow we die'** (15:32).

*Their ministry would be evil*

But it is not enough to say the bearers of the gospel have preached and suffered needlessly if Jesus did not rise from the grave. The truth is that in that case they have done great harm. They are actually **'false witnesses'** (15:15). The preacher of the gospel maintains his message is not one he has simply created in his own mind, but it is truth revealed by God himself. If, however, Jesus did not rise, the preacher has misrepresented and distorted the whole situation. He has attributed something to God that he did not do, and that is nothing short of blasphemous!

## The consequences for the hearers

What consequences befall the believing hearers of the gospel if Jesus did not rise?

## No standing before God

First, they have no present standing before God. The gospel message begins by declaring that all men stand guilty of sin before a holy God. It moves on to affirm that this holy God has himself graciously made a way for sinners to be forgiven and to stand clean and guiltless before him. He sent his own Son into this world to live in perfect obedience to God's laws and to take the punishment for their sins by dying on the cross. It further states that this Jesus arose from the grave, and his resurrection not only proves he was God in human flesh, but that the work he did for sinners was approved and accepted by God the Father. The gospel message also declares that all those who will turn from their sins in true repentance and place their faith wholly in what Jesus did for sinners will be forgiven of their sins and freed from God's just condemnation.

But if Jesus' body decayed away in that Palestinian tomb, all of this goes right out of the window! If Jesus didn't rise, the whole grand scheme of redemption comes crashing down, and believing the gospel message is senseless and meaningless. And if the gospel message is not true, the sinner is right back to square one. He is still standing before a holy God without any provision for his sins!

## No hope for their loved ones

In the next place, if Jesus did not rise from the dead, the believer has absolutely no hope for the future of his loved ones (15:18-19,29). Think about how many countless millions of people have walked away from graveyards with those familiar words ringing in their ears: 'We commit this body to the grave in the sure and certain hope of the resurrection.' What a comfort it is to know we shall see our Christian loved ones again! But if Jesus Christ did not rise, it is a false hope! Paul says if Christ did not rise, our loved ones are lost for ever! (15:18).

A little later in his discussion, Paul makes mention of a practice that had become popular among the Corinthians (15:29). Some of them were actually being baptized on behalf of their friends who had died without baptism. Nowhere does the Bible teach this practice, and Paul certainly doesn't condone it. He does mention it, however, to further support his argument for the resurrection of the dead. If Jesus did not rise from the grave, the dead are, as we have seen, hopelessly lost, and this practice made no sense at all. This practice was just another indication of the depth of the Corinthians' confusion on this vital matter of the resurrection. On the one hand, they were denying the resurrection. On the other hand, they were practising something that was senseless apart from it.

## *No hope for themselves*

Finally, without the resurrection of Jesus, the Christian not only has no hope for his dead loved ones, he also has no hope for himself. Those who have never embraced Christianity have been known to confess their envy of Christians. They see the serenity and tranquillity Christians have about what lies beyond death and wish they could have the same. But the Christian's confidence about death is groundless if Jesus is not alive and there is no reason for anyone to envy him. Without the resurrection, Paul says the Christian is **'the most pitiable'** of all men! (15:19). Take away the resurrection of Jesus and the Christian no longer has an endless hope, but a hopeless end!

## The influence of a pagan society

So Paul has, with unrelenting logic, shown the Corinthians that their denial of the resurrection of the body leads inevitably to a denial of Jesus' resurrection. That, in turn, leads to one wave after another of dire and dreadful consequences. Seeing Paul's forceful logic makes us wonder how the Corinthians could have ever got into the position of denying such a fundamental truth as the resurrection of the body. Paul gives us the answer by saying, **'Evil company corrupts good habits'** (15:33). T. C. Edwards states: 'The doubts of some in the Corinthian church concerning the resurrection of the dead was the consequence of their too intimate intercourse with their heathen neighbours.'[38]

In other words, they had done the same thing at this point that they had done in so many other areas. They had allowed the beliefs of their society to contaminate and corrupt their own thinking. Instead of allowing true doctrine to reform their sinful practices, the Corinthians had allowed their sinful practices to shape their doctrine. Instead of boldly declaring the undiluted message of the gospel to their society, they had tried to make the gospel more appealing by mixing pagan notions with it.

Paul, of course, recognized what they were doing. So he doesn't just tell them to get their doctrine straightened out. He says, **'Awake to righteousness, and do not sin...'** (15:34). If the Corinthians expected to win the unbelievers around them, they had to stop associating with them in their sinful practices and stop diluting the gospel so it would be acceptable to them. The Christian's success in reaching pagans lies not in minimizing the difference Christianity makes, but in maximizing it. The Corinthians were swimming in a sea of unbelieving pagans and, to their immense shame, the pagans were having more success in influencing them than they were in influencing the pagans. Paul wanted them to understand that the hope for reaching their society lay not in compromising the truth of the gospel, but in standing squarely and unashamedly for it.

# 47.
# Jesus' resurrection guarantees the resurrection of believers

*Please read 1 Corinthians 15:20-28*

A number of the Corinthians were having trouble believing in the resurrection of the body. They believed Jesus rose from the grave, but they didn't believe his resurrection was the guarantee of their own. Paul attacked their erroneous assumption by showing them they couldn't have it both ways. Either dead men do rise, or even Christ himself did not rise (15:13,16). And to make sure they would recoil in horror from the basic premise they had adopted, he began to heap one dire consequence upon another that would naturally and inevitably follow if Christ did not rise from the dead. He says, 'Look at all the terrible things you open the door for when you deny the resurrection of the body.' I can picture the apostle Paul, as he lists one vile consequence after another, feeling a deep inner protest rising higher with each one. Finally, he could sustain his litany of woe no longer, and he gives way to a sudden burst of triumph: **'But now Christ is risen from the dead'** (15:20).

Only after he takes the great flight of praise and triumph (15:20-28) does he return to finish his discussion of the consequences of denying the resurrection (15:29-34). Paul's sudden burst of triumph must have served as a tonic for the bewildered and beleaguered Corinthians. They were beset round and about with the everyday problems of family life, church life and social life. The glorious future awaiting them had been largely crowded out and covered up by these problems. In addition to struggling with the ordinary cares of life, the Corinthians had to live out their faith in a culture that was permeated with scepticism and doubt about the Christian message. That climate of opinion must have made it very hard for them to retain a firm grip on the eternal realities lying ahead. Don't we find ourselves in much the same situation? Don't we find ourselves so absorbed with 'coping' with everyday life that the future life seems faint and distant? Don't we also find ourselves intimidated by the cloud of doubt that hangs heavy over this generation?

Paul's sudden burst of euphoria ministers to all of us who are carried along by the tides of everyday cares and who are caught in the clutches of secularism and scepticism. It shows why Jesus' resurrection must be considered the guarantee of all those who belong to him. Two major reasons for this emerge in these verses.

## Jesus' original design in coming

In the first place, Jesus' original design in coming demands the resurrection of his people. Jesus came into this world for the specific purpose of being **'the firstfruits of those who have fallen asleep'** (15:20).

### The firstfruits

As one who was born and reared on a farm, I have no trouble understanding what Paul meant by using the word 'firstfruits'. Each autumn my father would bring three or four ears of corn into the house. He would show us those ears and say, 'There's a whole crop out there like that.' To my dad, the firstfruits showed that a crop was out there and what that crop was like. Paul had much the same thing in mind. He knew Jesus' resurrection was not just an isolated, solitary fact of history, but it was the first of a whole crop of resurrections!

The firstfruits were very important to the people of Israel. Because the firstfruits represented the whole harvest, they were offered to the Lord. A specific day was set aside for this, the day following the Sabbath after the Passover (Lev. 23). That happens to be the exact day the Lord Jesus Christ arose from the dead! No wonder Paul called him 'the firstfruits of those who have fallen asleep'.

### Adam and Christ

But why is Jesus the firstfruits of the dead? Why should his resurrection guarantee the resurrection of his people? Paul says it was by man that death came into the world in the first place; it is by man that death is defeated (15: 21). Doesn't it make sense for death to be ended in the same way it was started?

Adam was the man who brought death upon the whole human race. In God's scheme of things, Adam was no ordinary man. He was not only the first man ever to live, he was also the representative head of the human race. In other words, what Adam did counted for the whole human race. Of course, we know from the record in Genesis that Adam disobeyed God and the consequence of that disobedience was death.

Paul's point is that Jesus came into this world as the second and last representative head. There will never be another representative head for human beings. There are, however, some major differences between Adam's headship and Christ's. One is that while Adam represented every single human being without exception, Christ represents only those who belong to him. That is why Paul doesn't merely speak about all who have died, but those who have **'fallen asleep in Christ'** (15:18). And that is why Paul also reserves future hope only for those **'who are Christ's'** (15:23).

A second major difference between Adam and Christ is that while Adam's headship resulted in death for those he represented, Christ's headship results in life for his people (15:22). By denying the resurrection of the body, the sceptical Corinthians were, in effect, striking a blow at the very heart of the whole plan of redemption. In separating Christ's resurrection from their own, they were separating Christ from the very people he came to represent! And without Christ representing his people, the whole plan of redemption breaks down and falls to the ground.

## The final disposition of his kingdom

Paul's second argument is that Jesus' resurrection guarantees that of believers because the final disposition of his kingdom demands it (15:24-28). Paul makes three truths exceedingly clear in these verses: Christ has received a kingdom from the Father; he is now ruling and reigning in that kingdom until he has subdued all his enemies; he will at some point in the future hand that kingdom over to the Father.

Have you ever thought about what God's plan of redemption is all about? To redeem something is to buy it back, or to bring it back under original ownership. This is what God is doing in his plan of redemption. He is bringing all things back to the point at which human history began. Before Adam sinned, everything in this world was in perfect submission to God, but by that one act of sin, Adam introduced rebellion against God into the human race. God's plan of redemption, which existed even before Adam sinned, was designed to bring everything back into that state of submission.

How was this redemption to be accomplished? The Bible tells us God the Father commissioned his only Son to come into this world to set up a kingdom. This kingdom is both an accomplished fact and an ongoing process. When he died on the cross, Jesus encountered the forces of evil and won the decisive victory over them. His kingdom was established by his death on the cross, and he even now rules and reigns in the hearts of all who have placed their faith and trust in him. But even though the forces of evil have been decisively defeated, they continue their struggle against the kingdom of Christ to this present hour.

This struggle, thank God, is not going to last for ever. Paul says a time is coming when Jesus will finally put all his enemies under his feet (15:25). At that point, the goal of redemption will be realized. When all things are brought into subjection to Jesus, all that will be left for him to do is to hand the kingdom he has established over to the Father. And in the words of Paul, God will again be **'all in all'** (15:28).

In his discussion of the grand scheme of redemption, it is noteworthy that Paul makes special mention of one enemy in particular: death. This terrible enemy that was brought upon the human race by sin is going to be the very last enemy that is destroyed before the Lord Jesus hands his kingdom over to the Father.

The kingdom of Christ has many enemies. There is sin and all its various manifestations. Then there is Satan and all the hosts of demons. Why did Paul make specific mention of death? It was to show the Corinthians how foolish they were to argue against the resurrection of the body. By saying their bodies would not rise from the dead, they were essentially arguing that death was going to have the final word and that at least one of Christ's enemies would avoid subjection. Paul, on the other hand, says death is also going to be brought into subjection to Christ. This would be impossible if even one body belonging to him remains in the grave! For Jesus' victory over his enemies to be complete, the bodies of the saints have to be raised. Death must not have the final word! Thank God, it will not!

# 48.
# The character of the resurrection body

*Please read 1 Corinthians 15:35-49*

Two things are necessary to combat error. One is to show the logic of the truth; the other is to demonstrate the logical deficiencies of the error. Paul does both these things in the fifteenth chapter of his letter to the Corinthians. In the first half of the chapter, he unleashes a barrage of irrefutable logic against the belief of some of the Corinthians that their bodies would not be raised from the dead. In the last half of the chapter, he follows their error into its own den, ferrets it out and sets its fallacies in the clear light of day.

Paul goes to the heart of the sceptics' position by stating the two questions they continually asked when the subject of resurrection was brought up. The first question was: **'How are the dead raised up?'** This question focused on the seeming impossibility of decaying, disintegrating bodies being raised up. What about bodies that have been dead for thousands of years? What about bodies that have been devoured and digested by beasts? These were some of the possibilities the Corinthians had in mind when they asked, 'How are the dead raised up?' Resurrection sceptics today wonder how it is possible for a body that has been blown to bits in an explosion to be raised up.

The second question, **'With what body do they come?'**, sought to destroy the idea of the resurrection by suggesting that the kind of body that would come out of the grave was incomprehensible. Would it be just like this body? Would it be a heavenly body, or an earthly body? Would it be mortal or immortal? As far as the sceptics were concerned, the difficulty of these questions proved conclusively that the whole idea of a resurrection was absurd. For Paul, however, the perplexities associated with the resurrection were no reason to dismiss it. While not denying the complexity of the subject, he makes it clear that the problems were by no means insurmountable.

Let's look at how Paul deals with the question of how the dead are raised (15:36-41).


## Scepticism is folly

Paul begins his discussion of this question in a shocking fashion. He doesn't commend the doubters for their contributions to the ongoing theological discussion. Neither does he commend them for being sensitive to the intellectual trends of their society. He simply calls them 'fools'.

We may be sure Paul didn't use this word out of a hateful, malicious disposition. He did, however, want to wake them up to the reality of their situation. The Corinthians were very proud of their intellects, but on this particular matter, they had made a couple of assumptions that made them look anything but intellectual. They assumed the resurrection was totally unlike anything they were familiar with and, therefore, couldn't possibly happen.


## The example of the natural realm

All they had to do to see the principle of resurrection at work was to take a good look at the natural realm. There, life comes out of death on a regular basis. When a seed is planted, it dies and decays; however, from that dead, decaying seed springs a beautiful, fruitful plant! Job had taken note of the very same thing and said, 'For there is hope for a tree, if it is cut down, that it will sprout again, and that its tender shoots will not cease' (Job 14:7). Jesus also mentioned the same principle: 'Most assuredly, I say to you, unless a grain of wheat falls into the ground and dies, it remains alone; but if it dies, it produces much grain' (John 12:24).

The sceptical Corinthians, in their proud intellectualism, had walked right by the principle of resurrection on the way to the church meeting where they scoffed at it! No wonder Paul called them fools! But they were fools on another count as well. While they paid lip-service to the power of God in other areas, they had completely left it out of the equation in this matter of the resurrection.

## The power of God

Why does nature function as it does? It is because a powerful God is in control. He made all different kinds of seeds, and he decided that plants should come out of dead, decaying seeds. He is the one who created the human body, as well as the bodies for the animals, fish and birds (15:39). And if looking at these earthly bodies does not convince us of his might and power, all we have to do is look up to the heavenly bodies. How can we explain the vastness and the variety there? The only logical explanation is to say it all came from the hand of a powerful Creator.

The sceptics were in the ludicrous position of acknowledging that God had, in mighty power, created all these things, but denying that same power when the resurrection came up! If you believe in the power of God at every other point, why not believe it at this point?

Jesus emphasized the power of God in the resurrection in a debate with the Sadducees. Like these Corinthians, the Sadducees scoffed at the idea of the body being raised. So sure were they of their viewpoint that they rather enjoyed coming up with 'resurrection riddles' to discomfit those who believed in the resurrection. One day they decided to try one of them on Jesus. This riddle had to do with seven brothers. The first brother married a woman and died, leaving her, as the law provided, for the next brother. He also died, leaving her to the next brother, and so it went until all seven of the brothers had been married to the same woman. Their question was: 'Therefore, in the resurrection, when they rise, whose wife will she be?' (Mark 12:23).

The Sadducees fully expected their riddle to send Jesus into consternation, but he immediately shot back, 'Are you not therefore mistaken, because you do not know the Scriptures nor the power of God?' (Mark 12:24). It had never occurred to the Sadducees that the God who created everything that exists is capable of creating a whole new order in which the difficulties and complexities of this life hold no sway!

So how does Paul answer the question of how the dead are raised? He simply leaves it in the powerful hands of the same God who made all things, including making plants come out of dead seeds!

**The nature of the resurrection body**

Some of the Corinthians, as we have noted, were rejecting the idea of a resurrection because a resurrection body was inconceivable to them. They couldn't visualize it at all and they thought because they couldn't picture it, it couldn't happen. What does Paul have to say, then, about what the resurrected body will be like? (15:42-49).

The first point Paul makes is that the resurrected body will be vastly superior to the bodies we now have (15:42-44). It is apparent in these verses that Paul still has the analogy of the seed and the plant in mind. He likens these physical bodies to the seed that dies and decays in the ground and the resurrected body to the plant that springs up. Through a series of contrasts, Paul indicates that the resurrection body will be as superior to this body as the plant is to the seed!

Paul says this body is **'sown in corruption'** (15:42) and is subject to decay and deterioration. The body that is raised from the grave, on the other hand, will be incorruptible. It will never perish or decay. This body is also **'sown in dishonour'** (15:43). We try to make death look attractive and appealing, but our efforts are in vain. There is nothing attractive about death. 'Death with dignity' is a popular phrase these days, but there is nothing honourable or dignified about death. Thank God, the resurrected body will be different. The dishonour will be gone and the new body will be clothed in glory and splendour.

Furthermore, Paul says this body is **'sown in weakness'** (15:43). We know he is right. There is very little power in this physical body during life, and there is absolutely no power at all when death comes. The resurrected body, however, will not want for power. All limitations will be gone, and power will be just as characteristic of us then as weakness is now.

Finally, Paul says this body is **'natural'** (15:44). It was made for this natural realm and is ideally suited to it. But the next world is of an entirely different order. It is a spiritual world, and to live there, one must have a spiritual body. Needless to say, the resurrected body will be ideally suited to that spiritual world.

Not only will the resurrected body be superior at every point to the physical body, it will be modelled after Christ's resurrection body (15:45-49). Paul again reminds the Corinthians that there are two representative heads for human beings: Adam and Christ.

Adam was the first man, and we received the physical, corruptible body after the pattern of his body. He was our physical prototype, not because he had in himself the power to give life, but simply because God constituted him as the physical head of the human race. Christ is the other representative head. Paul doesn't call him the 'second Adam' because that implies there could be another. Instead, he calls Christ the **'last Adam'** (15:45) because there will never be another representative head for human beings.

Just as every man who has ever lived has received his physical body after the pattern of Adam, so everyone who belongs to Christ will receive his new body after the pattern of Jesus' resurrected body. Leon Morris put it like this: 'Just as throughout this life we have habitually borne the form of Adam, so in the life to come we shall bear that of our Lord.'[39]

The question we must each answer is whether we are connected to Jesus Christ. We are all connected by nature to Adam, but not all are connected to Christ. How do we become connected to this Christ who is heading up a new race of spiritual people? If that is your question, there is good news for you. The Bible tells us Christ has already done everything necessary for sinners to be connected to him. All that remains is for us to turn from our sins and place our faith and trust in his completed work, and we shall be forgiven and saved. Once we are connected with Christ we shall be able to say with the apostle John, 'We know that when He is revealed, we shall be like Him, for we shall see Him as He is' (1 John 3:2).

# 49.
# The character and comfort
# of the resurrection

*Please read 1 Corinthians 15:50-58*

The Corinthians had apparently equated the resurrection of the body with the resuscitation of the body and couldn't comprehend how mere physical bodies could inhabit eternity. When Paul talked about the resurrection, he had more than mere resuscitation in mind. He readily admits that **'Flesh and blood cannot inherit the kingdom of God'** (15:50). Yes, the physical body will be raised, but it will also be changed. The resurrected body will have continuity with the physical body, but it will be as superior to it as the plant is to the seed. So in this passage, Paul addresses himself to this great change. He deals with both the character of this change and the comfort that flows from it.

## The character of the change

Let's put some questions to Paul about the character of this change (15:50-53).

## 1. What does this change consist of?

Paul says it amounts to corruptible, mortal bodies being transformed into incorruptible, immortal bodies (15:53). The physical body is corruptible and mortal. It dies and decays. There can be no place in heaven for such a body! Heaven is an eternal place that, according to the apostle Peter, is 'incorruptible and undefiled and that does not fade away' (1 Peter 1:4). A body that is capable of dying and decaying just would not fit in there. The only body suited for such a place is one that has been clothed in immortality and one that is beyond the taint of corruption. The change Paul is talking about is one which ideally suits this body for that world.

## 2. Who are the ones included in this change?

Paul says, **'We shall not all sleep, but we shall all be changed'** (15:50). The word 'sleep' was, of course, the early Christians' favourite expression for death. Jesus himself used this term. When he received the news that his dear friend, Lazarus, had died he simply said to his disciples, 'Our friend Lazarus sleeps, but I go that I may wake him up' (John 11:11). What a tranquil, peaceful way to think of death!

So when Paul says we shall not all sleep, he means not all Christians are going to die! All Christians are going to receive a glorified body, but some will receive it without having to go through death! Who are these people? They are the Christians who are alive when Jesus Christ returns to this earth to rapture his church! When Jesus comes, these people will simply be 'scooped up' by him, and they will receive their glorified bodies in the process of that 'scooping'!

Paul goes into more detail about this in his first letter to the Thessalonians: 'For the Lord Himself will descend from heaven with a shout, with the voice of an archangel, and with the trumpet of God. And the dead in Christ will rise first. Then we who are alive and remain shall be caught up together with them in the clouds to meet the Lord in the air. And thus we shall always be with the Lord' (1 Thess. 4:16-17).

So who is going to be changed? Every single child of God! Those who have already died will be raised up first and will receive their new bodies as they come out of the grave. After these have risen and met the Lord in the air, all living Christians will be 'caught up' and will receive their glorified bodies in the process!

## 3. How will this great change take place?

Paul says it will happen **'in a moment, in the twinkling of an eye'** (15:52). The word 'moment' is translated from the word *'atomos'*, which is the word from which we get our word 'atom'. This word indicates that the change is going to take place in just a particle of time. It will take no longer than it takes the eye to blink.

*4. When will this change occur?*

'**At the last trumpet,**' is Paul's answer (15:52). That is the trumpet that is going to sound when the Lord Jesus Christ returns to rapture his saints. Did you notice in Paul's words to the Thessalonians that phrase about the trumpet? He said the Lord Jesus would return 'with the voice of an archangel, and with the trumpet of God' (1 Thess. 4:16). That is the same trumpet Paul refers to here in his letter to the Corinthians. The trumpet has always been associated with festive occasions, and no occasion could possibly be more festive than when the Lord returns to take his people home!

### The comfort of the resurrection

To many Christians, the second coming of the Lord Jesus is a doctrine for debate and speculation. Tragically, many Christians have fallen out with each other over some minute detail of prophetic teaching. Paul and the other apostles talked about the second coming in very practical terms. For example, when Paul told the Thessalonians about the second coming, he wrapped his teaching up by saying, 'Therefore comfort one another with these words' (1 Thess. 4:18). He does the same thing in this letter to the Corinthians. Before he closes this part of his letter, he emphasizes the comfort or confidence that flows from the change awaiting the children of God (15:54-58).

What Paul says about comfort can be divided into two parts. First, he talks about confidence regarding the future (15:4-57) and then about confidence regarding our work in the present (15:58).

*Confidence for the future*

As Paul thinks about that glorious instant of transformation for both the dead and the living, he can't help but taunt death itself: '**O Death, where is your sting? O Hades, where is your victory?**' (15:55).

Have you ever thought about how you will handle that grand moment when Christ's people meet him in the air? Surely, the very first thing we shall want to do is raise a tremendous chorus of praise to the one who purchased our souls with his own precious blood.

Perhaps the next thing we shall do is turn around, look back at those empty graves, and take Paul's words upon our lips: 'O death where is your sting? O grave, where is your victory?'

Death has played a monstrous role in each of our lives. It has deprived us of our loved ones, many of them taken well before their time. It has terrorized us, tyrannized us and caused our feeble hearts to tremble. It has diminished our joys, casting a dark cloud over our happiest moments. There has never been so much as a single hour in which we have not been in some way reminded of it hovering menacingly on the horizon. On that glorious day, it will finally be beaten once and for all, never to terrorize or tyrannize again. I believe I, for one, will want to thumb my nose at it and say, 'Reach me now if you can!'

Do you understand why death has been able to conduct such a reign of terror? Paul gives us the answer. He says, **'The sting of death is sin, and the strength of sin is the law'** (15:56).

Does any child of God need an explanation of 'the sting' of death? This is the anguish, the fear, the terror we feel in the face of death. What causes this anxiety and dread? Paul says it is sin. His point is not just that sin brought death into this world, but it is sin that gives death its power to terrorize us. Why? Each of us intuitively knows he must stand before a holy God and give account of himself and his sins, and that is such an awesome thought we cannot help but shrink from it.

But where does sin get its ability to terrorize us through death? Paul says, 'The strength of sin is the law.' Paul is talking about the law of God. He is not suggesting that the law in any way promotes sin. The law expresses the holy character of God, so it could not possibly encourage sin. But the law does state that death is the penalty for sin. Sin seizes on that pronouncement of condemnation and uses it against us. Every time we break God's law, sin whispers in our ear, 'You deserve to die!'

The glory of the gospel is that Jesus Christ came to receive the penalty for our sins and to fulfil the law of God perfectly. When he finally comes to rapture his waiting people, this gloomy triad of death, sin and the law will have absolutely no more hold over us. The truth is that we don't have to wait until that day to raise a chorus of praise to the Saviour. Even now we can take Paul's words as our own: **'Thanks be to God, who gives us the victory through our Lord Jesus Christ'** (15:57).

*Confidence for our work in the present*

What comfort and confidence the resurrection of the body gives us for the future! But we haven't got there yet. That glorious moment still awaits us. Meanwhile, we are still in this world of sin and difficulty. Does the resurrection of the body have any help to offer us for the here and now? Indeed it does! Paul indicates that reflecting on the reality of the future glory should yield two results in the here and now: it should make us firmly faithful and abundantly fruitful (15:58).

Being *firmly faithful* means we are **'steadfast'** and **'immovable'**. We are not to be like the Corinthians who were carried about by the latest fads of their culture and who were, therefore, constantly yearning to adjust and modify Christianity to fit the times. Instead of being thermometers which register the temperature, Christians are to be the thermostats that regulate it!

In addition to being faithful, we shall also be *abundantly fruitful*. Paul calls for the Corinthians to be **'always abounding in the work of the Lord, knowing that your labour is not in vain in the Lord'**. That word 'abounding' refers to being excessively, superfluously rich. In other words, Christians are to be really wealthy in their works.

How many of us can truthfully characterize our service to the Lord as 'always abounding'? There is a double jeopardy in those words. Most of us find it difficult to abound in our works for the Lord at any given time, but Paul says we should *always* be abounding. Isn't it true that most of us abound in our efforts to make money and to please and gratify our fleshly desires while our service to the Lord is halfhearted and miserly? If this is the case, how do we explain our lack of interest in serving the one who has guaranteed us such a glorious future?

Paul concludes his discussion of the resurrection with some very practical words and demonstrates in so doing that Christianity is not just a nice, neat set of doctrines for the mind. If we really grasp the doctrines of Christianity, we shall reflect it in our lives.

# 50.
# Thinking about missions

*Please read 1 Corinthians 16:1-12*

The last half of the letter to the Corinthians consists of Paul answering questions put to him by the church. They were confused about many things, so they looked to Paul for guidance. This last chapter of the letter brings us to a very practical matter. Paul had appealed to them to take up a collection for the church in Jerusalem. The believers there were in dire straits. Persecution by unbelieving Jews and periods of famine had combined to produce severe economic distress. Their situation weighed heavily upon Paul's mind and heart, and he made it a priority to appeal to other churches to come to their aid.

Paul's appeal for funds created some questions in the minds of the Corinthians. How should they go about receiving this offering? How would their money get to Jerusalem? These questions gave Paul the opportunity to talk specifically about their offering and as it were to think out loud about missions.

The truth is that the whole mission enterprise appears to have fallen on hard times. Statistics are still good, but there are alarming indications that the beliefs that fuel mission work are in jeopardy. What are those beliefs? One is that all people stand guilty before a holy God and must, therefore, have their sins forgiven. Another is that the work of Jesus Christ on the cross is the only means of forgiveness of sins.

For centuries, most professing Christians were in hearty agreement on these truths, but here and there some unsightly cracks have begun to appear in the foundation of the mission enterprise. Some have begun to question the validity of missions, hinting that it is really quite unethical for Christians to barge into other cultures and seek to convert people. Some have even gone so far as to suggest that faith in Christ is not the only means of salvation. They prefer to regard it as one way, but not the only way. Still others hold the view that Christ is the only way to God, but they believe him to be already present in other religions. They argue that the devotees of these religions are, in fact, already worshipping Christ but they don't know it. Mission work is, therefore, merely revealing the 'disguised' Christ.

Is it any wonder so many Christians have such scant interest in missions? Such views have almost completely severed the nerve of mission endeavours! When we read Paul's words, we get a totally different impression of the importance of missions. While our mission pulse is often so faint as to be almost undetectable, Paul's was throbbing with life and vitality. We can easily feel the throb by pondering his answer to the Corinthians' question.

## Systematic giving to missions

Two great conclusions about mission work are apparent here. The first is that Christians should give systematically to mission causes (16:1-4). Such a statement always sends some scrambling for cover. Excuses are always ready at hand: times are hard; the future is uncertain; jobs are scarce. All these excuses and umpteen more leap to our lips. Yes, we would like to give to missions but we just can't. Against all this, we have Paul's calm instruction: **'Let each one of you lay something aside'** (16:2).

The truth is that this command wasn't any easier for the Corinthians to follow than it is for us. They were far from being prosperous. Earlier in this letter Paul acknowledged as much when he noted there were 'not many mighty, not many noble' (1:26) in the church. But knowing all this didn't dissuade Paul from urging each one to contribute to this mission cause of providing help for the believers in Jerusalem.

But what if we don't give? Will it really make any difference? Won't the work of the Lord go on pretty much as usual?

A doctor who had served the poor citizens of a little French village for many years finally announced his retirement. The village leaders decided to ask each of the villagers to bring a pitcher of wine from their own wine cellar to make up a barrel of wine for the retiring doctor. The day the doctor's retirement became official the village honoured him with many speeches of lavish praise and presented their gift to him. That evening the doctor decided to sample his gift. He drew a glass and, much to his surprise, found that it was water! Each family had brought a pitcher of water, thinking it would go unnoticed when mixed with a whole barrel of wine!

What is it to give systematically? Both the individual Christian and the church have responsibilities here. First, the individual Christian is to give *as God prospers him*. Paul knew some wouldn't be able to give very much at all, but they must give what they could. Remember, Paul is talking here about a special collection. He is not dealing with the Christian's regular giving to his own church. For that, Scripture teaches us to give a definite proportion: the tithe. But for this missions offering, they were to give what they could.

Secondly, the individual church members were to bring what they were able to save up to the church **'on the first day of the week'** (16:2). Here we have evidence that Christians met on Sunday as a commemoration of Jesus' resurrection. Other Scriptures indicate the same (John 20:19,26; Acts 20:7).

Church attendance doesn't seem to have been nearly the problem in the early days of Christianity that it is today. To those early believers, it was simply unthinkable that one would choose to be absent when his fellow Christians were meeting.

What is the church's role in systematic giving? It is to ensure the money is handled with integrity. Paul says he wouldn't take the money to Jerusalem himself. Instead, he wanted them to designate certain representatives to take it. Paul anticipated the possibility that he might accompany these representatives, but he removed all possibility of creating a scandal by refusing to bear the money alone (16:3-4).

## Sympathetic understanding of mission work

Most Christians are in hearty agreement with all of this. Even those who don't give to missions know they should. But there is another part to Paul's mission emphasis. It is that Christians are to think sympathetically about individual missionaries (16:5-14).

What constitutes a sympathetic understanding of mission work? Two things. First, there must be an appreciation of the general nature of the work missionaries do, and, secondly, there must be an awareness of the special problems they face.

*The general nature of the work*

Two phrases capture for us the general nature of mission work. First, it is *the will of God,* as Paul makes clear with the phrase **'if the Lord permits'**, and secondly, it is what Paul explicitly calls **'the work of the Lord'** (16:10). Concerning the former, it is clear Paul considered his work to be God's will, even to the point of his most minute movements. This is illustrated by an experience he had earlier in his ministry. Luke relates how Paul was forbidden by God to preach in Asia and Bithynia (Acts 16:6-7). So they arrived in Troas not knowing where to go. The dilemma was resolved when 'A vision appeared to Paul in the night. A man of Macedonia stood and pleaded with him, saying, "Come over to Macedonia and help us."' Paul's response to that vision is also recorded by Luke: 'Now after he had seen the vision, immediately we sought to go to Macedonia, concluding that the Lord had called us to preach the gospel to them' (Acts 16:9-10).

In the light of such remarkable guidance, we must ask ourselves why God would exercise his will so strongly in the mission work of Paul if the whole mission enterprise is not his will. And if mission work is the will of God, how do we justify the low priority we so often give it? If it is God's will, shouldn't it be ours?

But we must also see mission work as *God's work* (16:8-11). At the time of writing this, Paul was in Ephesus. As far as the Corinthians were concerned, he was labouring on a foreign field. In regard to their own home field, Paul says Timothy was coming to work with them. All of this seems to be nothing more than mundane matters of church administration until we get a flash of insight from the words: **'For he** [Timothy] **does the work of the Lord, as I also do.'** What is so great about that? Both fields of labour, home and foreign, were equal. They were both the work of God, and one could not be ranked above another in terms of importance.

Is there a tendency among American churches to neglect the foreign field and to consume all our resources upon the home field? Isn't this tendency the result of failing to understand that both fields are the work of God? If you find your interest waning when the topic of foreign missions comes up, please reflect on what Paul has said about it being God's work. How can we be uninterested in what interests God? That is the general nature of the work of missionaries, and we must begin there if we are to think sympathetically about them. But we must also learn to think of special concerns of missionaries.

## The special concerns of missionaries

In addition to talking about his own ministry, Paul mentions the work of both Timothy and Apollos. It is interesting to note that each of these men had his own particular burden or problem. Paul himself was experiencing the trauma of having many opportunities and much opposition in his mission work. Many missionaries could truthfully say the same thing. Read the accounts in Acts and you will find the details about the adversaries Paul encountered in Ephesus. A false cult, the thorough-going secularists and materialists and the religious establishment all opposed him. But with so much error around, Paul saw a marvellous opportunity for the truth of the gospel to prosper (Acts 19).

Timothy had a struggle with a different kind of problem. He seems to have been the type who was given to fear, shyness and timidity. While Paul was as bold as a lion, Timothy was oftentimes intimidated. So Paul urges the Corinthians to refrain from doing anything to upset or disturb him (16:10-11).

Finally, Apollos seems to have been struggling with that old problem of too many demands and not enough time (16:12). He wasn't, of course, the only missionary to struggle with this, but this is what Paul mentions concerning him at this particular point. Paul had wanted him to go to Corinth, but his schedule was such that he simply couldn't do it.

Opposition, fear, shortness of time — these were the special concerns of the three missionaries mentioned in this passage. What should this mean to us? It should help us to understand that our responsibility to missionaries is not discharged when we bring an offering and throw it in the plate. Yes, by all means, do that. But as you do it, remember it goes to real people with real problems. Reflect for a while on what missionaries have been called to do. Make it your business to engage in mission studies so you can get better acquainted with some of the special burdens our missionaries are facing. I am confident that when we become keenly aware that our missionaries are doing the work of God according to his will and are facing enormous challenges in the process, our question will change. We shall no longer be content to ask ourselves how little we can give. We shall begin to ask ourselves what sacrifices we can make so we can give more.

# 51.
# Consecration and caution

*Please read 1 Corinthians 16:15-24*

The closing verses of Paul's letters are usually skimmed over in hurried fashion with scarcely a thought of encountering anything worthwhile. This tendency has robbed many of some very profound insights. Paul's closing words always abound with interesting information and throb with love for Christ and his church. It is certainly no different with his closing words to the Corinthians.

This may have been the most difficult letter Paul ever had to write. The Corinthian church was in a terribly low state, beset by contamination with the world and befuddled and confused by complex questions. In an earlier letter (which we do not have), Paul had addressed these twin perils of contamination and confusion, but his letter evidently had not brought about the desired effect. It had to be with a heavy heart, then, that he took up his pen again to write these words of correction and instruction.

At long last, we have reached his concluding words. I can picture Paul sitting in solemn reflection for a good while before closing this epistle. Just as he designed his opening words to be no mere formality but to drive right to the heart of their problems, so he undoubtedly wanted his closing words to be more than empty formality. He surely yearned for words that would make one final indelible impression on their foggy minds. At last, he shares the words we have before us.

As is the case with so much of what Paul wrote, they have both a positive and negative aspect. The positive aspect was designed to instil in them a desire to come away from the lowlands of selfishness to the higher plains of selfless service. The negative aspect was designed to shock them into seeing that repentance was not something they could ignore and neglect.

**The positive aspect**

The positive aspect of Paul's closing words comes in the form of five short, pungent instructions followed by the positive example of Stephanas, Fortunatus and Achaicus. The instructions call the Corinthians away from the sins that had polarized and paralysed them. Paul says, **'Watch, stand fast in the faith, be brave, be strong. Let all that you do be done with love.'**

He calls them to watchfulness because they had been heedless and had let all kinds of dangerous ideas and practices into the church. He calls them to firmness of faith because they had been extremely fickle and easily impressed with the thinking of the world. He calls them to courage and strength because that is what it takes to stand against the contamination of the world. He calls them to love because they had fallen into the trap of being selfish and critical.

Having given these instructions, Paul moves to give some positive examples. From what we have seen in this letter, we might have got the impression that there wasn't a single good person in the church at Corinth. Paul's words reveal that this wasn't the case. Some of the Corinthians were of such a spiritual calibre that Paul could safely use them as positive examples of consecration (16:15-18).

Paul mentions Stephanas and his household, Fortunatus and Achaicus. What was it about these that qualified them to be examples for the others? Two traits are spelled out by Paul. Of Stephanas and his household he says, **'They have devoted themselves to the ministry to the saints.'** And of Stephanas, Fortunatus and Achaicus he says, **'They have refreshed my spirit and yours.'** So these people were devoted to service and were refreshing to the spirit, and were, therefore, superlative examples of Christian living.

I wonder how many of us would dare claim these descriptive phrases for ourselves. Think about what is involved in them. The word 'devoted' is translated in the Authorized Version as 'addicted'. The word Paul used and the tense it is in give us to understand that at a certain point in their lives, Stephanas and his household decisively and deliberately dedicated themselves to serving others. They set themselves apart, not for positions of leadership, but for service.

We are quite familiar with the word 'addicted'. We know all about various addictions. Many are addicted to drugs and pleasure, fame and fortune. In other words, their lives are so controlled by this or that consideration they are powerless to do anything except pursue their addiction. It controls their thoughts, actions, time and energy. Everything is subjugated to satisfying their addiction.

When we put it like that, most of us realize we are in no position to claim this adjective for our Christian service. The truth is that most of us find it rather shocking to hear the word 'addicted' connected with Christian service. Our view of Christianity tends to be that it has its place, but it certainly shouldn't be an addiction. We think of Christian service as something rendered on Sunday morning for an hour or so. The thought of its controlling our thoughts, deeds and energy in an all-absorbing, all-consuming way is far too radical for the liking of millions who have made it a comfortable, convenient exercise. Paul is saying that Christianity existed in Stephanas and his household as an acute fever. For most of us, it is nothing more than a dull habit.

Paul also selects Stephanas, Fortunatus and Achaicus as examples for the church because **'They refreshed my spirit and yours.'** Paul was in Ephesus when these men visited him. They served as a connecting link between him and the church. This was refreshing to Paul and he trusted their return would be just as refreshing for the church. We might get the impression that anyone from the church would have accomplished the same and these men were not worthy of any special credit. But Paul specifically requests the church to **'acknowledge such men'** (16:18). So it wasn't just that these men served as the connecting link between Paul and the church but also how they served that made them refreshing to the spirit.

Most of us know of people like these men, people who are refreshing to be with. They possess the ability to lift our spirits, no matter how gloomy and depressed they find us. And we all know of those who do just the opposite, those who drag us down with them. We should each ask ourselves which of these groups we belong to. Are we among the refreshers or the depressors?

It is easy to see why Paul stressed these things. The Corinthians were by and large anything but addicted to service and refreshing to the spirit. They were addicted to childishness, selfishness, criticalness and permissiveness. When the church got together, instead of being refreshed, they were depressed and agitated. They really needed the examples Paul used. Therefore, he calls upon them to 'submit' to (16:16) and 'acknowledge' (16:18) these men. If we are to advance to higher levels of consecration, we also should seek to emulate those who are addicted and refreshing.

## Final words of greeting

From these positive examples of consecration, the apostle proceeds to share greetings from all the churches in the Roman province of Asia and from Aquila and Priscilla, that husband and wife team who were so mightily used of the Lord. Even as Paul wrote, Aquila and Priscilla were using their own home to nurture a church (16:19).

These simple words of greeting remind us of the deep interest and affections Christians have, no matter where they are found, in their fellow Christians and how heartily they desire their well-being.

The exhortation to greet one another with a holy kiss (16:20) is a reminder of the affection Christians are to have for each other and of the spirit of unity that is to prevail in their midst. A warm handshake and a hearty greeting express that same spirit of affection today.

At this point Paul takes the pen himself to sign his own name (16:21). It was his custom to dictate his letters to a scribe, and then sign his own name, a custom that may have been necessitated by his poor eyesight.

It would seem there was nothing more for Paul to do except sign his name. He has given the church five short exhortations (16:13-14) and urged them to learn from the example of Stephanas, Fortunatus and Achaicus (16:17). He has shared greetings from other Christians and exhorted the Corinthians to show affection for each other (16:19-20). The letter seemed to be complete.

But Paul wasn't content to simply tack on his name. With pen in hand, Paul not only signs his name but proceeds to write some surprising words. In these words we have the negative emphasis of his conclusion.

## The negative aspect

This negative aspect consists of two words of caution (16:22-24).

*Anathema*

The first is *'anathema'* which means 'accursed'. Paul writes, **'If any one does not love the Lord Jesus Christ, let him be accursed.'** Verses like this cause a good deal of hemming and hawing among many Christians today. Christians have always felt a bit uncomfortable about the psalms in which David called for a curse upon God's enemies. We have managed to get around that problem by saying the Old Testament saints like David did not enjoy full revelation, they didn't know about God's love for all people, and so on. But this is a New Testament verse. And to make matters worse, it is not the only verse which employs language like this. To the Galatians, Paul says, 'But even if we, or an angel from heaven, preach any other gospel to you than what we have preached to you, let him be accursed' (Gal. 1:8). And just to make sure we don't misunderstand what he said, he says essentially the same thing in the very next verse (Gal. 1:9).

Maybe it is time we stopped trying to explain away verses like these and simply accepted them at face value. In other words, let's accept what these verses teach: Jesus Christ has been given absolute pre-eminence by God and a curse rests upon all who do not recognize this and live accordingly.

If we have trouble here it is because we have imbibed too much of the modern spirit — a spirit which insists all religions are of equal value. Frequently, one hears it put like this: 'All religions are shooting for the same place and they will all make it in the end.' The Bible, however, will not allow us to think in this way. Jesus Christ says to us, 'I am the way, the truth, and the life. No one comes to the Father except through Me' (John 14:6). And in Acts, we find the same sentiment from Peter: 'Nor is there salvation in any other, for there is no other name under heaven given among men by which we must be saved' (Acts 4:12). Anyone who does not accept Christ has the wrath of God already abiding upon him (John 3:18,36).

This is not to imply we should be intolerant of other religions. Christians believe all men have the right to worship as they please or not to worship at all. But in granting this, we must not dethrone Christ, whom God has declared to be Lord of all (Phil. 2:9-11; Col. 1:15-20).

Perhaps someone will say Paul is not addressing unbelievers here but believers. The point is well taken and, in the light of it, there is only one conclusion we can draw: if the Corinthians continued in their sins, it was evidence they didn't really love Christ and, there-fore, were not truly saved. Are we clear on this? If the general tenor of our lives is disobedience rather than obedience, we don't love or know Christ, no matter how loudly we may profess to the contrary. And if we don't love Christ, we stand under his condemnation.

## Maranatha

The second expression of caution is the word *'Maranatha'*. It is an Aramaic word meaning, 'Our Lord come.' Scholars are uncertain whether it was used as a word of confession, 'Our Lord has come,' a word of expectation, 'Our Lord will come,' or simply a prayer, 'Our Lord, come' (Rev. 22:20). Most scholars are inclined to interpret it in one of the latter two senses, thus connecting it with the second coming of the Lord rather then with his first coming.

Why would Paul close this letter by making reference to the coming of the Lord? Was it to comfort the Corinthians? This is the conclusion most of us are inclined to draw. There can be no doubt the coming of the Lord has a tremendously comforting effect upon believers (1 Thess. 4:18), but I don't think that was Paul's primary purpose here. Throughout this letter, he has dealt with the Corinthians' sins, so it seems logical to regard this reminder of the Lord's coming as one final warning about their sins. It is a very solemn thing to think about meeting the Lord when our lives are falling so far short of his expectations.

So Paul ends his letter by appealing to the Corinthians for greater consecration and by cautioning them about their sins. He hammered on these themes throughout his letter so it isn't surprising to find him emphasizing them in his conclusion. Perhaps we find ourselves wondering what kind of impact Paul's pleas made on the Corinthians. We should be much more concerned about our own response to them. The Corinthians have passed away and now we occupy history's stage. What is our situation? Are we devoted to the Lord, or are we as contaminated and confused as the Corinthians? Let's make sure that Paul's pleas do not fall on deaf ears. If we have been 'Corinthianized', we need to face up to it and turn from it.

# Notes

1. John MacArthur, *The MacArthur New Testament Commentary, I Corinthians,* Moody Press, 1984, p.viii.
2. Warren Wiersbe, *The Bible Exposition Commentary,* Victor Books, 1989, vol.1, p.568.
3. David Prior, *The Message of I Corinthans,* Inter-Varsity Press, 1985, p.11.
4. MacArthur, *I Corinthians,* p.ix.
5. Prior, *Message of I Corinthians,* pp.24-5.
6. MacArthur, *I Corinthians,* p.36.
7. Steven F. Olford, *The Christian Message for Contemporary Man,* Word, 1972, pp. 65-6.
8. J. R. W. Stott, *The Preacher's Portrait,* Wiliam B. Eerdmans Publishing Company, 1961, p.101.
9. *Ibid.,* p.106.
10. *Ibid.,* p.118.
11. William Barclay, *The Letters to the Corinthians,* The Westminster Press, Philadelphia, 1954, p.29.
12. Matthew Henry, *Matthew Henry's Commentary on the New Testament,* Baker Book House, 1983, vol. 8, p.17.
13. Geoffrey Wilson, *I Corinthians: A Digest of Reformed Comment,* The Banner of Truth Trust, 1978, p.49.
14. *Ibid.,* p.53.
15. *Ibid.*
16. John Gill, *An Exposition of the New Testament,* The Baptist Standard Bearer, Inc., 1989, vol. 8, p.616.
17. Henry, *Commentary on the New Testament,* p.28.
18. R. C. H. Lenski, *The Interpretation of St Paul's First and Second Epistles to the Corinthians,* Augsburg Publishing House, 1961, p.161.
19. MacArthur, *I Corinthians,* p.98.
20. *Ibid.,* p.108.

21. *Ibid.,* p.116.
22. Leon Morris, *The First Epistle of Paul to the Corinthians,* Wm B. Eerdmans Publishing Company, 1975, p.86.
23. F. W. Grosheide, *Commentary on the First Epistle to the Corinthians,* Wm B. Eerdmans Publishing Company, 1974, p.119.
24. Wilson, *I Corinthians,* p.79.
25. Prior, *Message of I Corinthians,* p.78.
26. *Ibid.,* p.89.
27. Wilson, *I Corinthians,* p.89.
28. Wiersbe, *Bible Exposition Commentary,* vol. 2, p.589.
29. MacArthur, *I Corinthians,* p.151.
30. Prior, *Message of I Corinthians,* p.141.
31. Charles Eerdman, *The First Epistle of Paul to the Corinthians,* The Westminster Press, 1928, p.70.
32. MacArthur, *I Corinthians,* p.194.
33. Wilson, *I Corinthians,* p.135
34.  MacArthur, *I Corinthians,* p.359.
35. J. R. W. Stott, *Baptism and Fullness,* Inter-Varsity Press, 1976, p.112.
36. Gill, *Exposition of the New Testament,* p.712.
37. Morris, *First Epistle ... to the Corinthians,* p.202.
38. Wilson, *I Corinthians,*
39. Morris, *First Epistle ... to the Corinthians,* p.231.